Transcification Sequence Diagram

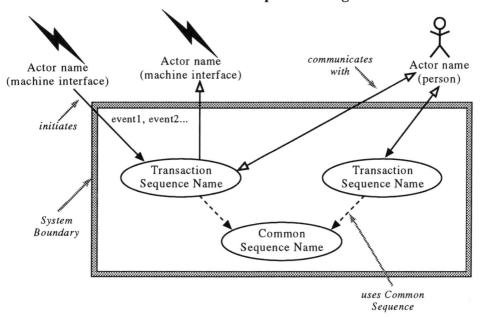

Actor name
(machine interface)

Actor name
(machine interface)

communicates with

Actor name
(person)

initiates

event1, event2...

Transaction
Sequence Name

Transaction
Sequence Name

System Boundary

Common
Sequence Name

uses Common Sequence

Activity Flow Diagram

Parallel or randomly sequenced Activities:

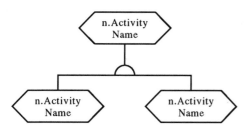

Selection of an Activity (decision point):

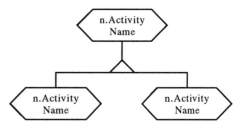

Iteration:

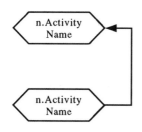

Synchronization Point:

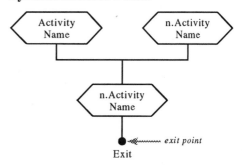

exit point

Exit

Mainstream Objects:
An Analysis and Design Approach for Business

Selected Titles from the
YOURDON PRESS COMPUTING SERIES
Ed Yourdon, *Advisor*

ANDREWS AND LEVENTHAL Fusion: Integrating IE, CASE, and JAD
ANDREWS AND STALICK Business Reengineering: The Survival Guide
AUGUST Joint Application Design
BODDIE The Information Asset: Rational DP Funding and Other Radical Notions
BOULDIN Agents of Change: Managing The Introduction of Automated Tools
BRILL Building Controls into Structured Systems
COAD AND NICOLA Object-Oriented Programming
COAD AND YOURDON Object-Oriented Analysis, 2/E
COAD AND YOURDON Object-Oriented Design
COAD WITH NORTH AND MAYFIELD Object Models: Strategies, Patterns, and
    Applications
CONNELL AND SHAFER Object-Oriented Rapid Prototyping
CONNELL AND SHAFER Structured Rapid Prototyping
CONSTANTINE Constantine on Peopleware
CONSTANTINE AND YOURDON Structured Design
CRAWFORD Advancing Business Concepts in a JAD Workshop Setting
DEGRACE AND STAHL The Olduvai Imperative: CASE and the State of Software
    Engineering Practice
DEGRACE AND STAHL Wicked Problems, Righteous Solutions
DEMARCO Controlling Software Projects
DEMARCO Structured Analysis and System Specification
EMBLEY, KURTZ, AND WOODFIELD Object-Oriented Systems Analysis
FOURNIER Practical Guide to Structured System Development and Maintenance
GLASS Software Conflict: Essays on the Art and Science of Software Engineering
JONES Assessment and Control of Software Risks
KING Project Management Made Simple
LARSON Interactive Software: Tools for Building Interactive User Interfaces
MCMENAMIN AND PALMER Essential System Design
MOSLEY The Handbook of MIS Application Software Testing
PAGE-JONES Practical Guide to Structured Systems Design, 2/E
PINSON Designing Screen Interfaces in C
PUTNAM AND MYERS Measures for Excellence: Reliable Softwware on Time
    within Budget
RIPPS An Implementation Guide to Real-Time Programming
RODGERS ORACLE®: A Database Developer's Guide
RODGERS UNIX®: Database Management Systems
SHLAER AND MELLOR Object Lifecycles: Modeling the World in Sates
SHLAER AND MELLOR Object-Oriented Systems Analysis: Modeling the World
    in Data
THOMSETT Third Wave Project Management
WANG (ed.) Information Technology in Action
WARD System Development Without Pain
WARD AND MELLOR Structured Development for Real-Time Systems
YOURDON Decline and Fall of the American Programmer
YOURDON Managing the Structured Techniques 4/E
YOURDON Managing the System Life-Cycle, 2/E
YOURDON Modern Structured Analysis
YOURDON Object-Oriented Systems Design
YOURDON Structured Walkthroughs, 4/E
YOURDON Techniques of Program Structure and Design
YOURDON, WHITEHEAD, THOMANN, OPPEL, AND NEVERMANN Mainstream Objects: An Analysis and
    Design Approach for Business
YOURDON INC. YOURDON™ Systems Method: Model-Driven Systems Development

Mainstream Objects:
An Analysis and Design Approach for Business

Edward Yourdon
Katharine Whitehead
Jim Thomann
Karin Oppel
Peter Nevermann

For book and bookstore information

http://www.prenhall.com
gopher to gopher.prenhall.com

YOURDON PRESS
Prentice Hall Building
Upper Saddle River, NJ 07458

Library of Congress Cataloging-in-Publication Data
Mainstream objects: an analysis and design approach for business /
   E. Yourdon ... [et al.].
       p. cm. -- (Yourdon Press computing series)
    Includes bibliographical references and index.
    ISBN 0-13-209156-9
    1. Object-oriented programming (Computer science) 2. Business--
Data processing. I. Yourdon, Edward. II. Series.
QA76 .64.M34 1995
650'.0285'511--dc20   95-7363
                                                         CIP

Editorial/production supervision: *Patti Guerrieri*
Cover designer: *Software AG*
Manufacturing buyer: *Alexis R. Heydt*
Acquisitions editor: *Paul W. Becker*
Editorial assistant: *Maureen Diana*

Published by Prentice Hall PTR
Prentice-Hall Inc.
A Simon & Schuster Company
Upper Saddle River, NJ 07458

The publisher offers discounts on this book when ordered in bulk quantities.
For more information, contact:

    Corporate Sales Department
    Prentice Hall PTR
    One Lake Street
    Upper Saddle River, NJ 07458
    Phone: 800-382-3419
    Fax: 201-236-7141
    e-mail: corpsales@prenhall.com

Printed in the United States of America
10 9 8 7 6 5 4 3

ISBN   0-13-209156-9

Prentice-Hall International (UK) Limited, *London*
Prentice-Hall of Australia Pty. Limited, *Sydney*
Prentice-Hall of Canada Inc., *Toronto*
Prentice-Hall Hispanoamericana, S.A., *Mexico*
Prentice-Hall of India Private Limited, *New Delhi*
Prentice-Hall of Japan, Inc., *Tokyo*
Simon & Schuster Asia Pte. Ltd., *Singapore*
Editora Prentice-Hall do Brasil, Ltda., *Rio de Janeiro*

Table of Contents

Foreword

Today, the role of IT in business is not simply to support existing administrative processes but to create competitive advantage through the innovative use of new IT and related technologies. Effective and efficient use of IT is a significant factor in the success or failure of businesses in all sectors.

At Software AG, we have solid experience in evaluating the benefits - especially the business benefits - of any new technology to mission-critical applications. We favor an evolutionary approach, which safeguards existing investments, while seeking to improve support for productive and high quality rapid application development.

We recognize object technology as one new technology with significant potential benefits for businesses. With this in mind, we have integrated elements of object orientation into parts of our product range and will continue this process in the years to come.

This book is one of the fruits of our object-oriented development program. Developed in collaboration with Ed Yourdon, *Mainstream Objects* describes a practical approach to object-oriented development. This approach, I believe, will help businesses introduce object technology into mainstream, productive use within their organizations.

Peter Schnell
President and CEO, Software AG

Preface

We see object technology as one of the major trends in software development. It promises advances in software development by offering higher productivity as well as improvements in software quality.

We think productivity is likely to be improved by the use of component-based software development. Components developed in previous projects will be put together to build new applications. And we expect it to be increasingly possible to buy components, or "business objects", from third parties, and use them as the basis for putting together customized, object-oriented applications.

We also believe the use of object-oriented techniques improves software quality. We discuss why this should be so in Chapter 1.

Client-server applications, with sophisticated graphical user interfaces, are of key importance in a world in which the integration of heterogeneous environments and data sources is becoming ever more significant. Client-server applications are often extremely complex and we believe an object-oriented development approach has great potential value in assisting in the building of such complex applications, as well as for providing encapsulated interfaces with existing systems and data sources.

Our belief in object technology as a major technology of the future provided the motivation for our search for an object-oriented development approach. At Software AG, we aim to incorporate new technology into our application engineering software as soon as it becomes mature enough for heavy-duty use in mainstream, commercial applications. This naturally led us to look for an object-oriented development approach for use in our own application development and for support in our range of application engineering tools.

Selecting an Object-Oriented Development Approach

We started our search for an object-oriented development approach in the same way as most people. We defined what we thought a suitable object-oriented development approach should be like. We then looked at the available methods with the aim of selecting the best method available.

We found a wide range of existing methods, many of which have much in common in their coverage of core concepts, with only superficial differences in notation. However, different methods had their own specific strong points and were strong in different areas. We concluded that no single method offered the best approach, whereas a combination of techniques, from the best of the methods available at the time of our survey, could be combined into an approach which would be very effective.

Because of this, although it hadn't been our objective to define a new approach, we decided we should combine the best techniques into an overall method, aiming at an approach which would be effective and complete, but not unnecessarily complex. Because we adopted techniques from various sources, we found it important to make sure that our techniques fitted together into a coherent, integrated whole, and we invested effort in ensuring we achieved this. Our approach to object-oriented development is thus positioned as a synthesis of the best of the currently existing techniques.

We chose techniques taken principally from two camps - Rumbaughand Coad/Yourdon on the one hand, and Jacobson on the other. Rumbaugh and Coad/Yourdon offer strong coverage of object structure and object behavior modeling techniques, while Jacobson's strength is his functionally-oriented "use case" approach, which we consider fills a gap in other methods with respect to the modeling of system requirements.

An additional influence on our approach was Wirfs-Brock's contribution of "object-think", conveying to the reader an understanding of how to structure the functionality of an object-oriented system. We also adopted aspects of her approach to the definition of subsystems and the definition of interfaces between subsystems.

We find it encouraging that since we embarked on this route, many other methodologists have also seen that there are benefits to be achieved by combining the strengths of the two major strands mentioned above. This can be seen, for instance, in Booch's second version of his approach to object-oriented development and in the articles of numerous methodologists in publications such as the *Journal of Object-Oriented Programming*.

Who Should Read This Book?

This book is aimed at practitioners. System developers and managers in mainstream, commercial environments should find it offers a practical approach to object-oriented development. It describes what to do and how to do it and is intended to be usable as a development handbook. It should also be of interest to managers and consultants responsible for application development strategy, and to consultants investigating object technology.

The book is concerned with analysis and design for effective system development, rather than with detailed programming issues. Individual developers who find the techniques useful can use them on an individual basis. However, we offer an approach which can be adopted for use throughout an organization, as an organization's chosen object-oriented development methodology. The approach is scalable - it can be used more or less fully depending on the size and requirements of individual projects.

We assume that readers are familiar with information technology, but we do not assume knowledge of object technology. Newcomers should therefore find the book of interest, while we hope that there is enough advanced material for experts to find the book interesting as well.

This book can be used as a textbook for a graduate or advanced undergraduate course on object-oriented system development.

Content and Organization

The book is divided into four parts:

PART I   offers an introduction to object orientation. It discusses the business case for object orientation and introduces the fundamental principles. It also discusses which object-oriented development techniques should be included in an object-oriented development methodology and why these techniques are useful.

PART II   provides an overview of the modeling techniques for analysis, design and construction of object-oriented applications. The contents and use of each modeling technique are introduced, together with associated diagramming techniques.

PART III   describes the *process* of object-oriented development. It emphasizes *what* is done *when* in the project life cycle, including steps, checklists and deliverables. It also discusses general management issues relating to the overall management of object-oriented development within an organization, including guidelines on how to organize, plan and carry out object-oriented development.

PART IV   discusses some of the less obvious conceptual issues of object-oriented analysis and design. It introduces some of the thought-processes required in order to produce a quality object-oriented design.

For managers, Part I and the early chapters of Part III will be of particular interest. Newcomers to object orientation, and those seeking a general overview, will find all the chapters of Part I useful. For system developers, Parts II and III will be of special interest, as they provide a thorough grounding in our approach to object-oriented application development. Advanced practitioners will also find Part IV of interest, as well as the discussion in Chapter 3 of the rationale behind our choice of techniques.

Appendix A includes brief notes on some of the methods we evaluated, including comments on their strengths and weaknesses.

Acknowledgments

We would like to acknowledge the assistance of various people at Software AG, on both sides of the Atlantic, who participated in the development and review of this methodology, as well as the members of our product development team who contributed their practical experience of object-oriented development and the application developers who tested the methodology for us. We are also grateful to the marketing managers who, in a manner of speaking, started the project and got Ed involved, the development managers who supported us throughout the process, and Scott Billings who managed the long process to get this book "out the door".

We would like to thank Steven Mrdalj, Gerald Pasternack, Haim Kilov, Richard Felsinger, Madhu S. Singh and Robert Glass for their helpful comments on the manuscript, and also Kathy Schiff, for editing our manuscript, and Chelle Hackett, for producing the diagrams and other illustrations.

Part I

Introduction to Object Orientation

Chapter Number and Title	Contents
Chapter 1 **Why Adopt an Object-Oriented Approach**	Summarizes the business case for adopting object orientation.
Chapter 2 **Fundamental OO Concepts and Principles**	Provides definitions and examples of the basic object-oriented concepts and principles.
Chapter 3 **Selected Object-Oriented Modeling Techniques**	Describes our choice of modeling techniques for object-oriented application development and the rationale behind this choice.

Chapter 1

Why Adopt An Object-Oriented Approach

Before an organization plunges into the technical details of object modeling techniques and new object-oriented programming languages, it needs to ask a very basic question: *why objects?* Most organizations already have a development methodology that they've evolved over the years, and it may not be obvious why that methodology has to be replaced. The purpose of this chapter is to summarize the benefits of object orientation and the business case that most organizations will be able to create for justifying the move to objects.

The Popularity of Object Orientation

By now, virtually everyone in the application development field has heard something about objects. Object technology is being used in real-time applications, insurance companies, banks, and a variety of industrial-strength applications. A survey in January 1994 by the Object Management Group[1] indicated that only about 3 percent of IT organizations in the U.S. were using object technology in 1994, but predicted the percentage would grow to approximately 40 percent by 1997, and 80 percent by 2001. Equally interesting are the spending plans of application development organizations over the next few years. The OMG survey indicated that IT organizations are planning to spend increasing amounts of money on object technology, as shown in Figure 1-1.

Another survey, conducted by Systems Development, Inc.[2] at the end of 1991 and again at the end of 1993, produced similar figures for OO. The survey covered a wide range of technologies, including OO, structured methods, CASE, etc. The number of projects using object technology increased from 3.8% in 1991 to 11.9% in 1993. Meanwhile, the usage of structured methods declined from 71.4% in 1991 to 60.7% in 1993.

But while OO is becoming more popular, it is still only used by a small minority of the software community. The trade magazines that report OO experimentation in 75 percent of the Fortune 100 companies don't emphasize, for example, that most of that usage consists of experimentation and pilot projects. Nor do they emphasize that most of what goes on in an object-oriented project is a lot of programming in C++, with little regard for the analysis, design, and other software engineering activities that should also be addressed from an OO perspective.

---

[1] "Corporate IS considers Object Plans," *Computerworld*, Jan 24, 1994

[2] Chris Pickering, Survey of Advanced Technology—1991 and Survey of Advanced Technology— 1993, (Denver, CO: Systems Development Inc., 1991 and 1993).

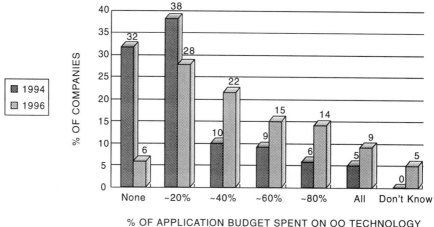

Figure 1-1: OO Spending Plans for IT Organizations

Reasons for Using OO Technology

In this section, we review the traditional arguments in favor of object technology, as well as the practical arguments in favor of abandoning an older methodology in favor of OO.

The productivity argument in favor of object technology

There are two primary arguments for object technology; productivity and quality. There are strong claims and some impressive anecdotal evidence in the computer trade magazines to suggest that a system built with object technology can increase the productivity of the project team by as much as a factor of ten, and that it can reduce the project's calendar schedule by as much as a factor of ten.

How can OO achieve such enormous productivity gains? Why is it that someone programming in Smalltalk or C++ can claim to achieve ten times the productivity of someone programming in COBOL? Part of the answer has to do with the level of the languages involved. The same claims have been made about 4GLs like NATURAL since the early 1980s, and most people are prepared to admit that a 4GL is likely to increase software productivity *during the programming phase of the project* by as much as tenfold over third-generation languages like COBOL or PL/I. We should not be surprised by similar claims for OO languages like Smalltalk or Eiffel. To the extent that the languages provide single-statement constructs that require 10-100 primitive statements in the older languages, they will naturally be more productive. This is particularly true for today's GUI-oriented applications, where it takes as much as six pages of code in C to simply open a window on the user's screen.

But there is more to the argument than the intrinsic power of the OO programming languages. Indeed, the primary reason why OO projects achieve dramatically higher levels of productivity comes from the extensive *reuse* of classes and objects. We have long known that reuse is one of those silver-bullet technologies with which some organizations have achieved near-miraculous results. In the worst case, a software organization steeped in the "not-invented-here" culture may achieve zero percent reuse. At the other extreme, a few organizations have reported as much as 94 percent reuse as they build applications from common components over and over again.

Object technology achieves reuse through libraries of classes and objects; in particular, through the concepts of encapsulation and inheritance. From a technical perspective, OO-reuse is easier to achieve than reuse in other software development methodologies. After all, objects tend to have a high cohesion because they encapsulate both code and data, so the chances are good that an object can be lifted from one program context and used in another.[1] However, reuse also involves some significant managerial and organizational issues (e.g., reward structures to encourage higher levels of reuse, groups of developers whose primary task is creation of reusable components, cultural changes to overcome the developer's typical attitude that a reusable component couldn't possibly be as good as one that he or she developed, etc.), so object technology cannot be said to guarantee reuse.

Developing applications more rapidly

If productivity in a software project is substantially increased, one would naturally assume that the project will be finished more quickly. But improved productivity is not necessarily synonymous with schedule reduction: is it possible, for example, that object technology might allow a project to be accomplished with three people instead of 30 people, but it could still drag on for three years? What is it about OO that could make it possible for a project schedule to be reduced from three years to three months?

The primary answer is the same as before, reuse. OO software engineers typically have available a robust library of reusable classes and objects, and they can easily create a specialized subclass of an existing object for their own unique needs through the mechanism of inheritance. This not only reduces the time spent for programming, but also for testing (because the reusable classes and objects have already been tested) and for design (because one doesn't have to spend time thinking about *how* to implement the classes and objects). Objects reduce redundant multiple specification of the same processing logic in multiple places in a system by encouraging the specification of each piece of logic only once; in addition, the concept of inheritance allows logic and attributes which are common to different but similar object types to be shared.

But there is an even more powerful reason for the dramatic reduction in OO project schedules: *prototyping*. The classical waterfall methodology, in which the life-cycle activities are carried out sequentially over a long period of time, was often required in structured analysis/design projects, but is typically ignored in OO projects. If you approach an OO application developer in the midst of a project and ask, "What are you doing now?", the answer is likely to be, "A little of everything: a little analysis, a little design, a little coding, and a little testing."

---

[1] A related point: encapsulation also contributes to making an OO component more understandable, because the specification of the object is more easily abstracted away from its possible implementation.

Prototyping and reuse go hand in hand. It is much easier to develop a prototype for the end-user if one has available a robust library of reusable objects. But it takes more than reusable objects to succeed with prototyping. As with reuse, there are significant management, cultural, and organizational issues involved in the change from a waterfall methodology to a prototyping or iterative approach; indeed, the first OO project won't show as much productivity gains as subsequent projects, and several such projects may be necessary before there are enough reusable components to make a significant difference in the organization's productivity. We discuss this further in Chapters 9 and 11.

Additional arguments for object technology

Productivity and rapid systems development are not the only arguments in favor of OO— but they are often the most commonly heard arguments in today's competitive business environment. There are two other justifications one often hears in veteran OO development shops: *quality*, and *maintainability*.

Quality has many dimensions, and it is beyond the scope of this book to explore the topic in detail. However, one important aspect of quality concerns the world view created by the methodology. As Wayne Haythorn[1] and others point out, business people (users) see the world in terms of objects; so a program developed in terms of objects should be more intuitive and understandable than a program organized around some other paradigm. In this book, we describe a systems analysis approach which starts from objects that exist in the user's world. If the design, coding, and maintenance activities can also be done in terms of objects, then the entire software development process will be governed by a single conceptual framework. The same objects which the user sees are present in the implemented system, improving the ease with which the implemented system can be related to the user's requirements. In other words, business professionals and developers should have a greater chance of speaking a common language throughout the project. We expect that this will also add greatly to the overall quality of the application software developed, because there will be fewer inconsistencies of the kind that are normally experienced in the transition from analysis to design to implementation, and greater traceability between user requirements and the implemented system.

There is another important aspect of quality: absence of defects. It can be argued that OO software is more likely to be bug-free than software developed using other methodologies. The greater emphasis on reuse is an important reason for experiencing fewer defects in an OO system. A component that has been reused hundreds of times is more likely to have had the bugs shaken out of it. The other reason is the strong emphasis on *encapsulation*: objects protect themselves and their associated data, so that if one object goes berserk, it is less likely to randomly clobber other objects in the same system.[2] For many OO applications, there is an interesting run-time

---

[1]   Wayne Haythorn, "What is object-oriented design?", Journal of Object-Oriented Programming, Mar-April 1994.

[2]   The degree to which this can actually be accomplished depends on the programming language and the run-time support provided by the compiler, operating system, and even the hardware. A similar degree of

consequence of this principle: if a bug *does* occur, an OO system is more likely to degrade gracefully than conventionally-developed software that often halts abruptly if something goes wrong. There is a tradition in many OO projects which says, "If my object receives a message that it does not understand, it simply replies to its sender that it is unable to process the message, rather than hemorrhaging, running amok, and destroying itself." And, of course, the principle of encapsulation also leads to higher quality during the design phase of the project, long before run-time behavior becomes an issue, by promoting robustness and correctness through modularity of the components.

What about maintainability? Because objects include both data and the behavior associated with that data, changes to data or behavior tend to be localized. The interface with other objects is small and well-defined, and because of encapsulation, the impact of any change on other objects is kept to a minimum. Advocates of OO point out that rather than basing the overall architecture of the system on a hierarchy of functions (which tends to be rather volatile, as end-users change their ideas about what functions they want the system to carry out), the architecture is based on a network of collaborating objects which tends, like data, to have a more stable structure, especially for business applications. Because of encapsulation, an object can be replaced with a new implementation—sometimes while the rest of the system is running—without affecting the other objects.[1]

Reasons for Abandoning Old Methodologies

In some elections, a politician is elected because everyone voted *against* the other candidate. Similarly, some organizations are adopting object technology because they have found that traditional methodologies no longer meet their needs. The reasons for this shift are:

- *Problems with older methodologies*—especially the structured or information engineering methodologies which separate the process (function) model from the data model. In practice, the two models are often developed by separate teams of people, using separate CASE tools. When it comes time to combine the two models, incompatibilities and contradictions are discovered—and the process often degenerates into a political argument about which of the two models will be accepted as the dominant (correct) one. The other model is often discarded, leaving the project to continue with only half of its essential characteristics documented in a formal model. One could argue

---

encapsulation could be accomplished in older methodologies like structured design but typically is not. The culture and the mindset of encapsulation tends to be stronger and more pervasive in OO projects.

[1] It should be emphasized that widespread use of OO methodologies is so new that we have few, if any, large OO-based applications that have survived a 5-year or 10-year maintenance period. Though there is some anecdotal evidence supporting the claim of improved maintainability, there are also some serious skeptics who argue that OO-based systems could turn out to be more difficult to maintain than conventionally-designed software, because of the relatively "flat" architecture involving hundreds of objects all sending messages to one another. See the discussion of "modules" in Chapter 8 to help deal with this issue.

that the problem here is not with the methodology, but rather with the organizational culture. But as a practical matter, if the methodology is incompatible with the culture, it will fail — and the organization is more likely to cast blame on the methodology than on itself.

An even more serious problem occurs in some organizations, because end-users don't understand *either* of the models that are being presented to them. Unfortunately, the traditional models that we've used for analysis and design (e.g., data flow diagrams and entity-relationship diagrams) are sometimes perceived as abstract or technical by the user. This has been a serious enough problem in some organizations that the traditional methodologies have been abandoned in favor of an OO approach, so that the systems analysts can talk to users in terms of objects which they *recognize* in their own world.[1]

It could also be argued that many organizations have abandoned older methodologies because it was too difficult to enforce consistency between the analysis model, design model, and implemented code. In the midst of a high-pressure development project, it's very difficult to keep the analysis/design models synchronized with the implementation. With the "single-model" approach used by OO methodologies, it's easier to retain an up-to-date analysis/design model, even when changes to the implementation are made.

- *Radically different types of systems being developed*—the earlier generation of methodologies was designed for the mainframe, batch, 3rd generation days. Today's systems involve PCs, client-server networks, distributed processing, and (perhaps most importantly) graphical user interfaces; some project managers have said, "We abandoned the old methodologies because, in this new world, they simply don't work. Our projects are guaranteed to fail unless we adopt an OO approach." In addition, today's systems are often ten times larger than the systems of the 1970s and early 1980s,[2] and they are taking place in a much more competitive environment that requires delivery of finished applications as quickly as possible; hence the issues of productivity and speed of development have become crucial, and concepts such as reuse have evolved from a whimsical Boy Scout virtue to a critical success factor.

- *Radically different programming languages, development environments, and CASE tools*— one reason we didn't use OO development technologies in the 1970s is that we didn't have any available. We didn't use them in the 1980s because we weren't aware of the early versions of Smalltalk and C++. Until recently, there were no OO CASE tools; there were no commercial libraries of reusable classes and objects. We tend to use the technology that is available to us. So when COBOL is upgraded to OO-COBOL and

---

[1] Of course, it's also possible that the problem was caused by the systems analyst's incompetence, or inability to model the system in the *user's* terms. If this was the cause of the problem, then it shouldn't be blamed on the older methodologies; and it should also be understood that the same problems could occur with object-oriented methodologies.

[2] Maintenance gurus such as Nicholas Zvegintzov have published reports showing that vintage-1990 legacy systems are 50 times larger than vintage-1980 systems.

NATURAL is updated to OO-NATURAL, it is reasonable to expect that the software development community will gradually take advantage of the new technology.[1]

Reasons not to Use OO Technology

Are there circumstances when one should *not* use object technology? The skeptics in a conservative DP organization—who often have a considerable investment in older tools, methods, reputations, and political empires—might well respond to this question, "If we wait for a couple of years, it will all blow over, and we can get back to business as usual!"

It's difficult to imagine that we will ever return to business as usual, if that means the kind of software development that often took place in the 1970s; moreover, the steadily growing popularity of object technology makes it increasingly difficult to dismiss it as a short-term fad. But this does not necessarily mean that OO should be the highest priority for a software development organization attempting to improve its productivity and quality.

In many organizations, for example, peopleware is the area where the greatest leverage can be obtained. Before concentrating on OO, it would be wise to ensure that the software development organization is staffed by talented people who are well trained, well motivated, and surrounded by a supportive infrastructure. In other organizations, the fundamental problem is the lack of a well-defined software process. The organization is populated by cowboy programmers who operate in a state of utter anarchy described by the Software Engineering Institute as "level-1."[2]

---

[1] If you *don't* have an object-oriented programming language available, should you still consider object-oriented analysis and design? In theory, it should be possible, for analysis/design activities should be independent of the programming language; in practice, it often doesn't work very well — inevitably, as linguists have pointed out, the way we form concepts in our mind is influenced by the language we have available to us. If you're going to do a good job with OOA and OOD, we recommend making the transition to an OOPL or implementation technology that supports object concepts.

[2] In other words, introducing object technology into an organization that operates at level-1 on the Software Engineering Institute's process maturity model is unlikely to bring any sustained improvement; indeed, many consultants advise that your organization should be at level-3 before attempting large-scale OO projects. For more details on the SEI model, see Watts Humphrey's *Managing the Software Process* (Reading, MA: Addison-Wesley, 1989) and more recent discussions in the July 1993 issue of *IEEE Software* and September 1994 issue of *American Programmer*.

The 1991/1993 survey by Systems Development Inc. that showed object technology was used by only 3.8% of projects in 1991 and 11.9% in 1993 also documented the reasons why the remaining majority chose *not* to use OO; their reasons are instructive:

REASONS FOR NOT USING OO TECHNOLOGY

Reason	1991	1993
Not aware of technology	31.0%	13.2%
Benefits not demonstrated	3.5%	19.3%
No business need	17.2%	3.5%
Technology too costly	0.9%	2.6%
Organization unprepared	19.8%	19.3%
Technology too immature	19.8%	36.8%
Other	7.8%	5.3%

The organizations who report that they have not seen a demonstration of the business benefits, and those who argue that there *is* no business need, may simply be following a conservative path, and (or) may still be living in a mainframe, batch-oriented, non-GUI world. The world *will* change for these people, and when it does, they will be more likely to embrace OO, even if that change occurs slowly. Indeed, this is evident from the changes in these two categories between 1991 and 1993.

The most sobering item in this survey is the group reporting that its organization is unprepared for object technology. The lack of preparation may involve training, familiarity with new concepts, "technology-transfer" problems, arguments over the advisability of introducing object technology in a revolutionary versus evolutionary approach, or a more fundamental problem involving the lack of a formal, standardized SEI level-3 systems development process. We discuss several of these issues in Part III of this book. Organizations in this category are realists. No matter how wonderful object technology may be, it will fail if the organization is not ready for it. Most sobering of all: this category remained virtually constant between 1991 and 1993.

Note also that nearly 20 percent of the respondents in 1991 argued that the technology is too immature, and that this figure has almost doubled between 1991 and 1993. The skeptics in this category often argue that there are too many OO analysis and design methodologies, each with its own vocabulary, rules, and diagramming notation. Others point to a lack of industrial-strength OO CASE tools, languages, class libraries, or other components of technology. While each of these points might be debated, it is difficult to argue that OO is a mature technology[1] in the same way that relational DBMSs, structured techniques, and information engineering is mature. For these organizations, the reaction to object technology is typically "not now" or "not yet." But from the surveys presented at the beginning of this chapter, a majority of application development organizations expect to be using object technology within the next few years.

Obviously, these issues are also of concern to software product companies, language developers, and tool builders like Software AG. A 4GL vendor has an advantage in this area, because object concepts can be added to the language in an evolutionary fashion, without requiring one's customers to go through the arduous process of learning an entirely new language like C++[2]. As a 4GL vendor, Software AG is also well-positioned to make object technology more accessible for mainstream commercial use, by delivering the kind of mature technology that is needed for OO to be adopted for serious use by mainstream commercial application developers.

Conclusion

Some organizations may indeed have valid reasons for postponing or even avoiding the transition from traditional methodologies to object-oriented methodologies. But for a larger and larger percentage of application development groups today, the potential benefits of productivity and quality improvements, coupled with the problems and weaknesses of older methodologies, makes the decision more and more inevitable. For most organizations, the question is no longer "if" they should adopt object technologies, but simply "when."

---

[1] Some organizations might argue that OO is mature. Ericsson made a fundamental commitment to an OO approach as early as 1976. Apple Computer has been using object technology for much of their systems software for over a decade. But these are isolated examples and do not represent the mainstream of DP organizations.

[2] Of course, C++ is just an evolutionary development from the original C language. But for the application developer who previously worked only in COBOL, it's quite a revolutionary change!

Chapter 2

Fundamental Object-Oriented Concepts and Principles

Since this book discusses object-oriented methods and processes in great detail, we felt that it would be useful to summarize some of the fundamental object-oriented concepts and principles. Readers familiar with the basics of OO may wish to skip to the next chapter, but most newcomers to the field should study these definitions and principles carefully, as they form the basis for the discussions that follow.

Definitions of Object and Object Class

Before we discuss the finer points of object orientation—e.g., inheritance, encapsulation, etc.—we need to begin with the basics. What is an object? What is a class?

From a business user's perspective, it is often sufficient to say that an *object* is a person, a place, or a thing. A **Customer** is an object, and so is an **Employee**. An **Invoice** is an object, but a **zipCode (postalCode)** probably is not. **BankAccount** sounds like a reasonable object, but **computeMonthlyInterest** probably is not. The key principle of object-orientation is the bringing together of data and function. An object contains a well-defined data structure together with a set of operations that specifically describe how the data can be manipulated.

In an object-oriented system (or application), objects are the basic unit that we use to modularize the system, rather than functional processing units. For business data processing applications, this usually means that the modularization is based on the data in the application. This is usually advantageous, because the data structure for a business application is more stable than its functional requirements. By contrast, the objects in a real-time system might not contain any data but consist only of some functionality that is invoked when the object receives a message.

Access to the data and functionality of an object is only available by using the operations associated with it. Each operation has a defined interface, consisting of its name (e.g., **changeCustomerCreditLimit**) and a list of input and output arguments. The operations provide the external view of an object, with which other objects can use the functionality that the object provides.

The internals of any object are private; some OO enthusiasts like to say that "objects encapsulate secrets." This encapsulation of the internal implementation details improves maintainability by minimizing the effect of any change to the internals of one object on other objects. Additionally, combining related data and function together in an object means that closely related information is likely to be found in the same object, thus increasing the likelihood that changes to an object will affect only that object.

When an object wishes to use the functionality provided by another object, it does so by sending a message which invokes one of the receiving object's operations. The message contains the name of the operation which is to be invoked, and a list of input and output argument values.

An object's data structure is described in terms of its attributes. For example, the attributes of a **Customer** object might include **name, address, creditLimit**, etc. *Attributes* are data values which are associated with and closely connected to the object. They describe the object, rather than having an independent existence of their own. In some applications, **address** might not be considered an attribute, because it might be meaningful to consider an "address" as an independent object by itself (which would imply that it has operations, and can receive messages, etc.). On the other hand, one would expect a relationship to exist between a putative **Address** object and a **Customer** object; relationships (e.g., a customer resides at address) represent information about an object which is similar to that represented by attributes. Relationships are regarded in our OO approach as a type of attribute.

Objects are grouped together into *object classes*, sometimes referred to simply as a *class*. An object class is used to describe a group of objects which can be considered to be of the same type. An object class can be viewed as a template for an object. Objects belonging to an object class have similar behavior and common attributes and semantics.

Alternative Definitions of Class and Object

As mentioned in the preface, the objective of our approach was to integrate the best concepts from all of the existing popular OO approaches. This was relatively easy to do in terms of basic definitions, for the authors of popular OO books and methodologies have only slightly different nuances in their descriptions of an object. For example, the Object Management Group (OMG), an influential non-profit consortium, offers the following definition:

> *An object is a thing. It is created as the instance of an object type. Each object has a unique identity that is distinct from and independent of any of its characteristics. Each object offers one or more operations.* [1]

Don Firesmith provides the following definition in his book:

> *An **object** is defined as a software abstraction that models all relevant aspects of a single tangible or conceptual entity or thing from the application domain or solution space. An object is one of the primary software entities in an object-oriented application, typically corresponds to a software module, and consists of a set of related attribute types, attributes, messages, exceptions, operations, and optional component objects.* [2]

---

[1] *Object Analysis and Design, Volume 1: Reference Model.* Draft 7.0, page 32 (Framingham, MA: Object Management Group, October 1, 1992).

[2] Donald G. Firesmith, *Object-Oriented Requirements Analysis and Design: A Software Engineering Approach* page 29. New York:John Wiley and Sons, 1993

Grady Booch offers a slightly different perspective:

> *From the perspective of human cognition, an object is any of the following:*
>
> •   *A tangible and/or visible thing*
>
> •   *Something that may be apprehended intellectually*
>
> •   *Something toward which thought or action is directed*
>
> *An object has state, behavior, and identity; the structure and behavior of similar objects are defined in their common class; the terms instance and object are interchangeable.*[1]

Pete Coad and Ed Yourdon defined object as follows in their first book on the subject:

> *Object. An* abstraction *of something in a problem domain, reflecting the capabilities of the system to keep information about it, interact with it, or both; an* encapsulation *of Attribute values and their exclusive Services. (synonym: an Instance).*[2]

Sally Shlaer and Stephen Mellor offer a similar explanation:

> *An* object *is an abstraction of a set of real-world things such that*
>
> •   *all the things in the set—the instances—have the same characteristics, and*
>
> •   *all instances are subject to and conform to the same set of rules and policies.*[3]

The definition provided by Ivar Jacobson, et al. is admirably succinct:

> *An **object** is characterised by a number of operations and a state which remembers the effect of these operations.*[4]

Finally, James Martin and James Odell offer an equally succinct definition of an object:

> *An object is any thing, real or abstract, about which we store data and those methods which manipulate the data.*[5]

There are common elements in these definitions that we use through the remainder of the book:

•   An object is a real-world thing *or* an abstraction of that thing. It is equally meaningful to talk about a real-world object like a pencil, or about a software representation of a pencil

---

[1]   Grady Booch, *Object-Oriented Analysis and Design with Applications* (Redwood City, CA: The Benjamin/Cummings Publishing Company, 1994)

[2]   Peter Coad and Edward Yourdon, *Object-Oriented Analysis*, 2nd edition, page 53 (Englewood Cliffs, NJ: Yourdon Press/Prentice Hall, 1991)

[3]   Sally Shlaer and Stephen J. Mellor, *Object Life Cycles: Modeling the World in States.* (Englewood Cliffs, NJ: Yourdon Press/Prentice Hall, 1992)

[4]   Ivar Jacobson, Magnus Christerson, Patrik Jonsson, and Gunnar Övergaard, *Object-Oriented Software Engineering: A Use Case Driven Approach.* (Reading, MA: Addison-Wesley, 1992)

[5]   James Martin and James J. Odell, *Object-Oriented Analysis and Design.* (Englewood Cliffs, NJ: Prentice Hall, 1992)

which we intend to specify, design, and eventually program. Computer people tend to deal almost exclusively in abstractions; thus, we automatically think of a pencil in terms of how we will represent it in some binary format, how we will arrange lists and arrays of pencils, etc. But during the analysis portion of a systems development project, we are dealing with users for whom abstractions are often irrelevant, confusing, and difficult. To a user, a pencil is more likely to be the physical object, consisting of a stick of graphite surrounded by yellow-painted wood. Please remember that while most of the objects that *we* talk about are abstract objects, many of our users prefer to think in terms of real objects.

- A real-world object can be tangible or intangible. Embley, Kurtz and Woodfield make a similar distinction between physical objects and conceptual objects[1], as does Firesmith. A pencil, as discussed above, is clearly tangible: we can touch it, bite it, and use it to make markings on paper. But there are many other objects that are far less tangible, but nevertheless important and meaningful to our end-users: plans, strategies, styles, directions, etc. It might be convenient to classify these intangible objects as "abstract," in the sense used above—but *our* abstractions are typically quite different from the user's abstractions. An end-user might think of a plan in terms of a textual description or a series of flowcharts and diagrams; a software engineer might have a very different abstraction of that same intangible object.

- An object is a single occurrence, or instance of a real-world thing or abstraction. Thus, when discussing people, we recognize that John is an object and Mary is a different object. Implicit in this statement—but quite essential to an OO methodology—is the assumption that each object/instance can be uniquely identified, and distinguished from other objects.

In many discussions of basic OO principles, it doesn't matter whether we refer to an object class, or the objects within the object class. Our choice of object or object class will sometimes depend on what sounds more natural in the context of the discussion.

The Key Characteristics of Object-Orientation

From the previous discussion, it is obvious that any OO software development methodology must be based on objects and classes. But what else is involved? What are the key features of the OO paradigm? In this book, we emphasize four fundamental characteristics of an object-oriented method for developing systems.

Abstraction

Abstraction is a mechanism that allows us to represent a complex reality (e.g., a set of detailed components) in terms of a simplified model (e.g., a single higher-level component), so that

---

[1]   David W. Embley, Barry D. Kurtz, and Scott N. Woodfield, *Object-Oriented Systems Analysis: A Model-Driven Approach.* (Englewood Cliffs, NJ: Yourdon Press/Prentice Hall, 1992)

irrelevant details can be suppressed in order to enhance understanding of the overall system.[1] Of course, all software development approaches incorporate some kind of abstraction—e.g., a "top-down design" methodology is usually based on the concept of decomposing functions into smaller, simpler sub-functions. OO methods are based primarily on the notion of abstracting *objects* into *classes*. However functional abstraction does play a role in some OO methodologies.

Encapsulation

Encapsulation is any mechanism that allows us to hide the implementation of the object, so that other components of the system will not be aware of (or be able to take advantage of) the innards of the data stored in the object.[2] As a practical matter, this means that an object's data (or attributes) and the functions that operate on the data (whose external, visible manifestation constitutes its operations) are packaged together. Not only is this important as a programming mechanism, but also as a design and analysis concept. Most earlier methodologies went to great lengths to separate the data and functional components of a system. The other practical consequence of this concept is that an OO system depends heavily on communication between objects. The communication takes the form of messages which are sent to specific operations within the receiving object.

Inheritance

Inheritance is a relationship between object classes which allows one object class to include (reuse) the attributes and operations defined for another more general object class. The more general class is called the superclass, and the more specific class is called a subclass. The subclass/superclass relationship structures the object classes of a system into an inheritance hierarchy. In practical terms, this usually means that OO systems involve hierarchies of objects, with subordinate objects inheriting all or part of their definition (i.e., the definition of their attributes and their functional behavior) from higher-level parents or superclasses. Some OO methods allow a subclass to have only one superclass; this is called single inheritance. Others allow an object class to have more than one superclass; this is called multiple inheritance.

Polymorphism

A subclass may override the implementation of an operation that it inherits from a superclass. When the operation is invoked, the caller does not need to know which implementation of the operation to select. Instead, the object-oriented system selects the version of the operation appropriate to the object in question. This is known as *polymorphism*, which refers to the fact that the same operation (or object type) may have many forms. This means that an object can send a

---

[1]   A good discussion of this perspective on abstraction can be found in *Basic Reference Model for Open Distributed Processing - Part 2: Descriptive Model* (ISO/IEC JTC1/SC21/WG7, DIS 10746-2, Feb. 1994)

[2]   Veteran software engineers will find this a familiar concept: techniques such as David Parnas's information hiding have been well known since the 1970s. But what makes the OO approach different is that such concepts are typically enforced (through CASE tools and/or OO programming languages) and combined with the other OO concepts of abstraction and inheritance.

message to another object without necessarily knowing (or caring about) the precise class to which the object belongs. Thus, the message move might be sent to an animal object, without knowing whether that object is a fish, a bird, a snake, or a mammal. Each of these different types of animals knows how to interpret the move message—e.g., by swimming, flying, wiggling, or walking—thereby eliminating the necessity of the sending object to first ask, "What kind of object are you?" and then sending a specific message like swim.[1]

It is hard to imagine any software engineering methodology—or any of the CASE tools, languages, and packages that application developers use to build systems—that do not have some form of abstraction. For object-oriented methodologies and systems, the key point is that the abstraction used is objects and object classes. In addition to this, the presence or absence of encapsulation, inheritance, and polymorphism determines the degree to which the methodology/tool/language can legitimately be called "object-oriented."

Some vendors describe their products as object-based, or object-compatible, or object-like in order to associate the magical marketing properties of the "O" word without actually lying. Object-based, for example, is frequently used to describe programming languages like Ada83 or Visual Basic which have the fundamental property of encapsulation but lack the fundamental property of inheritance.[2] As for other marketing terms, the best advice is *caveat emptor*.

Additional OO Concepts

Does the term object-oriented imply anything above and beyond the fundamental characteristics of abstraction, encapsulation, inheritance, and polymorphism? One concept that is quite useful, and which will be discussed in more detail in later chapters of this book, is *aggregation*, which allows a composite object to be described in terms of the objects of which it consists (e.g., a **Person** consists of a **Head**, two **Arm**s, and two **Leg**s). Aggregation can be regarded as a relationship which is looser or less close than the relationship between an attribute and the object it describes. On the other hand, aggregation is tighter than the type of relationship between two independent objects such as **Customer** and **Order**. Attributes have no independent existence apart from the object they describe. Objects, on the other hand, have an independent existence apart from any aggregate, but can be brought together via aggregation into assemblies or composite objects, which then appear externally to be like a single object.

What about reuse? Many of the earlier methodologies treated reuse as a Boy Scout virtue (like loyalty, bravery, and thrift) without offering any specific strategies or techniques for accomplishing it, while the OO concept provides a technical basis for reusability, through its emphasis on encapsulated, single-purpose objects, and through the mechanism of inheritance. We

---

[1] In a software environment, a similar example might be the "display yourself" message sent to an object in the "figure" class, or a "compute your current balance" message sent to an object in the "invoice" class.

[2] Peter Wegner's more technical definition has gained some acceptance: an *object-based* approach (or language) supports abstract data types, while an *object-oriented* approach (or language) also supports inheritance and polymorphism. See "Concepts and paradigms of object-oriented computing," Peter Wegner, *OOPS Messenger*, Vol. 1, No. 1, 1990.

can't say that an OO methodology guarantees that an organization will enjoy higher levels of reuse, because, as mentioned earlier, it also involves significant management support and organizational issues. On the other hand, we can say that OO guarantees the technical ability to reuse components; in a technical sense, reuse is free with OO.[1]

Not included on our list of key characteristics of object-orientation are two items identified by Grady Booch: concurrency and persistence. Booch defines concurrency as "the property that distinguishes an active object from one that is not active." He goes on to argue that:

> *One of the realities about concurrency is that once you introduce it into a system, you must consider how active objects synchronize their activities with one another as well as with objects that are purely sequential. In the presence of concurrency, it is not enough simply to define the methods of an object; we must also make certain that the semantics of these methods are preserved in the presence of multiple threads of control.*

For obvious reasons, emphasis on the concurrency characteristics of a system typically occurs in the realm of programming and design. For real-time and on-line systems, it may also be a sufficiently important issue that it will be represented in the analysis model, after discussions with the user. On the other hand, there is one respect in which concurrency is a key object-oriented concept. This is because objects are conceived as relatively independent entities that interact, and maintain their state, between calls to them. Thus, objects *exist* concurrently with other objects, even if in most OOPLs only one object can be active at any one time.

Similarly, the concept of persistence is often discussed within the context of OO methodologies: some objects are transient, and disappear shortly after they are created, while other objects persist long after the execution of the associated program that created them.

Booch defines persistence as follows:

> *Persistence is the property of an object through which its existence transcends time (i.e., the object continues to exist after its creator ceases to exist) and/or space (i.e., the object's location moves from the address space in which it was created.*

Traditional programming languages typically deal only with relatively transient data—e.g., variables which exist only within a block of code, or during the execution of the program. Data that survives between different versions of the same program, or from one transaction to the next, or that outlives the very existence of the program, has traditionally fallen under the control of database management systems (DBMS). In OO systems, such a distinction between the programming language and the DBMS is typically blurred considerably.[2] Persistence is an issue of

---

[1] From an organizational perspective, reuse is *not* free: it requires a substantial investment in an organizational infrastructure to encourage, support, maintain and manage the reusable components.

[2] Conventional DBMSs have always provided for the storage of persistent data, but have rarely provided any mechanism for storage of the methods associated with that persistent data. This is changing with recent DBMS products that allow stored procedures or triggers to be stored along with the data; but since an OO approach encapsulates data and function together, it is important to indicate which objects are transient and which are persistent.

concern in the design and programming stages of a project, and typically not discussed in great detail during the analysis stage (where it is usually assumed that all objects are persistent). We don't consider persistence to be one of the key characteristics of an OO approach so much as a necessary secondary concept. The issue of how an OO methodology deals with persistence at the design and implementation stage will be discussed in Part IV of the book.

Finally, we mention the concept of *visibility*, which is particularly relevant in the design and implementation of object-oriented systems. Objects, and particularly the operations they contain, may be treated as public or private. Some OOPLs, such as C++, have additional mechanisms for describing the degree of visibility associated with an object. An object's public operations can be invoked or accessed by any other object within the system. Private operations can only be invoked by other operations within the same object; and it may also be desirable to define operations that are visible to members of a class hierarchy, but *not* to objects outside the hierarchy. During discussions with the user in the business analysis and requirements definition phase of a project, it is typically appropriate to regard all of an object's attributes as private, and all of its operations as public. During the design and implementation phases of the project, these decisions need to be re-examined.

While many commercially available OOA and OOD methodologies address the OO issues differently, all of them provide some mechanism for implementing the fundamental concepts.

Chapter 3

Selected Object-Oriented Modeling Techniques

A review of the current OO textbooks and vendor marketing literature indicates that the term "object-oriented" is used, at various times, to describe programming techniques, or analysis techniques, or combinations of design and programming, etc. Before we plunge into the details of our approach, we have devoted this chapter to explaining which modeling techniques we believe should be included in an object-oriented development approach. The emphasis in this chapter is on explaining *why* we include the different techniques rather than providing details about them. The details of each technique are described later in this book. Part II provides an overview of each type of model introduced in this chapter and Part III describes how the models are used during the different phases of the development life cycle.

Coverage of the Project Life Cycle

A complete object-oriented development approach should include coverage of the following life cycle phases:

- Project definition and planning
- Analysis
  - Business analysis
  - System requirements analysis
- Design
  - Logical design
  - Physical design
- Construction
  - Development
  - Test
  - Documentation
- Acceptance and Cutover
- Operation, including application support.

Despite the popular focus on programming languages like C++ and Smalltalk in the marketplace, we strongly believe that object-oriented techniques have a special relevance during analysis and design, as well as construction. Indeed, from the methodological point of view, analysis and design are the most significant phases to be addressed, and we therefore concentrate on these areas in this book.

The Evolution of Object-Oriented Analysis and Design Techniques

The initial focus of object-oriented methodologies and approaches, historically speaking, was on programming issues. Only recently have we begun to see a recognition of the importance of using an appropriate, and relatively formal, analysis and design approach when developing a system to be implemented in an object-oriented programming language. Although the importance of this is increasingly recognized, object-oriented analysis and design is still seen, in many organizations and many development projects, as a side-issue relatively speaking. Because of this historical context, many of the earlier object-oriented analysis and design approaches have naturally taken the basic concepts of object-oriented programming as their starting point and have then gradually extended or adapted these in the light of requirements which are specific to systems analysis and design. See Appendix A for notes on some of the other current object-oriented analysis and design approaches.

Many of the earlier object-oriented analysis and design approaches have also demonstrated strong links with traditional structured analysis and design techniques. This has led some OO purists to reject them, claiming that they are not object-oriented.

In an object-oriented development approach, the object structure model—which we describe in the next section—is the fundamental model that provides a common way of modeling the system from analysis through to implementation. For specific analysis and design activities, however, additional techniques are useful, and these can be arranged around this core model. We explain in this chapter which techniques we regard as useful, starting with the object structure model.

The Object Structure Model

The object structure model identifies the object classes that are involved in the application development project; it identifies inheritance, aggregation and relationships between objects, and it also identifies the attributes and operations of objects. The ability to describe these aspects is clearly essential, and must be covered in any object-oriented analysis and design approach.

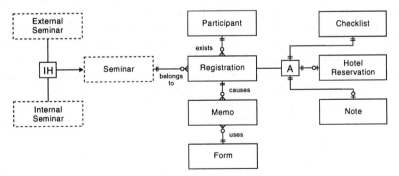

Figure 3-1: Extract from an object structure diagram

One of the basic principles of object orientation is the bringing together of data and function in objects. Another basic principle is that the implementation of the system should also be structured in terms of objects. So objects, as a building block or atomic unit, naturally occupy center-stage in an OO approach, and the object structure model—which illustrates the basic organization and architecture of the objects in an application—has pride of place in our object-oriented development approach, as indeed in all popular OO methodologies.

The object structure model reduces the gap between the user's business requirements and the developer's technical model of the system's implementation by describing these two in a compatible way. During the process of analysis and design, the object structure model is defined in increasing detail, until the level of detail necessary for implementation is reached.

For the analysis phase of a project, object orientation offers specific benefits because it facilitates discussions with users, who can talk in terms of objects which they can recognize in their own world. This is in stark contrast to what we see in many projects today, where users are required to articulate and negotiate their requirements in terms of functional DFD "bubbles" and normalized data structures,where objects are broken up into constituent parts.

Object orientation also offers a single development paradigm which allows the application to be described in the same terms (i.e., in terms of objects) from analysis through to implementation. The same objects which the user sees in the real world are present in the implemented system. Even though the implemented system typically requires additional objects, beyond those the user understands and works with in the real-world, the objects the user understands are still visible and recognizable in the end result. This makes it easier to relate the implemented system to the user's requirements.

Two aspects of the object structure diagram which are not handled in the same way in all OO analysis and design approaches are the modeling of static relationships between objects and the modeling of constraints. With respect to static relationships, for example, Jacobson's approach uses unidirectional relationships, while most others choose to model bidirectional relationships. We prefer to regard relationships as inherently bidirectional. Chapter 19 provides more information on this topic.

Like Rumbaugh[1] and Coad/Yourdon, we also include constraints among our object structure modeling techniques. This is a way of specifying declaratively, as part of the object structure model, constraints on the values an attribute or a relationship may take. This means that important information affecting the integrity of the structure and data of objects can be clearly and separately specified, and is not unnecessarily buried in the detail of the operations associated with each object class. It also means that constraints can be specified before the decision has been made as to how the constraints are to be enforced. Constraints could be enforced by checking of user input or via database-level triggers as well as (or instead of) in the operations of the object classes they affect.

---

[1]   J. Rumbaugh, M. Blaha, W. Premerlani, F. Eddy, W. Lorensen, *Object-Oriented Modeling and Design.* (Englewood Cliffs, NJ: Prentice Hall, 1991).

Like Jacobson, we distinguish between three types of object class:

- Entity objects which are usually directly recognizable in the business domain,

- Interface objects which contain logic relating to the system's external interfaces, and

- Control objects that contain logic that does not naturally belong in entity and interface objects.

We distinguish these three types because it makes explicit the different possible uses of objects in the object model. It reminds the developer that the obvious real-world objects are not the only ones required when building a system and encourages a clearly thought-through allocation of functionality to appropriate object classes. If the developer has these issues in mind, the result should be a more robust object structure. Any later changes to functionality should have minimal impact on the object structure and be restricted to a small number of object classes.

Why Additional Models are Required

The first generation of object-oriented analysis and design approaches concentrated primarily on the object structure model. While the object structure model has the central role in any object-oriented analysis and design approach, additional models are necessary for a complete, practical analysis and design method. These additional models feed information into the core object structure model and assist with tasks which are specific to analysis and design, such as:

- eliciting requirements,

- acquiring a clear understanding of system requirements including how objects change dynamically over time,

- documenting requirements in a form such that the customer can check that the system developers have understood the requirements,

- specifying requirements in sufficient detail that developers can build a system which fulfills the customers' requirements and the implemented system can be checked to ensure it does indeed fulfill those requirements, and

- handling the development of systems which are large or complex enough to require breaking down into more manageable units.

We regard the following model types as essential to handle these tasks:

- the transaction sequence model, extended with business process modeling during business analysis and enhanced with object interaction modeling during logical design, for mapping of system requirements to the operations that support these requirements.

- the object life cycle model, which plays an essential role when modeling objects with complex behavior patterns.

- system-wide modeling, which breaks down a complex problem into manageable or presentable units and allows the interfaces between these units to be described.

We discuss each of these additional models in the sections that follow.

Business Process Modeling and the Transaction Sequence Model

Modeling system requirements

One important aspect of an application development project which the object structure model does not cover adequately is the modeling of system requirements. If we consider the object structure model on its own, all of the functionality is defined at a very fine level of granularity. In an object-oriented system, the processing logic is to be found in operations embedded within objects, and each operation is typically concerned only with a single "microscopic" aspect of the user's requirements.

To appreciate just how microscopic the operations are, here is an interesting observation: when an operation is eventually implemented in a programming language, it frequently consists of fewer than ten lines of code. There is nothing wrong with this as a way of structuring an implementation. However, it makes it difficult to see exactly what system functionality is supported by looking only at the operations in the object structure model. It is also difficult, in the early stages of a project, to bridge the gap between the identification of the user's requirements for the system (which are typically expressed in rather broad generalities) and the identification of fine-grained operations.

If we use the object structure model on its own, we fail to even acknowledge that requirements exist, and that there must be some way of documenting these requirements and some way of verifying that the system meets these requirements. The object structure model can express how requirements will be fulfilled (in terms of objects and operations), but it provides no backward traceability. It is not possible to identify any given requirement in the model or to check that a specific requirement is satisfied by what is contained in the model.

For these reasons, we take the view that a model of the required system functionality should be included in an object-oriented development approach, and included explicitly, not simply assumed to exist prior to starting development as it is in some methods. For this purpose, we use what we call the transaction sequence model. This provides a means of modeling system requirements at an appropriate level of granularity. As we explain next, it also assists with the identification of operations and with traceability.

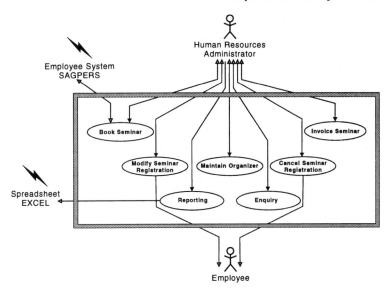

Figure 3-2: Example of a transaction sequence diagram

Our transaction sequences are effectively what Jacobson calls "use cases". We think the term use case is a very powerful metaphor: it links the idea that we should model the possible ways of using the system with the idea that these ways should be partitioned into separate cases. However, use case is an awkward phrase in conversational English. We prefer to use the term transaction sequence. Transaction sequence expresses the content of what is modeled and harmonizes with Jacobson's own definition, since Jacobson often defines a use case as a "sequence of transactions".

Each transaction sequence describes a service which the user requires from the system. A transaction sequence includes the whole sequence of interactions between the user and the system that is required to complete an item of work which is a meaningful whole from the user's perspective. Such a sequence of interactions might involve separate interactions with the system on different days. It might also involve more than one user.

Transaction sequences are valuable in providing users and developers with a means of communicating which addresses system requirements from a standpoint that is meaningful to the user. Transaction sequences focus the development of the system on the specific requirements for that system.

An analysis of transaction sequences can be used to derive the object structure model. Often the two models will be derived in parallel, as we will discuss later in this book.

Transaction sequences, supported by the use of object interaction diagrams also offer a powerful starting point for the identification of operations. Object interaction diagrams show how messages, which are passed between objects to invoke operations, can provide the processing required for a given transaction sequence. This way of using object interaction diagrams to model transaction sequences, which we take from Jacobson, offers a convincing technique for bridging the gap between requirements and operations, by providing assistance with the identification of required operations. Moreover, once a system has been developed, object interaction diagrams offer a way of finding what objects and operations are used to provide specific system functionality, thus providing traceability.

Rumbaugh (in common with several other writers) has a similar concept to a transaction sequence which he calls a scenario. Scenarios are used to describe a "typical dialog between user and system to get a feel for expected system behavior". These scenarios are used to check that the objects and operations which have been specified are able to meet the requirements of the system. Scenarios differ, however, from transaction sequences in that they describe a *specific* possible course of events. As Rumbaugh puts it in an article in the June 1993 *Journal of Object-Oriented Programming*, a use case (transaction sequence) can be seen as a "group ... of prototypical scenarios that describe different ways for external actors to use the system". Transaction sequences describe more generically a sequence of interactions between the user (or users) and the system that enables the user to carry out some business activity. And we think that these general cases should be modeled in order to adequately model requirements.

Modeling object interactions

When an object wishes to use the functionality provided by another object, it does so by sending a message which invokes one of the receiving object's operations. This is what we call an *object interaction*. A whole series of object interactions is typically required in order to provide any significant service to the user. Figure 3-3 is an example of an object interaction diagram.

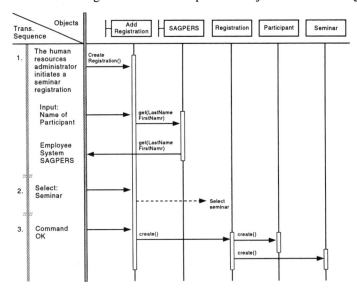

Figure 3-3: Example of an object interaction diagram

Object interaction diagrams provide a useful technique for modeling the series of object interactions that are required to support transaction sequences, assisting in the identification of operations and the validation of the design. In our view, they should be included in every object-oriented analysis and design approach. They also assist in understanding how a system which has been developed actually works, making it possible to see how control is transferred between objects as they interact.

Modeling business processes

Few, if any, object-oriented analysis and design methods provide good support for business analysis at the beginning of a project. The scope of most methods is restricted to the system development process itself—and the modeling of the business, which should usually precede system development, is ignored.

We regard business analysis as an important aspect of the full development life cycle. Because of its importance, we have found it necessary to introduce techniques for use during business analysis. We describe business analysis in detail in Chapter 12.

Most of the techniques which are relevant for system development generally are also useful for business analysis. In addition to these standard techniques and models, we consider the modeling of business processes to be relevant for business analysis.

A *business process* describes the sequence of events, from start to finish, which is required to produce a significant business result, product or service. It takes one or more kinds of input and creates an output that is of value to the customer. This process-oriented view is significantly different from a typical function-oriented view, in which a business function (e.g., accounting) describes an activity included in one or more business processes, which is carried out by a specific department within the organization.

Modeling of business processes usually emphasizes sequences of events. This is a good fit with transaction sequences, since they also describe those sequences of actions within a business process that the system under development is to support. The same basic concepts and modeling techniques can be used in the two contexts, with only a change in emphasis. With business processes, the emphasis is on understanding the business. With transaction sequences, the emphasis is on defining the computer system support for the business processes.

The Object Life Cycle Model

In addition to the object structure model and the business process and transaction sequence model, the modeling of object life cycles has an important part to play in the process of defining the required functionality of an object-oriented system.

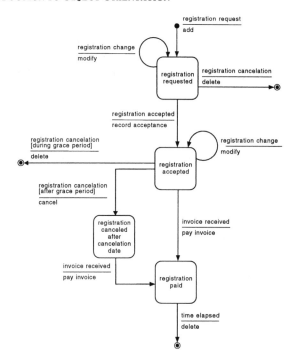

Figure 3-4: Example of an object life cycle diagram

While the object structure model addresses the data-oriented kernel of an object-oriented system and the transaction sequence model addresses the analysis of the users' functional requirements, the object life cycle model addresses the question of how objects change through time.

The importance of this (both for object-oriented and for non-object oriented system development) should not be underestimated. Often, a system's complexity is underestimated until behavior that varies depending on time and state has been recognized. At this point, estimates of development effort, cost, and schedule will tend to increase dramatically. Obviously, the sooner such complexity is recognized the better, both in terms of producing a system which meets the users' needs and of managing the process effectively.

The analysis of object life cycles ensures that all aspects of object behavior have been thought through. Object life cycles can be cross-checked against operations to ensure that operations support the different processing required at different stages in an object's life.

Object life cycles are also a concept with which users can identify. The diagramming notation can actually assist the process of communication between the business professional and the system developer.

System-Wide Modeling

When developing systems of any size, the question of controlling complexity arises. Once a problem reaches a given size, it needs to be partitioned in order for it to be handled effectively.

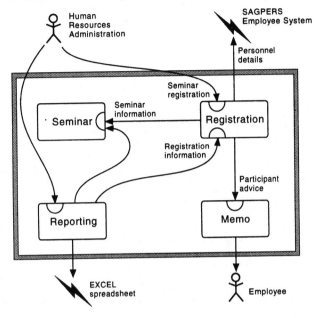

Figure 3-5: Example of a system overview diagram

System-wide modeling assists in controlling complexity by breaking a target system into parts (submodels or subsystems). Breaking a system down into submodels assists in a number of different ways. Subsystems can be allocated to different teams or used to define delivery units or units for distribution. They can also be useful for validating that a system is well-designed to support change and for use when presenting overviews of system functionality.

It is also important to be able to model the interfaces between subsystems. This can be achieved by grouping the operations one subsystem offers for use by other subsystems into *services*. This area is not well-covered in most object-oriented analysis and design methods and we are indebted to Wirfs-Brock[1] for her concepts of contracts and collaborations between subsystems, documented using CRC-cards, from which we have derived our concept of services.

---

[1] R. Wirfs-Brock, B. Wilkerson, L. Wiener, *Designing Object-Oriented Software*. (Englewood Cliffs, NJ: Prentice Hall, 1990).

Model Usage and the Project Life Cycle

Figure 3-6 summarizes the models introduced in Chapter 3. It shows the life cycle phases in which each type of model is used. Note the central role of the object structure model, which the other models feed into.

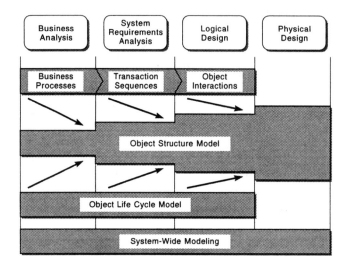

Figure 3-6: Model usage during the application development life cycle

See Part III for a detailed account of how each model is built up during the development process and how the models feed into one another and into the central object structure model.

Part II

Overview of Modeling Techniques

Part II provides *basic* information on each of the model types. It is organized as follows:

A Description of This Model Type...	*Is Found in...*
Object Structure Model The object structure model is the core model. It contains the object classes and associations required to construct an application.	Chapter 4
Business Process and Transaction Sequence Model The business process model describes the business processes to be supported by the application. The transaction sequence model takes this high-level understanding of what the business needs to do and translates it into the requirements for an application.	Chapter 5
Object Interaction and Activity Flow Diagrams Object interaction diagrams show the interactions between objects that are required so that the application can provide the services to the user described in the transaction sequence model. Activity flow diagrams are used to analyze and present complex activity flows in business processes and transaction sequences.	Chapter 6
Object Life Cycle Model The object life cycle model is used to describe how an object changes over time and what causes those changes.	Chapter 7
System-Wide Model The system-wide model is used to subdivide an application's object structure model for the purpose of managing complexity.	Chapter 8

The following information is provided about each model:

- The purpose of the model,
- An overview of the model and its usage,
- Comments on when the modeling technique is useful in the development process,
- An example of the model's usage,
- A detailed description of the components of the model, and
- Notes on advanced modeling techniques, where appropriate.

Chapter 4

Object Structure Modeling

Object structure modeling is central to object-oriented development. OO brings a common language and structure to the entire process of building an application to meet business needs. Objects and object classes are at the core of this common language. The object structure model is used to document object classes as they are identified during the development process and to associate them with object classes that are already present.

The object structure model is worked on throughout the analysis, design and development of an application. Once the development process is complete, the model fully documents the components needed to implement the application. It provides an application blueprint. It identifies:

- the object classes in the application,
- how the object classes are associated with each other,
- how objects communicate,
- the details of each object class, including attributes and operations.

All the models used for analysis and design have their own role to play in allowing different types of information to be captured, understood and used to help in building an application. All the other models, however, feed into this central model. One attractive feature of OO is that it allows every aspect of the application (data, processes and communications) to be represented in one all encompassing model: the object structure model.

Overview of Object Structure Modeling

Object structure modeling is an additive process. The application's object structure model is added to and modified throughout the entire process of building an application. Object classes are added progressively to this model and thus to the application. Each stage in the process adds more detail to the object classes in the model. Some object classes may also be removed from the model as analysis and design progresses.

During business analysis, the objects that are key to the business are discovered and abstracted into the appropriate object classes. These objects represent the tools used by the business to accomplish a specific set of objectives.

During system requirements analysis, structural associations between objects are identified. Inheritance or aggregation structures are used to more fully describe the object classes that have already been identified. Any missing business object classes and any additional application object classes relevant for a specification of requirements are added, and any object classes that are no longer necessary are removed. The model may also be divided into logical partitions called subsystems or subject areas.

Until logical design, the focus is on business objects (entity objects). During logical design, the object structure model expands to include all the object classes required for the application including the interface and control objects. Addition of logical design object classes completes the basic design of the application.

Finally, during physical design, any remaining implementation details are defined for each object class.

Determining what to include in the object structure model is a challenging task. Chapters 16-18 and 21-24 discuss in detail how object structure modeling can be carried out.

Object Structure Diagram for a Seminar Registration System

Figure 4-1 shows a subset of the object structure model for our seminar registration system example. It shows an extract from the full diagram that was produced during Logical Design. The application was built to assist a company's training coordinator in the booking of training for employees. It supports a business process that is triggered by a request for a specific type of seminar (or training event) and is completed when the invoice for the chosen seminar has been paid. We have used this application in many examples throughout the rest of this book.

The diagram shows the most important object classes for the application. It includes examples of most of the possible types of association between object classes. The next section describes the components of the object structure model in detail.

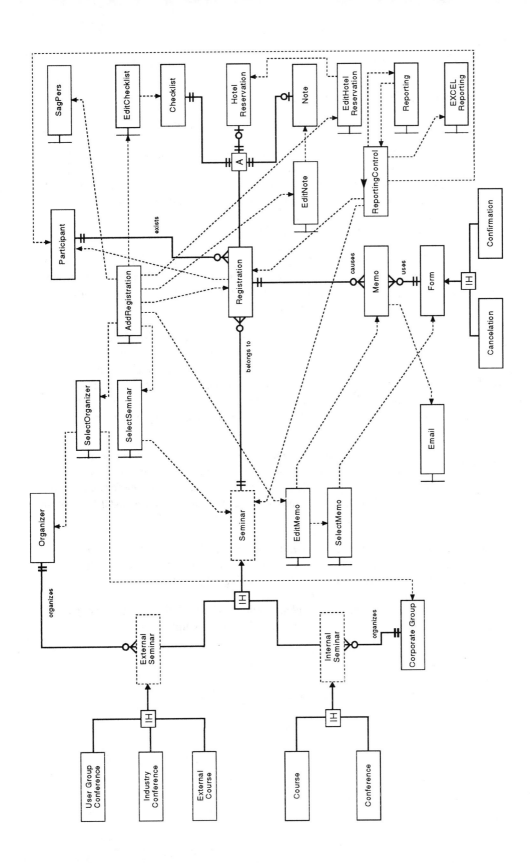

Figure 4-1: Seminar registration system

Object Structure Model Components

The most basic component of the object structure model is the object class.

An object class is used to provide a description of a group of objects which can be considered to be of the same type. Objects belonging to an object class have similar behavior and common attributes and semantics. An object class can be viewed as a *template* for an object. Objects are sometimes referred to as instances, while an object class is sometimes referred to as a class.

We find it useful to distinguish three types of object classes.

 Entity objects represent something real or abstract about which the business needs to store data. They represent the essential business memory. Business objects are usually entity objects. In Figure 4-1, Seminar, Participant and Organizer are examples of object classes of this type.

 Interface objects represent the technical objects required to link the application with outside sources or receivers of the information the application manages. These include user-interface screens and interfaces to other applications. It is through this object type that data, most importantly that contained in entity objects, typically enters or leaves the application. In Figure 4-1, the object class EditorNote represents a user-interface screen, while the object class EXCELReporting provides the interface to Microsoft EXCEL.

Control objects contain behavior which does not naturally belong in entity and interface objects. They are usually transient. In Figure 4-1, the object class ReportingControl is responsible for packaging the necessary data for an EXCEL report from a number of different objects, and sending the package to the object EXCELReporting which handles the interface with EXCEL.

Note: We use the term entity object rather than entity object class because the latter is too long and unwieldy for general use. The same applies to interface object and control object. The context generally makes it clear whether a class or an instance is being referred to.

For each object class, the behavior, attributes and semantics of objects belonging to the object class are defined. This definition includes a description of the following:

- Operations
- Attributes
- Constraints

Additionally, the object structure model describes associations between objects or object classes. These associations can be of the following types:

- Static relationships
- Inheritance
- Aggregation
- Communication (via messages)

These object structure model components are described in more detail next.

Operations

An *operation* defines a service offered by an object together with the information which must be supplied when it is invoked, its name and input and output arguments. It may also contain a method specification, which specifies an implementation for the operation. Typically, free text or other specification notations (e.g., pseudocode) are used to specify operations during analysis and logical design and an object-oriented programming language is used to define the method during physical design and/or construction.

Some operations can be assumed to exist for each object class and may not need to be formally identified. These are called *implicit operations.* The most important implicit operations are Create, Destroy, Read and Update. In your development environment, there may be other operations which you choose to regard as implicitly available. An implicit operation should be formally identified and defined when its pre- and post-conditions are not trivial.

Identifying and specifying operations is the key task during logical design. (See Chapter 14.)

Attributes

Attributes are data values which are associated with objects in an object class. They are values that are closely associated with the containing object class such that they have no independent existence or object identity. Whether an item should be considered as an attribute or an object may vary from system to system, depending on how the information is to be handled. What is modeled as an attribute in one system may be modeled as an object class in another. Color, for instance, will usually be handled as an attribute. In an application in which the characteristics of each color are significant, however, color would be modeled as a separate object class.

Each attribute identified should be atomic in the sense that it is either a single value or a group of values that always belong together, e.g., address. Objects can include arrays of a single attribute or arrays of a structure which itself consists of a number of attributes. Note that this means that objects need not be in first normal form. During physical design, a decision may be taken to handle complex data structures or attributes as objects, where this is a sensible design decision in the target implementation language.

Attributes can be based on *attribute type* definitions, which provide a standard definition for the format, length and range of values of attributes of the same type. For example, quantity, price, name, address, zipcode are typically defined as attribute types.

Constraints

Constraints may be specified on the values an attribute or relationship may take. Constraints can be specified as part of an object structure model before it has been determined how they are to be enforced. The implemented system may then enforce constraints by various means, including validation during user input, implemented as part of the user interface, database-level triggers or logic contained within one or more operations.

Static relationships

Static relationships describe how objects can be associated with each other, in the same way as in Entity Relationship modeling. They also identify dependencies between objects; whether an object requires the existence of another object, either in a different object class or in the same object class. Static relationships are usually between Entity objects.

Like attributes, relationships model information about an object (the things an object knows about itself). These are object properties. Attributes have data values which are literals, while relationships have values represented by references to other objects. In an object structure model, relationships are often mirrored by message communications. This does not make the modeling of relationships any less important in ensuring that all the business information associated with an object is captured during the development of an object structure model.

A static relationship is represented by a solid line with cardinality symbols superimposed on the line. Relationships are modeled as binary; two object classes are always involved in the relationship[1]. Static relationships are named. Depending on the modeler, the diagram may show:

- a name for each direction of the relationship,
- a name for one direction of the relationship,
- a single name that represents both directions, or
- no name.

The name should identify the purpose of the association. Chapter 19 discusses naming conventions for static relationships.

It is possible that more than one relationship may exist between the same pair of object classes. When this occurs, the actual objects participating in each relationship are probably different and the purpose of each relationship is different. In this case, it is essential that the relationship's name clearly identifies its purpose.

---

[1] A recursive relationship is sometimes called "unary" because there is only one object class involved. This is still a binary relationship; it just so happens that the same object class is at both ends of the relationship. Chapter 19 discusses recursive relationships as well as n-ary relationships, attributed relationships and much more.

Cardinality identifies the minimum and maximum number of objects in one object class that can be related with a single object in the second object class. (This set of possible source objects may include the target object itself, when both ends of the relationship are connected to the same object class.) Note that for any relationship there will be two cardinalities and both cardinalities must be defined in order to define the relationship.

In this book, we use the crow's-foot notations for cardinalities, but other alternatives are equally acceptable, and we illustrate one alternative in our diagram notation, at the front of this book.

The following cardinalities can be shown:

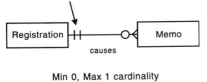

Minimum 1, maximum 1.
A **Memo** object **is caused by** *one* and *only one* **Registration** object.

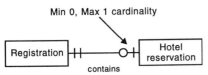

Minimum 0, maximum 1.
A **Registration** object **contains** a *minimum of zero* but *at most one* **HotelReservation** object.

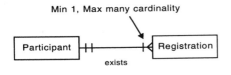

Minimum 1, maximum many (n).
A **Participant** object **exists for** *at least one* **Registration** object, but may **exist for** *many* of the **Registration** objects.

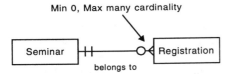

Minimum 0, maximum many (cn).
A **Seminar** object **belongs to** a *minimum of zero* **Registration** objects, but may **belong to** *many* of the **Registration** objects.

Now look at Figure 4-1 again. The relationship between **Memo** and **Form** is read as follows:

- A **Memo** object must **use** *one and only one* **Form** object.
- A **Form** object may **be used by** *no* **Memo** objects or may **be used by** *one* **Memo** object or *more than one* **Memo** object.

Inheritance

A square symbol with an arrow identifies an inheritance structure. Note that the arrow always points to the parent object class, the *superclass*. Object classes can inherit from a superclass, using single inheritance. *Single inheritance* means that any object class has no more than one superclass. The inheriting object classes are called *subclasses*.

Attributes, operations and constraints defined for a superclass are inherited by all its *subclasses.* The subclass may redefine inherited attributes and operations. Additionally, new attributes, operations and constraints may be defined for a subclass.

Each object class that inherits an operation may include its own method specification, which specifies how to implement the operation for the individual class. This method specification overwrites any inherited method definition. A Create operation, for instance, might be redefined in a subclass to add initialization of attributes introduced in the subclass.

In Figure 4-1, the object class **Seminar** is the parent of two object classes: **ExternalSeminar** and **InternalSeminar**. Each of these subclasses is also itself a superclass.

Each subclass is mutually exclusive. An object can belong to only one subclass. It can also belong only to the superclass, without belonging to any of the subclasses.

Inheritance structures also allow the definition of *abstract classes*. These classes are superclasses which do not contain any objects themselves. All the objects belong to subclasses. As abstract classes are used solely for inheritance, the definitions in an abstract class do not have to be complete. They can be completed in the subclasses which inherit from the superclass. In Figure 4-1, **Seminar**, **ExternalSeminar** and **Internal Seminar** are all abstract classes.

In object-oriented programming languages generally, an object belongs to a single object class from the time of its creation to the time it is deleted. Because of this, it is sensible to model such that this is true during analysis and design as well.

Aggregation

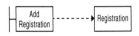

A square symbol identifies an object class that consists of one or more components - an aggregate. Aggregation is depicted using associations between the object representing the aggregate and its components. The cardinality of components in an aggregate can be defined and is used to identify how the objects of each of the object classes participate in the aggregate.

Figure 4-1 shows that **Registration** is an aggregate object class. It is made up of three object classes: **Checklist**, **HotelReservation** and **Note**. The cardinalities for **Checklist** show that every **Registration** object must have one **Checklist** object and that each **Checklist** object must be part of one **Registration** object. On the other hand, a **Registration** object does not have to have a **Note**. If it does, there can be no more than one. If a **Note** object exists, it must be part of a **Registration** object.

Communication (via messages)

Communication associations can be used to show that objects of a class send messages to objects of another or the same class. The association shows that there is a communication path in a single direction. Thus there is a maximum of one communication association between object classes in each direction. A communication association effectively corresponds to the set of messages which are sent by objects of one object class to objects of another. Messages implement the communication association. Figure 4-1 shows examples of communication associations between **AddRegistration** and **Registration**, and between **Registration** and **Participant**.

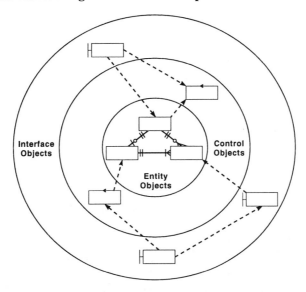

Figure 4-2: Communication associations and the three object types

Typically, the communication association is the only association which exists between objects of the three different types (entity, interface and control). Figure 4-2 illustrates this.

Advanced Object Structure Modeling Techniques

Some more advanced object structure modeling components are described in this section.

Visibility defines which objects may access and use the attributes and operations of any given object. The visibility of attributes and operations can be defined as private, protected or public. Private attributes and operations may be accessed only by the object to which they belong, and moreover may not be accessed by operations defined in subclasses. Protected attributes and operations are like private attributes and operations except that they can be accessed by operations defined in subclasses. Public attributes and operations may also be accessed by other objects.

Identifying attributes are attributes or groups of attributes which uniquely identify an object. They indicate how objects can be accessed other than by their internal object identifier. Identifying attributes are often needed for entity objects, enabling the relevant object to be selected according to criteria supplied by a user. For instance, a user may need to be able to select orders for a specific customer. Not all objects have identifying attributes. Some objects can be referenced only via objects which know of their existence, by means of the internal object identifier.

Attributes can be identified as *derived*. Derived attributes are attributes the value of which can be calculated from other attribute values. For persistent objects, a decision must be taken as to whether to store the derived attribute, the attributes used to calculate it or both. This decision is made during physical design, based on the usage the information will be put to and on how often its value changes as compared with its frequency of use.

Similarly, some static relationships are redundant in that they can be derived from other relationships. For example, the relationship 'grandparent' can be derived from the relationship 'parent'. It is often not necessary to include such *derived relationships* in the object structure model, as it just adds complexity without adding useful information. Sometimes, however, a derived association is particularly meaningful for the application domain, and in this case it can be included in the object structure model, marked as derived.

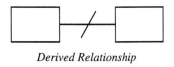

Derived Relationship

Inclusion of a derived relationship in the object structure model may also be useful in cases in which the decision as to which relationship should be considered as derived is, for requirements analysis purposes, arbitrary.

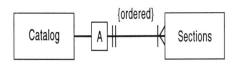

Objects at the "many" end of a relationship can be *ordered*. It is particularly useful to be able to specify that the objects in a component of an aggregate are ordered. By ordered, we mean that the component objects will be accessed in a specific, pre-defined sequence. Ordering is noted when it is necessary for the correct understanding and usage of the aggregate object. As an example, the ordering of components in a catalog may be considered significant and can be noted.

Class attributes and operations define the behavior of the class itself rather than the behavior of its instances. Class attributes are used for values which are the same for all objects in a class. Class operations operate on the class as a whole and can be used, for instance, to access or modify class attributes. The classic example is the Create operation which is by convention carried out by the class. It cannot be carried out by the instance to be created since this instance does not yet exist, and, from an object-oriented perspective, no other instance should take over responsibility for this, since each object should take care of its own responsibilities. (Putting this colloquially, each object should mind its own business.)

Chapter 5

Business Process and
Transaction Sequence Modeling

The requirements for a business application should be based on the actual business activities it will support. The business process model is used during business analysis and provides a means for describing the business. The transaction sequence model is used during system requirements analysis and provides a means for describing the required application functionality for the business processes.

Purpose of Business Process and Transaction Sequence Modeling

As discussed in Chapter 3, object structure and object behavior[1] models are not sufficient for the specification of an object-oriented application. Looking only at operations, it can be difficult to see exactly what functionality is really required in the application. Equally, when first developing the application, it can be difficult to bridge the gap between required functionality and the operations needed to provide this functionality.

Because of this, our approach explicitly includes modeling of business processes, and the required application functionality to support those business processes, and includes guidelines for the mapping between these requirements and the object structure and behavior models.

The object structure model is usually defined in parallel with business processes and transaction sequences. As types of objects are identified, these are added to the object structure model.

Business process modeling is used to understand and document the high-level activities performed by business professionals to accomplish specific business objectives. A clear understanding of the objectives and the business procedure to accomplish them assists in determining exactly how the application should support the meeting of these objectives.

The focus on business processes during business analysis provides a starting point for determining what is required for the application. During system requirements analysis, we decide which parts of the business processes require computer support and describe these requirements using one or more transaction sequences.

---

[1] The object behavior model includes object life cycle diagrams and object interaction modeling.

Transaction sequences model what the user requires from the application (its functional content). Transaction sequences provide traceability from the user requirements to the objects and operations which implement the required functionality. Transaction sequences are also useful for communication with users because they address application requirements in a way to which users can relate.

As part of the logical design process, transaction sequences can be analyzed to identify how objects and their operations provide the functionality required by the transaction sequences. Later, during testing, transaction sequences will also provide the basis for defining test cases.

Overview of Business Process and Transaction Sequence Modeling

A *business process* is defined by Hammer and Champy as a collection of activities that takes one or more kinds of input and creates an output that is of value to the customer. A second aspect is that a business process describes from start to finish the sequence of events required to produce this significant business result. It covers the whole process required to produce the product or service. Focus on seeing a business process as a whole to counter the tendency to break the process up and see parts of it in isolation.

Business processes typically cross organizational boundaries and any drastic changes to the business process could require a major shift in the organizational structure of the business. Business analysis could lead to a need for large scale business reengineering being identified. More often, it will result in improvements in support for business processes and associated computer support, without major business reorganization.

The following actions summarize how to identify and define a business process:

- the significant products and/or services that the business is responsible for are identified, and associated with one or more business processes;
- the inputs and triggering event(s) that initiate each business process are identified and the business processes are named;
- each business process is described by specifying the high-level activities that are required to produce the products and/or services.

The concept of business processes, as used in business analysis, is carried over into system requirements analysis in the form of transaction sequences. Transaction sequences are used in system requirements analysis to describe the services the user requires from the planned computer system. This definition of planned computer support may to some extent redefine the business process. It defines how the business process will be carried out in the future.

Transaction sequences have the same scope as a business process, or a significant subprocess of a business process, because the aim is to describe a sequence of interactions with the application which enables the user to accomplish an objective which has a meaning from the business point of view. There is a difference in focus in that in business analysis the emphasis is on understanding the business whereas in system requirements analysis the emphasis is on defining the application support which is to be provided.

It is important to note that the scope of a transaction sequence is defined by the user's perspective on requirements, rather than by any computer-oriented unit of processing. A transaction sequence is not, for instance, restricted to a single use of a single system function. It can involve the user (or more than one user) sitting down at a computer terminal on more than one occasion, perhaps over a period of time which exceeds a day. A transaction sequence should include the whole sequence of interactions between the user and the application that is required to complete an item of work which is a meaningful whole from the user's perspective and produces a significant result.

Obviously the core products and services the user requires from the application are business-related and most transaction sequences will therefore be business-related. In addition to these business-related transaction sequences, which describe support for business processes, there will be transaction sequences required purely for administration of the computer system itself, e.g., change user's access rights.

A transaction sequence normally starts when a human user or another system (an actor) chooses to initiate it by selecting some relevant application option or sending a message. Once the transaction sequence has started, it usually proceeds as a dialogue between the application and the actor who initiated it, or with other actors.

A productive way of identifying transaction sequences is to start with a business process and ask the users to describe their jobs within the context of that business process. The discussions provide an understanding of system requirements which are then described using transaction sequences.

The process of identifying users' requirements and describing transaction sequences can be assisted by producing prototypes of user interfaces. While there is a risk that prototypes will encourage too much attention to detail too early in the development process, the use of early user interface prototypes tends to speed up the process of clarifying requirements.

Next is an example of a prototype from the Seminar Registration system.

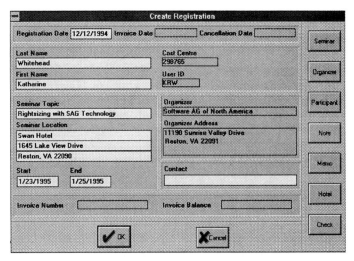

Figure 5-1: User interface prototype

Transaction Sequence Diagrams for the Seminar Registration System

We use the same diagram types and documentation templates for both business processes and transaction sequences. For this reason, we only show examples of transaction sequences here. Figure 5-2 shows the overview transaction sequence diagram for the seminar registration system as a whole and Figure 5-3 shows the diagram for the **Book Seminar** transaction sequence. Following this, the detailed description of the **Book Seminar** transaction sequence (Figure 5-4) is shown.

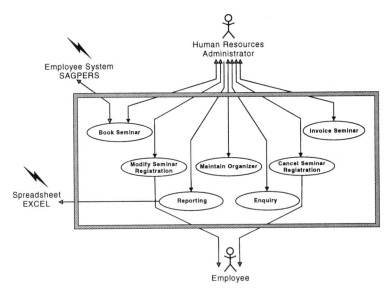

Figure 5-2: Overview transaction sequence diagram for the seminar registration system

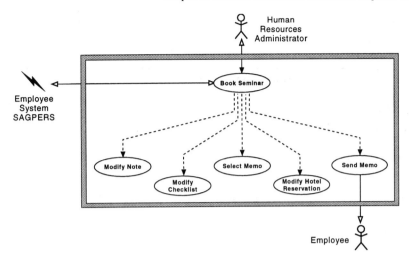

Figure 5-3: Common sequences for Book Seminar

The following symbols are used in the transaction sequence diagram:

 Actor. Persons are shown as stick people and machine interfaces, including interfaces with other systems or subsystems, are shown using a communications symbol, which looks like a bolt of lightning.

System border. A box is used to show the boundary of the business area or system. Actors are shown outside the boundary. Business processes or transaction sequences appear inside the box.

 Business process or transaction sequence. These are shown using an oval.

 Initiating actor and event. An arrow can be drawn from an actor to a business process or transaction sequence to indicate which actor initiates it. The arrow can be labeled with the initiating event(s). (The example diagrams do not include an example of an initiating event.)

 Communication between an actor and a business process or transaction sequence. This is shown by a double-headed arrow between the actor and the transaction sequence.

 Common sequences. Common sequences used by more than one transaction sequence can be shown on the diagram. Arrows show which transaction sequences use them. Figure 5-3 shows the common sequences used by **Book Seminar**. **Send Memo** is a common sequence.

As an example, the transaction sequence description for the **Book Seminar** transaction sequence is shown on the next two pages:

Book Seminar Transaction Sequence

Abstract

The Human Resources administrator registers an employee for a seminar.

Business context

An employee is to be registered for a seminar to be held by an external or internal organizer.

The most important organizational details must have been previously clarified by the administrator:

- The seminar must be going to take place and the interested employee must be able to participate,
- The employee's manager must approve the employee's participation.

Standard path

1. The user (administrator, Human Resources) selects the 'Create' command in the 'Registration' menu, in order to register an employee for a seminar.

2. The 'Create Registration' window is displayed. The current date is set automatically in the 'Registration Date' field. This default entry can, however, be modified if necessary.

3. The registration always refers to an employee in his or her capacity as a participant at the seminar. The user enters the last name and possibly the first name of the participant; all the related employee data (user ID, cost center) is then added automatically by the system. The employee data is taken from the external SagPers system.

4. A seminar can be selected from the set of seminars which already exists, or a new seminar can be created. If an existing seminar is edited, the system generates new seminar data from it.

5. Organizers must be entered in the 'Maintain Organizer' subsystem. They cannot be entered via the 'Create Registration' screen, but must always be selected either from the existing entries or in conjunction with a seminar.

6. A hotel reservation can be entered optionally for each registration. Clicking on the 'Hotel' button opens a window in which the reservation data can be entered (see also Edit Hotel Reservation).

7. The user edits the checklist in order to document the current status of the registration. The checklist consists of preformulated questions, which must either be answered by typing in information or ticked off as appropriate. The checklist can be opened by clicking on the 'Checklist' button (see also Edit Checklist).

8. The user can click on the 'Note' button to open an editor window, in which a note relating to the registration can be saved (see also Edit Note).

9. A confirmation should be sent to the participant. Clicking on the 'Memo' button opens the 'Select Memo' window. The user can either select one of the forms offered by the system or deselect the default form, i.e., he or she can either request that a confirmation be sent or cancel this request (see also Select Memo).

10.   The new registration can be confirmed by clicking on 'OK'.

11.   If a confirmation has been requested, it is sent to the employee via e-mail using the selected form (see also Send Memo).

Alternative path

1.   The user can stop the registration procedure at any time by clicking Cancel button

Actors

Initiated by: Administrator, Human Resources

Common sequences

1.   Edit Hotel Reservation

2.   Edit Checklist

3.   Edit Note

4.   Send Memo

5.   Select Memo

*Figure 5-4: Transaction sequence description for **Book Seminar***

Business Process and Transaction Sequence Model Components

Abstract

This can be used to provide a brief description of the business process or transaction sequence. It should identify the purpose, actors and expected results.

Business context

Business context the area of primary emphasis during business process modeling, and of secondary emphasis in transaction sequence modeling. Here the business process and transaction sequence are put into context and described.

When describing a business process the following components should be described, validated and fully understood:

- the result(s) of the business process,
- the customer of the business process,
- the value the customer gains from the result(s),
- the event(s) that initiate the business process,
- the inputs required by the business process to produce the result(s),
- a high-level description of the business process, and
- any special requirements that control the execution of the business process.

When describing a transaction sequence it is only necessary to include a description of the environment surrounding the transaction sequence and any pre-conditions which must be satisfied prior to its initiation by an actor.

Standard and alternative paths

The primary emphasis of each transaction sequence and secondary emphasis of the business process is on a description of the standard course of events, defined as the standard path. This is a sequential description of all the activities that need to take place in order to achieve the result(s). Exception processing is not described in the standard path description. For a transaction sequence, the standard path describes the actors' activities and what the application must do in order to service those activities. For a business process, this path describes the high-level set of activities for the process.

Alternative courses of events (called alternative paths) are described separately but still as part of the transaction sequence. These paths describe what is necessary to process unusual cases and also exception handling. The alternative path description also indicates where the deviation from the standard path takes place.

The advantage of this separation of the standard path and alternative paths is that the standard path can be read and understood without the reader being distracted by the detail of how error and unusual cases are handled.

Actors

In the description of a business process, the actors represent the business professionals and computer systems involved in producing the product or service. In a transaction sequence, actors are external agents who interact directly with the application. They may represent human users or may represent interfaces with other systems. Each actor is used to model a role which a human user or another system may play with respect to the application.

Any given role may be played by more than one user and any individual user may play a number of roles and may be represented by a number of different actors. An inheritance hierarchy may be defined for actors, so that actors may share parts of their role with other actors.

Common sequences

Sequences common to multiple transaction sequences should be described separately and only once. Such sequences are called common transaction sequences, common sequences for short.

Advanced Modeling Techniques

Subdividing business processes

Business processes can be divided into subprocesses. There are two major ways of subdividing business processes:

- *Specialization* of the business process into a number of variant types that produce the same result but have different sets of activities.

- *Partitioning* the business process along the time axis into a sequence of subprocesses.

If the business process requires the use of both specialization and partitioning, then it is better to try to specialize first. This is discussed in more detail in Chapter 12.

Diagramming the standard path and alternative paths

A graphical display of the standard and alternative paths can be useful for a number of reasons. First, it can be helpful when presenting the paths to others for validation and communication purposes. Second, the more complex the activities involved in a business process or transaction sequence, the more likely a diagram will be needed to work them out in the first place. Two diagrams can be used for these purposes. These are the object interaction diagram and the activity flow diagram. Either diagram can be used on its own, or they can be used together. Chapter 6 describes the use of these diagrams to document the standard and alternative paths of business processes and transaction sequences. Chapter 6 also discusses the use of the object interaction diagram as a tool for logical design.

Chapter 6

Object Interaction Modeling

Object interaction modeling is one technique which can be used to model object behavior. Object behavior is also modeled using object life cycle diagrams (described in Chapter 7). Where object interaction modeling describes interactions between objects, object life cycle modeling describes how any individual object of a given object class changes through time.

The primary use of object interaction modeling is during logical design, when it is used to model the way objects collaborate to provide the functionality described in each transaction sequence.

Object interaction diagrams also assist in understanding how a system actually works. They make it possible to see how control is transferred between objects as they interact. They also help with traceability, as they show which operations support specific system requirements.

While used mainly in logical design, object interaction diagrams are also used in business analysis as part of business process modeling. The diagrams show the sequence of interactions between actors (human or machine) required for the business process to achieve its results.

Activity flow diagrams are also used in conjunction with object interaction diagrams to describe business processes and transaction sequences.

Overview of Object Interaction Modeling

When an object wishes to use the functionality provided by another object, it does so by sending a message to the other object to invoke one of the receiving object's operations. This is what we call an *object interaction*. A whole series of object interactions is typically required in order to provide any significant service to the user.

Object interaction diagrams, as used in logical design, provide the link between transaction sequence descriptions and object-level operation specifications. Modeling object interactions assists in determining how object classes can be used to support the requirements described in transaction sequences. It assists in identifying the object classes and operations required, in considering how functionality should be distributed between operations in different object classes and how the object classes should collaborate to provide the functionality described in the transaction sequence.

Transaction sequences are usually initiated by an actor external to the system. Object interaction diagrams usually start with this initiation request. They show the operation which is invoked in response to this request and the messages it sends and so on down a whole chain of further interactions in different object classes. Normally one diagram is used for each transaction sequence for which object interactions are modeled. This object interaction diagram concentrates on the standard path.

Alternative paths can be included in this main diagram, elaborated in further object interaction diagrams, or left out. If you feel confident that operations adequately cover the alternative paths, then there is no reason to use object interaction diagrams. The value of object interaction diagrams is as a tool to help with design and they are obviously only required when they actually assist with this.

Object interaction diagrams are used differently in business analysis from the way in which they are used in logical design. When object interaction diagrams are used in logical design, they show how the system functions internally and how the objects used to model or implement the system interact. For business analysis, it is not usually interesting to consider system internals, or to consider what object should be responsible for what operation. For this reason, it is often useful to represent the system as an actor (a machine interface), to which requests are sent and from which results are received. We represent the system to be developed as a black box. When we come to system requirements analysis and logical design, we use a white box approach, looking inside the proposed system and defining the details of how it is to operate.

Object interaction diagrams show events and object interactions as if they occur in a linear sequence. Often groups of events can occur in alternative sequences, or in parallel, or there can be iterations or groups of events which do not always occur. Activity flow diagrams in combination with objects interaction diagrams can be used to represent this logic in a diagrammatic form. We describe these diagrams in the section on activity flow diagrams.

When is Object Interaction Modeling Useful?

During business analysis, the use of object interaction diagrams is an optional technique which can be useful to help gain an understanding of a particular business process.

Object interaction modeling is not generally useful during system requirements analysis. The objective during system requirements analysis is to define the requirements not to design the system. Object interaction diagrams, however, show in detail how objects interact to support the system's requirements.

During logical design, object interaction diagrams are usually produced for transaction sequences when a new part of the system is being developed and details of each operation and the responsibilities of each object class are not yet clear.

When reuse is involved, you will usually wish to restrict the scope of object interaction diagrams used for logical design. The use of object interaction diagrams in logical design involves a white box approach. For each operation considered, you consider what objects and operations that operation will use in order to provide its functionality and look into a whole chain of operations in various different object classes.

This is appropriate when you are designing a new subsystem. However, when reusing object classes from a class library or existing system, it is generally irrelevant to look into those fully tested object classes in order to understand how their operations work. Indeed, it is contrary to the object-oriented principle of encapsulation which says that the details of an object are private to it and that knowledge of its internals should not be needed by users of the object class. It should be clear from the operation's description whether it supplies the required functionality.

In this case a different approach is possible. The completed object classes can be regarded as black boxes. There is no need to explode the operations of a completed object class to show its internal workings. In these cases object interaction diagrams may not be needed, or you may choose only to expand, on the object interaction diagram, operations in the part of the system currently under development. Other uses for object interaction diagrams are for verifying that a transaction sequence can be supported by the existing object classes (in which case you choose to use a white box approach even for existing object classes) and for presentation/documentation purposes.

Activity flow diagrams can be useful during business analysis and logical design in combination with object interaction diagrams to clarify the logic flow of business processes and transaction sequences. They can also be used to clarify the logic of transaction sequences during system requirements analysis, when the standard and alternative paths are defined, although this is not their primary purpose.

Object Interaction Diagrams for the Seminar Registration System

We show two examples of *fence*-style object interaction diagrams. The first example shows a diagram produced during business analysis, modeling a black box view of the business process **Seminar Registration to Invoicing**. The second diagram shows an object interaction diagram for the transaction sequence **Book Seminar**, developed during logical design.

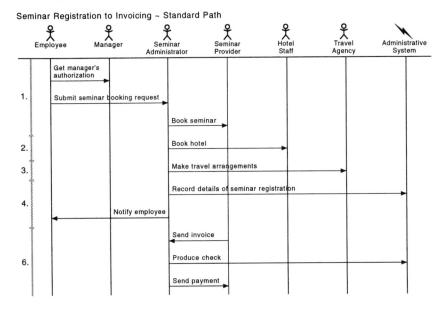

Figure 6-1: Seminar Registration to Invoicing - object interaction diagram

This diagram can be read a little like a spreadsheet. You start at the top left and read from left to right and from top to bottom.

Across the top of the diagram, we show the actors who interact to produce the results required by the business process.[1] In the diagram above, most of the actors are human. We also show our planned computer system as an actor - a machine interface labeled *Administrative System*. We are treating our planned computer system here as a black box. It is too early for us to consider how we might support the required functionality using object classes. Our objective during business analysis is to understand the process, not to specify computer support for it.

Associated with each actor, underneath the actor symbol, there is a vertical bar which represents the actor shown above the bar.

The arrows on the diagram represent requests which are sent by one actor (represented by one vertical bar) to another actor (represented by the vertical bar at the end of the arrow). In Figure 6-1, the first request is sent by the **Employee** to his or her **Manager** to request authorization to go to a seminar. We label the arrow with a name that explains the nature of the request from the sender's point of view, e.g., **Get manager's authorization**.

Notice that we show no return arrow for this request. Normally the actor who receives the request also responds to it by replying to the sender of the request. A less cluttered diagram results if you use a single arrow to show such a single request/response pair. One actor requests a service from another actor and we normally assume that that service is supplied and therefore don't show it explicitly on the diagram.

The second request on the diagram is the request or message, *Submit seminar booking request* which the *Employee* sends to the *Seminar Administrator*. In this case, the actor who receives the request needs to send further requests to other actors before it can respond. In cases like this one, it can be clearer to show the request and the response to the request separately. We have chosen to do that with the response to the request labeled *Notify employee*.

The numbers shown on the left-hand side of the diagram represent links with an activity flow diagram and will be explained in the section on activity flow diagrams below.

---

[1]Actors can also be regarded as a type of object class. When we are modeling the business, we are modeling a system in the real world rather than a computer system. We could recognize the actors as objects and represent them using the object class symbol. However, it is friendlier and more intuitive to represent people as actors - especially on a diagram which may be shown to the people it represents.

An object interaction diagram for the transaction sequence Book Seminar

Our second object interaction diagram shows the planned computer system support for part of the business process described previously. The business process is supported by these transaction sequences:

- Book seminar
- Change seminar registration
- Pay invoice
- Cancel seminar registration.

Figure 6-2 is an object interaction diagram for the transaction sequence **Book seminar**. A description of this transaction sequence, with its standard and alternative paths, can be found in Chapter 5.

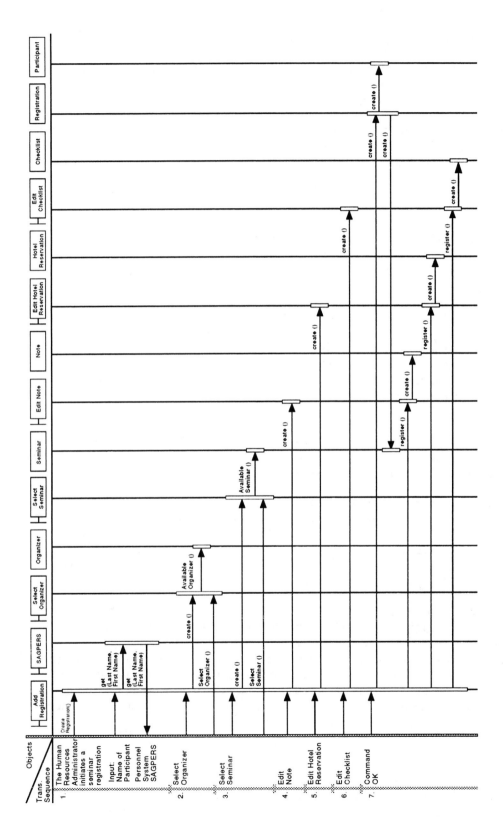

Figure 6-2: Book Seminar ~ object interaction diagram

Where Figure 6-1 treated the planned computer system as a black box, Figure 6-2 explores the object classes which will be used within the system. For this reason, some of the symbols on this object interaction diagram are different from those on the previous diagram.

To the right of the text description of the transaction sequence, there is a bar which represents the system boundary. Actors who communicate directly with the system send messages across this boundary. In our case, most communications are with the Human Resources Administrator. There is also a communication with another computer system - the Employee system which supplies the details of the staff member who is booking the seminar. This is noted in the description in the left-hand margin.

Because Figure 6-2 shows the internal workings of the system, no actors are shown across the top of the diagram. Instead the object classes are shown, with different symbols used to represent entity, interface and control objects.

Figure 6-2 also shows operations as elongated boxes on the vertical bar which represents the object class. Messages go to a specific operation in the object class and this operation may send a series of requests to other object classes before it terminates. Showing the operation explicitly makes it easier to see which operation is responsible for each message. The length of the bar is only proportional to the number of messages it sends and therefore the space it has to occupy on the diagram. It makes no statement about the execution time the operation is expected to take or any other such details.

Because the length of the operation box clearly shows whether the operation is active, we only use a single arrow to show request/response pairs for communications between object classes. The arrow shows which operation requests the operation and which operation is invoked. It is assumed that the invoking operation will receive a response.

Messages are labeled with the name of the request from the sender's point of view. One convention is to show the name of the operation which is invoked in the receiver, as we do in our example. Often this is adequate to explain the sender's purpose. Sometimes a more specific label is useful. For instance, if a number of different memos are sent for different purposes and you action the sending of these memos by sending messages to a **Memo** object class, then you may find it useful to label the different messages with the type of memo to be sent.

For communications which cross the system boundary, i.e., are sent or received by actors, it can be useful to show a response explicitly, separately from the request. However, if you avoid showing return response arrows, you will find it easier to pick out cases where the system itself initiates an interaction with an actor. We have an example of this in Figure 6-2 where the interface object **SagPers** (which lies within the system scope) sends a request to the Employee System. You can see that the arrow goes to the system boundary. The actor representing the machine interface is not shown explicitly on this type of object interaction diagram. A comment in the description is used to make it clear which actor sends or receives a request.

While an object interaction diagram shows events occurring in a linear sequence, the order in which events are received from outside the system may be random. For instance, the Human Resources administrator can choose to select a seminar before entering a hotel registration or vice versa. This is not shown explicitly on the diagram. Effectively, the order in which requests come across the system border is not defined and this needs to be considered when interpreting object interaction diagrams where more than one event can be received from outside the system.

Blocks of events which always occur in sequence can be marked on the object interaction diagram. Each block is identified with a number down the left-hand side of the diagram. In our case each such block begins with a request from the Human Resources Administrator. Where it is important to analyze in detail whether such blocks of logic occur in parallel, conditionally, or repeatedly, an associated activity flow diagram can be drawn. We show an example of an activity flow diagram for this transaction sequence later in this chapter.

Additional object interaction diagram components

We have described the main object interaction diagram components in the previous sections. In this section, we explain some detailed points which may be of interest.

Invoking an operation in "self"

Often an operation in an object class invokes another operation within the same object. This can be shown as depicted below:

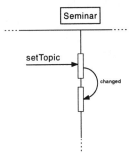

Figure 6-3: Object interaction diagram notation - invoking an operation in "self"

Such internal operations within an object are often used in order to structure the logic of a complex operation. Depending on the level of detail required, internal operations can often be omitted from object interaction diagrams.

Multiple objects of the same object class

Sometimes, different objects belonging to the same object class can be involved in a single transaction sequence. This can be shown on an object interaction diagram by representing the object class more than once.

Common sequences

You usually draw separate diagrams for common sequences. You show the point at which a common sequence is invoked using the following notation:

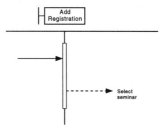

Figure 6-4: Object interaction diagram notation - invoking a common sequence

When drawing an object interaction diagram for a common sequence, the system boundary line represents the point across which messages from outside the scope of the common sequence arrive, which the common sequence has to handle. For a common sequence, the system boundary is thus interpreted as meaning "common sequence boundary".

The "net" form of object interaction diagram

In the preceding sections we used *fence*-style object interaction diagrams. This format is similar to Jacobson's object interaction diagram and Rumbaugh's Event Trace diagram. There is an alternative form of this diagram, called the *net* diagram. This shows the object classes between which messages are exchanged using the same symbols as on an object structure diagram. Figure 6-4 illustrates the net form of an object interaction diagram.

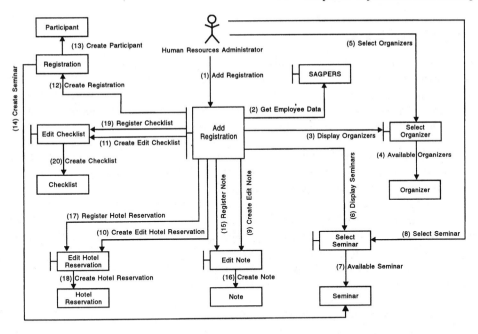

Figure 6-5: Book Seminar - object interaction diagram (net form)

The numbers on the message lines indicate the sequence in which the messages are sent and can be cross-referenced with the relevant parts of the transaction sequence's standard path.

Net form object interaction diagrams are easy for users familiar with object structure or ER diagrams to understand. However, for a transaction sequence with more than a very small number of messages, the fence-style diagram is easier to read and most people find they prefer it, even if they found it unfamiliar at first.

Net-style diagrams can be useful when you want a diagram that shows object classes in the same positions as on an object structure diagram (although the object structure diagram layout does not usually make it easy to pick out the sequence of messages). Animation can help with these diagrams. For instance, each message can be highlighted in turn, making it easier to walk through the sequence in which messages are sent. Without animation, it is often difficult to pick out the message sequence.

One way of organizing a net diagram that makes it easier to read is to position the first message at the top left of the diagram and draw subsequent messages radiating clockwise around the center of the diagram. Keep them in the order in which they occur to the extent that the message sequence allows this. We followed this rule in the organization of Figure 6-5.

Activity Flow Diagrams

Object interaction diagrams do not show decisions, iterations or the possibility that parts of the processing can take place in random sequences or in parallel. You can use text in the left-hand margin of a fence diagram to record these aspects of a business process or transaction sequence. An alternative is to use an activity flow diagram in combination with object interaction diagrams, to provide another form of documentation of the business process.

Activity flow diagrams are used specifically to document decisions, iterations and parallel/random processing. An activity groups a sequence of interactions. The scope of each activity is normally defined by the fact that the given sequence of interactions is conditional, iterated or can occur either before or after other interaction sequences. That is to say, the scope of an activity is artificially determined by any point at which the sequence of interactions can potentially branch. Naturally, such diagrams could be used to document logic flow at a very detailed level. However, very detailed activity flow diagrams are not recommended, either in business analysis where too detailed a level of analysis should be avoided, or in logical design, where it serves no useful purpose.

The following symbols are used in the activity flow diagram:

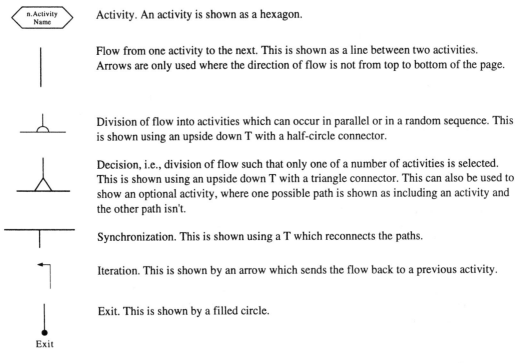

Activity. An activity is shown as a hexagon.

Flow from one activity to the next. This is shown as a line between two activities. Arrows are only used where the direction of flow is not from top to bottom of the page.

Division of flow into activities which can occur in parallel or in a random sequence. This is shown using an upside down T with a half-circle connector.

Decision, i.e., division of flow such that only one of a number of activities is selected. This is shown using an upside down T with a triangle connector. This can also be used to show an optional activity, where one possible path is shown as including an activity and the other path isn't.

Synchronization. This is shown using a T which reconnects the paths.

Iteration. This is shown by an arrow which sends the flow back to a previous activity.

Exit. This is shown by a filled circle.

We show next an example of an activity flow diagram for staff training as produced during business analysis.

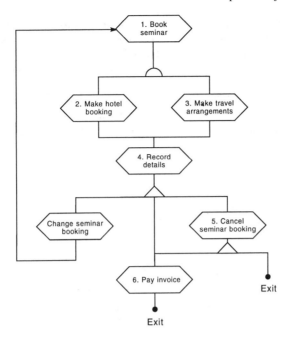

Figure 6-6: Seminar registration to invoicing - activity flow diagram

In Figure 6-6, the activities **Make hotel booking** and **Make travel arrangements** can occur in an undefined sequence or in parallel. After details of the seminar registration have been recorded, there are three alternative paths. Normally the seminar will take place and the next activity will be **Pay invoice**. However, one of two alternative activities, **Change seminar booking** or **Cancel seminar booking**, may be the next required activity.

The activity flow diagram can include activities which are not shown in the standard path but in alternative paths. In the case above, the activities **Change seminar booking** and **Cancel seminar booking** are not included in the standard path on the object interaction diagram we used to model this business process, but we show them here.

If we cancel a seminar booking, we may still have to pay. We show this decision explicitly in Figure 6-6. It is not necessary, however, to show every decision. Some decisions can be hidden within activity boxes.

The numbers in the activity boxes provide cross-references with any associated object interaction diagrams. Each number references a group of interactions, on the object interaction diagrams, which occur as a straightforward sequence, at least at this level of analysis.

As a convention, the interaction which results in a decision belongs in the activity which precedes the branch.

Another convention is that activities with no associated processing can be shown. In our example, these are the activities with no numbers. These activity boxes are used to make the logic flow easier to understand by showing for instance why an iteration may occur. The activity **Change seminar booking** is a marker explaining why **Book seminar** is to be repeated.

Figure 6-6 is an example of an activity flow diagram as used during business analysis to describe a business process. These diagrams can also be used during system development to describe transaction sequences. We show an example below for the transaction sequence **Book Seminar**.

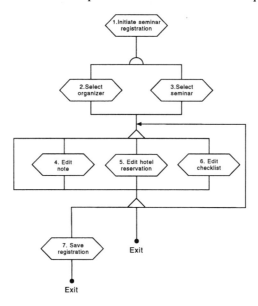

Figure 6-7: Book Seminar - activity flow diagram

Figure 6-7 illustrates the possible sequences in which the user can interact with the system when entering a seminar registration. The numbers can be used to cross-reference this diagram with the object interaction diagram.

It is also possible to use an activity flow diagram without an object interaction diagram to make clear the flow of logic described in the standard and alternative paths for a transaction sequence. You may find it interesting to compare Figure 6-7 with the textual transaction sequence description for **Book Seminar** in Chapter 5 to see how the two correlate.

Advanced Modeling Techniques

Generally, one object interaction diagram is used to model each transaction sequence. It is possible to use more than one object interaction diagram per transaction sequence and we describe two alternative approaches below.

Using activity flow diagrams for modeling system operations

Activity flow diagrams can be used in combination with object interaction diagrams. On an activity flow diagram each block normally represents a group of events which always occurs as a sequence. Another option is to show one block on an activity flow diagram to represent each possible external stimulus for the transaction sequence. Such external stimuli (or system operations as they are called in the Fusion method[1]) can often occur in random sequences or in alternative sequences. One object interaction diagram can be developed for each such block or system operation. Note however that we favor using a single object interaction diagram for the whole transaction sequence where possible, since this gives a less chopped-up view of the processing required.

Object interaction diagrams, transaction sequences and scenarios

We generally develop only one object interaction diagram per transaction sequence. This single diagram shows the general case omitting unusual and alternative paths. It does not show an execution scenario that might occur on a specific occasion. In complicated cases, it can be useful to develop alternative object interaction diagrams showing typical alternative execution paths.

---

[1] See Derek Coleman, Patrick Arnold, Stephanie Bodoff, Chris Dollin, Helena Gilchrist, Fiona Hayes, and Paul Jeremaes, *Object-Oriented Development: The FUSION Method.* (Englewood Cliffs, NJ: Prentice Hall, 1994)

Chapter 7

Object Life Cycle Modeling

Object life cycle modeling is used as a way of describing the dynamic aspects of objects. Whereas object interaction modeling is used to model what goes on between objects - what messages one object sends to another, object life cycle modeling is used to describe what happens within objects belonging to a given object class. In other words, how an object changes and what causes the changes to the object.

Object life cycle diagrams assist in gaining a better understanding of the behavior of objects with complex behavior patterns. One of the most difficult things to understand and analyze is the behavior of an object over time. The passage of time alone can cause an object to change, and these changes are among those we need to uncover.

Cross-checking object life cycles with other information can also assist in ensuring that state-dependent behavior has been recognized and is handled in the planned implementation.

Overview of Object Life Cycle Diagrams

Object life cycles are used to represent:

- how objects are created,
- how objects are deleted,
- how objects change through time,
- what states an object typically goes through,
- what events cause an object to change its state, and
- what actions an object takes when it receives an event which causes it to change state.

It is especially important to recognize object behavior which is dependent on time and state because this can add significantly to the complexity of an application. In fact certain operations and/or attributes may only be valid in certain states. Some of the key processing in a system, forming significant parts of business processes, is likely to relate to changes of state in the key business objects.

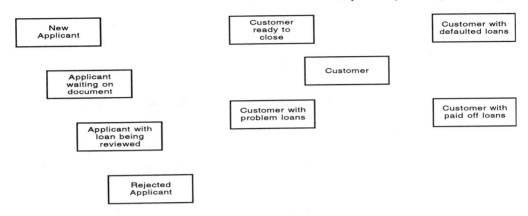

*Figure 7-1: Possible states for the object class **customer***

Customer is an example of an object class. A bank would not automatically grant a loan to everyone who applies. Prior to the loan being granted, there are a number of states that the person must go through, such as new applicant, applicant waiting for arrival of all pertinent documents and applicant under review. Depending on the outcome of the review, the person either receives the loan or does not. Once a customer, there are again a number of states that can occur like customer in good standing, customer behind on payments, and, past customer. Having decided that these states are needed, we want to determine exactly what events cause the state to change and what temporal events affect the applicant/customer.

Many objects in commercial data processing have a large number of potential states. Therefore, object life cycle diagrams should show only those states which are significant in determining the behavior of the object based on the needs of the business, and a clear business definition of each state should be written.

Each object life cycle diagram applies to a single object class and shows the different states the object may be in and the possible transitions between these states. Transitions are caused by the object receiving an event. Such an event may be an external event, received from outside the system, or may be sent by another object or indeed by the object itself. The subsequent state of the object depends on its current state, the event it has received and, optionally, the value of a guard condition. When the object receives the event, it executes an action (which usually corresponds to an operation) associated with the transition. Either at the end or during the course of executing this action, the object makes the transition into its subsequent state. It is possible that the subsequent state may be the same as the starting (current) state.

When is Life Cycle Modeling Useful?

Whenever new object classes are added to the object structure model, it is important to examine the new object class to see if there are any significant states for the objects in that object class. If there appear to be any, then a life cycle diagram should be drawn for the object class in order to be sure that the life cycle is fully understood.

Life cycle modeling is useful during the analysis phases, both for business and system requirements analysis. Object life cycles are a concept with which users can identify. The use of object life cycle diagrams can enable the communication of knowledge about objects which is sometimes difficult to verbalize without the assistance of a graphical representation.

Life cycle diagrams can be very useful when analyzing business processes and transaction sequences. Determining the key object class(es) involved in the business process or transaction sequence and analyzing their life cycles helps give a basic view of what the standard and alternative paths are. In addition, the standard and alternative paths of a business process or transaction sequence may also help ensure that all the significant states have been identified for the objects involved.

During logical design, object life cycles are useful in identifying the operations that are required. Events trigger actions. These actions are carried out by operations.

During the analysis phases and logical design, object life cycles are used to model life cycles for entity objects. During logical and physical design, object life cycle modeling can be useful for interface and control objects. In a GUI environment, the meaning of different user actions may be very context-dependent, and modeling the life cycle of key interface objects is often useful in capturing and clarifying these complex behavior patterns.

Some examples of interesting dynamic behavior, taken from Shlaer/Mellor, are as follows:

1. Cases where objects accumulate values for their attributes as they progress through their life cycle.

2. Equipment that has an operational cycle, e.g., mixers or robots.

3. Objects that come into existence step by step, e.g., during manufacture.

4. Objects that represent tasks to be done.

5. Objects that move dynamically in and out of relationships.

6. Objects whose life cycles interact with the life cycles of other objects.

7. Cases where objects may change their subclass.

Static data does not usually have complex behavior and life cycle modeling is not usually necessary for these types of object class.

Object Life Cycle for the Seminar Registration System

Let's look at the object life cycle for the object **Registration** in the object structure diagram for the seminar registration system.

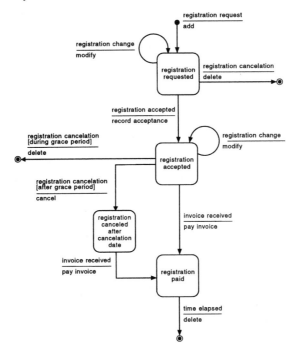

*Figure 7-2: Object life cycle diagram for the object **Registration***

This diagram shows the states that a **Registration** object goes through while it exists. Note that the event that triggers the object's creation is the receipt of a **registration request**. The object is deleted under two circumstances: first, if the participant cancels the registration during the grace period or second, after it is paid and a certain period of time has elapsed.[1]

Object Life Cycle Diagram Components

The basic components of an object life cycle diagram are:

- Entry and exit points (shown as terminators),
- States (shown as rounded boxes),

---

[1] If you compare this life cycle with the business process and transaction sequence **Book Seminar** illustrated in Chapter 5, you can see how the life cycle of this object roughly parallels the actual activities that need to take place for someone to be registered in a seminar.

- State transitions (shown by arrows connecting two states). The state transition should be labeled. The label may include any or all of the following:

    - Event identifier

    - Guard condition (shown following the event identifier in square brackets)

    - Action or operation name (shown under the event).

The **entry point** represents the time before the object comes into existence. The state transition line from the entry point to the first state identifies the event that brings the object into existence. In Figure 7-2, the entry point is the event **registration request** and the first state is **registration requested**.

The **exit point** represents the point at which the object ceases to exist from the point of view of the system. It is at the end of the final transition and represents a transition into 'no state'. Not all objects cease to exist. Some objects remain forever within the scope of the system, and the object life cycles of these objects will have no exit point. There may also be multiple exit points from the life cycle. These occur when there is a certain event that always causes an exit in any or all states, or when an event combined with a certain state causes the exit. Figure 7-2 illustrates three exits from the life cycle. The first two occur when the event **registration cancellation** is received. The last occurs when the state **registration paid** determines that a predetermined time period following invoice payment has elapsed, shown by the event **time elapsed**.

registration
paid

The **state** of an object is often described as the set of values the object has at a given point in time. For instance, in the Seminar Registration system, the state **registration accepted** means that there is room in the requested seminar and the participant has been confirmed as registered by the seminar provider. It is only in this state that the operation **pay invoice** will be carried out as a result of the event **invoice received**.

invoice received
pay invoice

A brief event definition can be used to define the nature of the **event** which causes a state transition. Events may be external, arising from outside the system, or internal, arising within the system. External events are not normally associated with a sending object class. An internal event is implemented as a message which one object sends to another. In Figure 7-2, the event **registration accepted** causes an actual change of state, but the event **registration change** only triggers a specific operation that does not change the object's current state. It is shown because it was important to document which states the event could occur in and that the event did not cause a change in state. Temporal events which occur at intervals or at a given time may also be relevant. In the example, the temporal event **time elapsed** is one of the events that triggers an exit from the life cycle.

registration cancelation
[after grace period]

Guard conditions are used when the object's current state and the event received cannot adequately determine the object's next state.

An example of when to use a guard condition is a stack where a **pop** event can result in the stack reaching the state **empty**, but it is not possible to define a previous state such that the previous state and the event are sufficient to define the subsequent state, unless you define a state for every possible size of stack. (Try it!) In this case, it may be necessary to evaluate some other item of information in order to decide the object's next state. This check can be formulated as a guard condition, which is an expression which is either true or false. The event may then be associated with more than one possible state transition from a given state, with each possible transition being associated with a guard condition. All guard conditions for an event must be mutually exclusive. The state transition which actually occurs when the event is received is that for which the guard condition is true. If no guard condition is true, then no transition occurs and no action is performed. The guard condition is implicitly ANDed with the occurrence of the event. It can be expressed as a combination of conditions including time conditions.

We show an example of the use of guard conditions for a stack object in Figure 7-3.

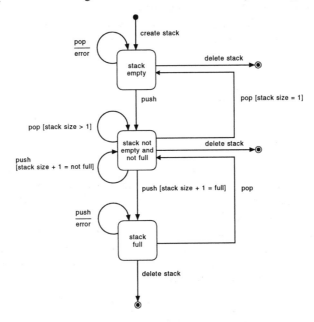

*Figure 7-3: Object life cycle diagram for a **Stack** object*

In Figure 7-3, there are two guard conditions associated with the event **pop** and the state **stack not empty and not full**. The **pop** event causes the removal and return of the top item from the stack. The guard conditions determine what state the stack is in following the occurrence of the event. When the condition **stack size = 1** is true prior to the event, then the stack returns to the **stack empty** state. When the condition **stack size > 1** is true prior to the event, then the stack does not change as a result of the event since, following the event, the stack is still not empty and not full.

In many cases, an alternative to specifying a guard condition is to introduce a new object state so that object state plus event adequately determine what state transition is required.

The **action label** identifies the action an object takes on receiving an event, during which it makes the transition into its destination state. The action is carried out by an operation and can be described within this operation. Or, at an early analysis level, a reference can be made to a transaction sequence which fully describes the action, instead of to an operation.

Note that an object may be in one of a variety of different states when it receives a given event. The action it takes in response to the event may vary depending on its state, or may always be the same, regardless of its state. In Figure 7-2, the event **registration change** causes the same action regardless of the state. In Figure 7-3, note that both the events **pop** and **push** result in different actions depending on the state. If the stack receives the event **pop** when it is in the state **stack empty**, it triggers the action **error**, at all other times it triggers the action **pop**.

Any given event always invokes the same operation in an object, regardless of the object's state. This is because an event comes from outside the object and the world outside the object has no knowledge of the object's state - what events the sending object sends can only depend on the sending object's own state, not on that of the receiver. Therefore, in cases where the action that should be taken by the receiving object varies depending on the object's state, the operation must handle the decision as to which action to take.

State-dependent behavior can (optionally) be implemented using state machines. Chapter 23 discusses this topic in much greater detail.

Advanced Life Cycle Modeling Techniques

The scope of an object life cycle diagram is restricted to one object class and the events shown on the diagram are thus normally those which the object class receives and which affect its life cycle. It is possible to show relationships between the life cycles of different objects by showing, on an object life cycle diagram, an event which the object class sends to objects of another object class and which then affects the other object's life cycle. This event is shown as a dashed line from a state transition line to another object and it shows that as part of the object's reaction to the event it has received (in Figure 7-4, a modification to a booking which has been confirmed), the object sends an event to another object (to the audit log, in this example).

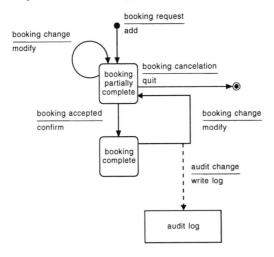

Figure 7-4: Example of an event sent to an object of another class

For superclasses and subclasses, it has to be considered whether to model the life cycle of the superclass or of the subclasses. This depends on the extent to which the subclasses have a common life cycle. The same life cycle may apply to all subclasses, in which case it is logical to model the life cycle for the superclass. Alternatively, the life cycle of each subclass may be different, in which case the life cycle of each subclass can be modeled separately. Or the subclasses may have a common life cycle for part of their life and distinct life cycles for other parts of their life. In this last case, the part of the life cycle which the subclasses have in common can be drawn for the superclass and the parts which are subclass-specific are drawn separately. This can be handled by depicting the superclass object as sending an event to the relevant subclasses, at the point at which the life cycles diverge, and by depicting the subclasses as sending an event to the superclass when the life cycles converge.

Cases where an object changes its class can also be shown on life cycle diagrams, although we recommend avoidance of such objects: see the section Time-Dependent Specializations in Chapter 20. For an object to change its class, an object of the new object class must be created and the object of the old object class must be deleted. This can be shown as a transition to an end state for the object class from which the object is switching, with an event being sent to the object class for which a new object instance should be created.

Diagrams may be nested, with a lower-level diagram being used to explode activities which take place within a state. In this case, the states shown in the lower-level diagram are subtypes of the state which is being exploded. There are a number of reasons to use nested diagrams:

- in the design phases you may need a finer breakdown of one or more states in order to properly design the operations and attributes of the object;
- the life cycle may be too complex to work with otherwise;
- different groups of users may see the life cycle in more or less detail so that you need to work differently with each group.

Nested life cycles allow precision to be added to a life cycle without making it overly complex and enable a top-down approach to the development of the life cycle. The same problems arise, however, as with nested data flow diagrams, for example. It becomes necessary to work with a number of different diagrams in order to deal with the entire life cycle. For this reason, we recommend avoiding the use of nesting unless it is really necessary.

Chapter 8

System-Wide Modeling

System-wide modeling makes it possible to produce overviews of the object structure model, assisting with the handling of complexity.

Purpose of System-Wide Modeling

The major reasons for using system-wide modeling are as follows:

- It makes it possible to partition an analysis or development task, something which is necessary for all but the most simple development tasks. For large systems, subsystems can be allocated to different teams or subprojects.

- It can be used to define delivery units, i.e., units of functionality which can be delivered to customers on successive delivery dates, or product components.

- It can be used to define units that are distributable.

- It can be used to validate the design of a system to ensure that it is well-designed to support change.

- It includes a diagram type - the system overview diagram - that can be used to produce overviews of an analysis model or a subsystem, assisting with the presentation of the model or subsystem at an overview level.

One important feature of the system-wide model is that it allows the modeling of the interfaces between subsystems. This is achieved by modeling the *services* one subsystem offers for use by other subsystems.

Overview of System-Wide Modeling

System-wide modeling involves subdividing the problem space into components. In an object-oriented development approach, this is achieved by grouping object classes together. (Object-oriented system modeling differs here from structured techniques, in which subsystems usually group functions together, rather than objects.)

Transaction sequences do not have to reside within a single component or subsystem. They can require support from object classes in more than one component.

The problem space and its components

How we think of the problem space and the types of component we divide it into, changes as we move through the development life cycle.

During business analysis, the problem space is a business domain and we can choose to subdivide the business domain into subject areas. Each subject area contains object classes which are semantically related to each other - deal with the same subject.

Before starting on system development, it may be necessary to divide large systems into subsystems which will be developed separately, by separate teams or in more than one phase, as separate delivery units. In this case, subsystems are defined when the project or projects are defined. A system overview diagram can be used to show how the different subsystems are related to one another. Even for a development project involving a system which is not broken down into components, it is useful to use a system overview diagram during project definition, to define the scope of the project. [1]

During system development, the problem space is the system or subsystem which is being built. This system or subsystem can itself be subdivided into submodels or subsystems. Submodels are used mainly for presentation purposes, as a way of providing overviews of the functionality the system will provide. The criteria governing what should be included in a submodel are not hard and fast. Subsystems, on the other hand, are defined for technical reasons, and there are quality criteria which can be used to decide how to subdivide into subsystems or to validate that the subsystem definition is good. The technical reasons for dividing a system into subsystems include the definition of delivery units, the definition of distributable units and the definition of modules - which are important for validating and preserving the maintainability of the system. Since these aspects relate to the logical design phase, they are discussed in detail in Chapter 14, Logical Design. We provide a short overview of quality criteria for subsystems in the section on Advanced System-Wide Modeling Techniques at the end of this chapter.

A further use for partitioning is an architectural one which is particularly relevant during physical design. We recommend dividing all systems into six architectural subsystems. The main architectural subsystem, the problem domain component, is the area which is concentrated on during system requirements analysis and logical design. The human interface component and external interface component are introduced during logical design. The remaining components, the data management component, task management component and utility services component are introduced when required during physical design. These components are described further in Chapters 10 and 15.

Defining the scope of a subsystem

Basically, object classes that have a high level of interdependency and serve a common purpose should be allocated to the same subsystem. Subsystems should be such that they can be allocated a sensible name. They should be coherent and consist of tightly coupled objects.

---

[1] Delivering separate subsystems in separate phases is one way of delivering a system in stages. An alternative way of phasing delivery is to deliver reduced functionality first and increase the functionality delivered with each subsequent release. See Chapter 11 for a discussion of how to plan an object-oriented development project.

For the parts of the inheritance hierarchy that fall into the problem domain component, a whole inheritance hierarchy branch or aggregation structure is usually allocated to a single subsystem.[1]

Note that if objects are always required and are needed by multiple subsystems, they do not have to be in a subsystem.

Services

A subsystem provides its services via an interface, which is the set of operations which clients of the subsystem may use. It is useful to group these operations into services, which can be documented with a name and a short description. Each service groups related operations which have a common purpose, for instance drawing pictures or sending e-mail.

Services provided by one subsystem to another, or to actors, can be identified by looking at what communications are possible between subsystems and grouping these into services. This is best done during logical design, when the operations have been defined. It can also be done, tentatively, before the operations to be included in each service have been defined, as a way of sketching out the overall architecture of the system.

Whether subsystems have a client-server relationship with one another or a peer-to-peer relationship can be seen from their usage of the services of other subsystems. A client subsystem uses a service provided by another subsystem, while a server provides the service. In a peer-to-peer relationship, a subsystem is both a client and a server for the subsystem it has a peer-to-peer relationship with. Looking at system overview diagrams assists in identifying dependencies between subsystems such that when one subsystem is delivered another is required.

Vertical and horizontal partitions

A system may be partitioned horizontally (into layers) or vertically. Vertical partitions are used for partitioning application functionality, while horizontal partitions are particularly useful to isolate applications from knowledge of the operating system or database or hardware. Such a layered approach assists in safeguarding portability.

---

[1] The parts of the inheritance hierarchy in the problem domain are normally developed during analysis and logical design. During physical design and construction, these inheritance hierarchies are often attached to a single overall inheritance hierarchy with a single root class. The superclasses towards the root of the inheritance hierarchy are usually abstract object classes which are interesting in terms of physical design, but not in terms of the problem domain. They are usually included in a physical design component.

Figure 8-1 is a simplified block diagram for the seminar registration system. It shows only the problem domain component and the data management component.

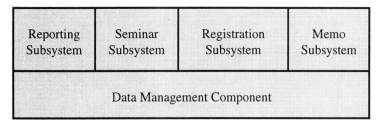

Figure 8-1: Block diagram of subsystems in the seminar registration system

The problem domain component is divided into four vertical partitions. The data management component is a horizontal partition, which exists to isolate the application from knowledge of the database software used. Horizontal partitions are discussed further in Chapter 15.

Using subsystems for defining distribution units

Each subsystem defines a group of object classes which has a small interface with other object classes. A subsystem is, therefore, a good unit to use when defining the distribution of a system. Typically, the subsystems identified at the lowest level in the subsystem definition tree (the smallest units) will also be the smallest unit used for distribution to different processors.

Multiple layers

With a large system, it can be desirable to be able to subdivide subsystems into further subsystems. For this reason, components can be further divided into sub-components. Donald Firesmith recommends that no subsystem include more than 20 components (either object classes or further subsystems) and should typically contain between 5 and 15 components.

Multiple views of the problem space

There is more than one possible reason for subdividing the problem space. A different subdivision of the problem space may be required for each of these different purposes. A subdivision you use for presenting an overview of the system to the users may not correspond to the technical subsystems you develop. Normally, any one partition of the problem space will result in one object class being included in only one subsystem. (This is a good rule of thumb which there may sometimes be reasons for not observing.) However, the same object class may be included in different subsystems in partitions of the system produced for different purposes.

System Overview Diagram for the Seminar Registration System

Our seminar registration system is a small system which was delivered as a single delivery unit. We drew a system overview diagram (Figure 8-2) to provide ourselves with an overview of the capabilities of the system.

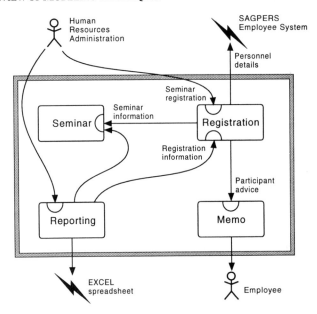

Figure 8-2: System overview diagram for the seminar registration system

In Figure 8-2, we show that the seminar registration system consists of four components:

- the **Registration** subsystem, which is the main subsystem and is used by the **HumanResourcesAdministrator** to maintain details of seminar bookings, including a note as to whether the invoice has been paid.

- the **Seminar** subsystem which includes details of the seminars attended by employees, together with details of seminar organizers. This subsystem is used by the **Registration** subsystem to obtain and maintain details of seminars. The subsystem is also used by the **Reporting** subsystem, which requests information from it in order to produce its reports.

- the **Reporting** subsystem, which is used to produce reports on seminar registrations, optionally exporting data to an **EXCEL spreadsheet**. This subsystem is used by the **HumanResourcesAdministrator**.

- the **Memo** subsystem, which is used to send e-mails to **Employee**s to notify them that their seminar has been booked or canceled.

The **Registration** subsystem uses a service from the **SagPers** employee system, which is outside the scope of our system, in order to obtain the details of individual members of staff.

Note that we show only the problem domain component in Figure 8-2. This is typical. It is often only during physical design that it becomes important to partition object classes in the other components into subsystems.

System Overview Diagram Components

The following symbols are used in the system overview diagram:

 Actor: Persons are shown as stick people and machine interfaces, including interfaces with other systems or subsystems are shown using a communication symbol (which looks like a bolt of lightning).

 System border: A box is used to show the boundary of the system, subsystem or subject area which is the subject of the diagram. Actors are shown outside the boundary. Subsystems or submodels appear inside the box.

 Subsystem or subject area: A subsystem or subject area is shown as a rounded rectangle.

Services: Services are shown as semi-circles on the edge of the subsystem rectangles. Each service has an associated service name which is shown near it.

 Actor or subsystem uses service: Arrows are used to show which services an actor or subsystem uses. The arrow points at the service which is used. The system may use services offered by systems outside the system boundary, represented as a "machine interface" actor.

Advanced System-Wide Modeling Techniques

Quality criteria for subsystems

As we mentioned earlier in this chapter, in the case of subsystems that are defined for technical reasons, rather than for organizational or presentation purposes, there are quality criteria which can be used to decide whether the subsystem definition is good.

These quality criteria can be described as follows.

- Subsystems should have high internal cohesion and low external coupling. High internal cohesion means that the object classes in the subsystem are related and have a coherent function. By low external coupling, we mean that their interface with other subsystems should be small. Chapter 24 provides more information on cohesion and coupling.

- Each subsystem interface is defined as one or more services, where each service groups functionality which the subsystem offers to other subsystems.

  The size of the interface of the subsystem should be small in relation to its internal communications. Most of a subsystem's communications should occur within the subsystem. The subsystem should have a relatively small interface with the outside world, both in terms of number of services and of the number of objects communicating with the outside world. The amount of data crossing the interface should be small.

Subsystem interfaces define the information which is passed across the subsystem boundary, without defining any subsystem-internal implementation details. This is useful where subsystems are to be developed independently, by different project teams. Provided subsystem interfaces can be clearly defined in advance, each system can then be designed independently, without affecting the other subsystems.

The quality criteria can be used in multiple ways such as:

1. Validates that a subdivision into subsystems, made for any of a number of reasons (e.g., for definition of delivery units or definition of distributable units), is a good one.

2. A system can be subdivided into subsystems in order to test the quality of a design. If the system divides into "good" subsystems, then it passes one check on design quality.

3. It is possible to adopt as a standard practice the division of a system into modules. Modules contain object classes directly and are defined as the next grouping level which is larger than an object class. They typically contain between 5 and 15 object classes and should not normally include more than 20. They should also conform to the quality criteria for subsystems, i.e., they should have high internal cohesion and low external coupling, and most communications should occur internally within the module rather than with other modules.

Defining modules is beneficial for maintainability. These modules can be used to provide a unit for maintenance and release purposes which is larger than individual object classes. Like object classes, they should have high internal cohesion and low external coupling. Maintainability benefits are gained from the use of modules which have high internal cohesion and low external coupling because changes are often localized to a single subsystem. Also, the number of object classes that have to be checked when a change is made is reduced, including normally only object classes within the module. As we have already mentioned, a benefit of object orientation is its encapsulation into object classes with the consequent localization of change. If uncontrolled communication between all the object classes in a system is allowed, however, this creates dependencies between object classes which damage maintainability. This is why we strongly recommend having a module layer with carefully defined module interfaces.

Using an object class to encapsulate a subsystem

It is possible to encapsulate systems using an object wrapper. This can be very useful for allowing the use of non-object oriented systems from an object-oriented system. It is done by defining an interface object which can be called to invoke functions provided by the encapsulated system. Only this interface object needs to be aware that the system that is used is not object-oriented and to convert object-oriented operation invocations into the appropriate form. Chapter 15 contains examples of the use of object wrappers.

It is also possible to use an object class to encapsulate access to an object-oriented subsystem. Without such an object class, all messages from outside a subsystem go directly to an object class within the subsystem, which means that the senders of messages must have some knowledge of what object classes the subsystem contains.

An alternative is to enforce a rule that all messages to object classes in the subsystem should be sent in the first place to a subsystem object which will then delegate by forwarding each message on to the relevant object class. As for an object wrapper for a non object-oriented system, this can be achieved by defining an interface object class to implement the subsystem. This interface object class has by default a set of operations that is the set of all operations offered via the subsystem's services. The object class has the task of resolving polymorphic references. That is to say, where more than one object class within the subsystem offers a given operation, it must select which object class to forward an operation to.

Whether to use subsystem objects or not depends on the circumstances. It is always a good idea to ensure that access to the operations of a subsystem requires the knowledge of as few object classes as possible. Using a subsystem object is not usually necessary for subsystems that are internal to a system. On the other hand, when building a subsystem for use by unknown third parties, it can be useful to define a single object class that is used specifically to encapsulate access to the subsystem.

Part III

The Object-Oriented Development Process

Part III describes the *process* by which object-oriented development is carried out. It emphasizes what is done in what sequence. It also describes the focus appropriate at each point in the life cycle—e.g., the focus of business object modeling as compared with object modeling in system requirements analysis, etc. Part III builds on the model information contained in Part II.

Chapter Number and Title	Contents
Chapter 9 **Managing an Object-Oriented Development Initiative**	Discusses how to introduce object-orientation into an organization.
Chapter 10 **Overview of Object-Oriented Project Life Cycles**	Introduces the basic elements of the object-oriented life cycle.
Chapter 11 **Planning an Object-Oriented Project**	Discusses how OO affects project managers responsible for scheduling, estimating, managing and controlling projects.
Chapter 12 **Business Analysis**	Reviews business analysis, the life cycle phase where many organizations today are carrying out business reengineering and/or business process reengineering.
Chapter 13 **System Requirements Analysis**	Discusses system requirements analysis, where the details of user requirements are modeled and documented. This corresponds roughly to the structured analysis phase in traditional, non-OO projects.
Chapter 14 **Logical Design**	Discusses logical design, where the process of translating user requirements into a software architecture begins. This corresponds roughly to the phase of structured design and logical data modeling in traditional, non-OO projects.
Chapter 15 **Physical Design**	Discusses physical design, which is concerned with the impact of hardware, distributed processing, GUI technology, and database technology upon the logical design. This corresponds to equivalent physical design activities in other methodologies.
Chapter 16 **Development of Object-Oriented Applications**	Discusses the options for implementation, ranging from object-oriented programming languages (OOPLs) to OO 4th generation languages to CASE tools. This corresponds to the programming, or construction, phase of any other methodological approach.
Chapter 17 **Testing, Acceptance, Cutover and Operation**	Summarizes the issues involved when testing an object-oriented system.

Chapter 9

Managing an Object-Oriented Development Initiative

It is important to realize that introducing OO into an organization will cause a major change to the way it does business. For all practical purposes, this must be treated as a business re-engineering project for an IT organization. It will probably not be the only change that an organization is trying to handle, but it may very well be the most complex. The complexity is due to the need to shift our mindset completely into what is called "Object Think".

If such changes could be faced one at a time, the situation would be more manageable. Guidelines, reference documents, and evolving methods offer help in adopting most new directions. The problems occur with the combination of several simultaneous changes whose effects are compounded and are sometimes of a conflicting nature. For example:

- Each new direction seems to depend on some or all of the others to be successful. "Can I achieve rightsizing goals without mastering client/server technologies? Or build client/server applications without understanding objects? Where do I start?"

- Every new direction calls for new technologies, and demands new job roles and responsibilities. "While my staff is shrinking, the range of technical skills that must be mastered continually increases. The gap between the leading-edge and trailing-edge of technology seems to be an ever-widening gulf. The capacity of the organization to absorb and apply new technologies appears to be a resource with finite limits."

- Each success magnifies the problems associated with legacy systems: they aren't integrated, they don't readily distribute, they lack the look and feel users have come to expect. When success increases pressure and adds to the workload, motivation and morale are difficult to maintain.

- Yesterday's solutions become today's problems. Each new direction is only partially implemented when a new cycle of change begins.

The real problem is change, especially *revolutionary* change. Information technology is a rapidly changing field. Application of that technology in a dynamic and volatile business environment compounds the issues. Continuous, complex and ever-accelerating change is a fact of life in the IT organization.

The challenge, then, is to harness change; to understand the nature of change and actively employ it as a business tool. Attempting to stop change is a futile exercise. And learning to cope with change is a victim's tactic. Winning in this set of circumstances demands that you develop a program to actively manage change. Accept that change is inevitable, then work to ensure that you achieve desired, planned change at a pace your organization can absorb.

An effective change management program determines what changes are implemented, regulates the timing and pace of change, and commits the resources necessary to ensure that planned changes are successfully implemented. Change management begins with a solid business foundation. Changes under consideration should each be evaluated on the basis of contribution to business goals. Technology is viewed as a means of meeting business objectives and is not itself an objective.

Finally, change management demands special attention to the human factor. Change is always met by fear and resistance. Understanding the roles, perspectives, and motivators of everyone, whether they are formally involved in the change project or not, is a significant contributor to the success of change projects. The changes will only be as successful as the ability of the people in your organization to overcome their fears and resistance, and commit to the changes.

Success with OO requires a commitment and a plan of action. Application developers, who are likely to be excited by the new technology, are often ready to make the commitment with no planning at all. And software managers, wary of yet another silver bullet technology, are sometimes prone to plan forever, without ever making a commitment.

Some of the necessary actions for implementing object technology are obvious: acquiring CASE tools, training the staff, etc. But there is more: risk management, pilot projects, and a host of other related activities. Introducing OO is like introducing any other major new technology, and it must therefore be planned carefully. And while some technology innovations may have a relatively limited scope—e.g., changing the programming language from Natural to Natural OO, or from C to C++—others can have a ripple effect that extends beyond the ranks of the technicians, into the wider arena of users and managers. A full-scale introduction of object technology can have as momentous an impact as the introduction of client-server technology.

This chapter summarizes the major management planning activities required for successful implementation of OO and is based on a series of planning steps articulated by Don Firesmith[1]. It begins with a discussion of the choice between revolution and evolution. The activities will be familiar to most managers, and details are available in a variety of other sources. The concern at this point is simply that we not forget any of them.

Revolution Versus Evolution

Changing from an older methodology to OO is not like going from a 386 PC to a 486 machine. It is more like going from an MS-DOS system to a Macintosh or from an IBM MVS operating system to a UNIX environment. It is abrupt change, a discontinuity from older habits. The OO paradigm is seen as a revolutionary change by some application developers, and by others as an evolutionary step beyond the older methodologies. Whatever the personal biases of the application

---

[1] Donald D. Firesmith, *"Take a Flying Leap: the plunge into OO Technology,"* American Programmer, October 1992.

developer or the software manager, the choice of approach must be made carefully in order for the OO paradigm to succeed in the organization.

The argument for revolution

In some software organizations, OO is regarded as so different from the old way of developing systems that it is hard to describe it as anything other than a revolution. The programming languages are different, the terminology is different, the notation is different, and (most importantly) the mindset is different.

Sometimes the revolutionary aspect of object technology is unavoidable, for it comes along with a number of other revolutionary buzzwords: downsizing, client-server technology, cooperative processing, GUIs, etc. Whether or not OO improves software productivity by an order of magnitude, it has rarely, if ever, been the direct cause of a tenfold reduction of staff in the software organization. Downsizing, PCs, and client-server technology, on the other hand, *do* tend to have this brutal effect. Since the late 1980s, the computer trade magazines have been filled with stories of million-dollar mainframes being replaced with $10,000 PCs, and stories of hundred-person DP empires being sacked en masse and replaced with three PC programmers (though it remains to be seen whether these traumatic upheavals will have the long-term benefits and cost savings that the revolutionaries are promising).

So if someone begins talking about OO as a revolution, it's a good idea to see if they mean OO will be *leading* the revolution, or will just be part of a larger revolutionary army. If OO is the primary topic of discussion—i.e., the issue is whether OO analysis/design methodologies should replace SA/SD or IE methodologies—then the question of revolution versus evolution is an interesting one to consider. Even within this narrow domain, revolution may turn out to be necessary—for the same reason it's necessary on the hardware side. A heavily-entrenched culture that has spent the past 20 years doing things a certain way might not embrace a different approach that may threaten its security and its very jobs. Application development organizations in some companies have become enormous bureaucracies, so involved with their committees and procedures and paperwork that they have forgotten the job they were supposed to be doing. A revolution—whether it's based on OO or something else—may be the only way of shaking the organization up and getting it to make some dramatic changes.

A revolution may also be necessary to avoid letting the OO paradigm become more and more corrupted by the older methodologies. One sees this phenomenon especially often in organizations trying to use old CASE tools to carry out OO analysis and design. "Well," says the analyst, "I know the XYZ tool calls this an entity-relationship diagram, but it's pretty close to an object diagram—so we'll just fake it." On the one hand, this spirit of flexibility is commendable, and application developers know that sometimes they have to do the best they can with the tools available. However, what happens if the analyst discovers that the XYZ tool doesn't support multiple inheritance ... or *any* inheritance ... or some way to graphically represent the encapsulation of data and function within an object ... or messages between objects? At some point, we have to 'fess up and admit it: the OO paradigm has gotten lost in the morass of old methodologies, old tools, and old thinking. Sometimes, it seems, maybe the best thing to do *is* to burn the old methodology manuals and throw the old CASE tools out the window (or send them to our fiercest competitor).

Aside from the politics involved, the idea of throwing old manuals and tools out the window involves only money. The real problem with the revolutionary approach comes when someone suggests throwing the old people out the window, too. There is a common, though unspoken, feeling that "old" software engineers (who may or may not be old in biological years, but who are old in their ways of developing software) are obsolete, and can't be salvaged. Someone who has spent the past 20 years writing COBOL or FORTRAN, using a functional decomposition design methodology, will never successfully learn an OO methodology and an OO programming language—or so the argument goes, from the mouths of the revolutionaries.[1]

Sometimes the argument involves money, power, and various aspects of classical political struggles. The older generation, that may still favor SA/SD, is the generation in power in the typical software organization. These are the folks who may still be defending COBOL and the mainframe. These are the folks that typically earn twice, or three times, as much as the younger generation of hotshot C++ programmers. Is it any wonder there should be a conflict; and is it any wonder that many of the methodological arguments have a hidden agenda, and seem to have no technical basis whatsoever?

The argument for evolution

What does the older generation have to say for itself? The arguments tend to fall into two categories: (a) there are a lot of old ideas that still have merit, and which can be salvaged in a brave new world of OO, and (b) there is a lot of old legacy software and data which mus*t* be salvaged in the brave new world of OO. This generation is also more likely than the younger revolutionaries to identify a third theme: (c) there are a lot of old software engineers who not only should be salvaged for humanitarian reasons and because of the enormous investment the company has made in them, but who *can* be salvaged, for they can eventually be converted into OO-people.

The issue of salvaging old methodological ideas into the new OO methodologies is primarily a question of degree and priority—it's not an either-or, black-and-white world. There are a number of fundamental software engineering principles that remain valid in the OO world; however, they might not have the same emphasis or dominant theme. And while principles such as striving for a system of highly cohesive, loosely coupled components remain the same, the strategies for accomplishing those principles have changed drastically. The older generation recalls that encapsulation was described rather elegantly by David Parnas in the early 1970s as information hiding, but it will usually admit that the methodologies of the 1970s typically didn't do a very good job of accomplishing information hiding.

---

[1] The deeper, and more subtle, problem in many of these organizations is that the old-timers never *really* learned any formal methodology; changing from an ad hoc approach to *any* formal approach, whether object-oriented or not, is often the biggest part of the problem.

As for salvaging the legacy systems, the older generation is likely to argue that that's non-negotiable. Most organizations have tens of millions of lines of old code, and disk farms full of DB2-based databases. The thought of all of this disappearing is simply inconceivable. Of course, this discussion can get us into the broader techno-political arguments of downsizing, reengineering, etc.—and depending on the organization, we may find a spectrum of choices, ranging from one extreme of scrapping all the old software, to the other extreme of scrapping nothing. Realistically, though, most organizations simply can't afford to throw out a 25-year investment in legacy applications—nor can they scrap their databases overnight.

Whether the OO revolutionaries like it or not, their new OO systems will have to operate in some kind of harmony with legacy software and legacy data built with older methodologies. Indeed, the vast majority of OO methodologies accept this without argument, and there are a number of straightforward strategies for interfacing object-oriented software with flat-file and relational-file databases. As for the legacy software itself, it is becoming more and more common to see object-oriented wrappers which surround the old code without throwing it away; this issue is discussed in Chapter 8.

What about the third issue—i.e., scrapping the older generation of application programmers and systems analysts, weaned on older methodologies? Here again, the older generation will argue that it is not a binary issue. The ability of a large group of software engineers to learn, assimilate, and practice object technology will probably follow a normal distribution: some will make the transition right away, some will never learn, and the vast majority will muddle along and slowly make the transition over a period of several years. The older generation also notes that OO is not the first new technology to come along—and while it may appear radically new and different from the other software methodologies du jour, those commonplace methodologies and technologies were once equally strange and alien. When entity-relationship diagrams and relational database technology was first introduced, it was a major culture shock for most organizations, but we gradually assimilated it. Structured design and structured programming were as radical and controversial in the early 1970s as OO is in the early 1990s. Ten years from now, OO will seem commonplace and boring, and we'll all be arguing about some new controversial idea.

The likely future

Smaller application development organizations may wish to consider the revolutionary approach. This is a practical approach if there is not much history that needs to be thrown away—e.g., very little legacy software, very little accumulated experience of old methodologies and practices. As noted above, there is something to be said for making a clean sweep. If nothing else, it generates an air of excitement, and gets the adrenaline flowing.

For larger IT shops, the issue of OO revolution is likely to be subsumed into the larger revolutionary issues of the day. If the former Director of Systems Development was lukewarm about OO, it's a good bet that the new Director—who was also responsible for throwing out the mainframe and introducing the first GUI-based client-server system—will be outspoken in its support[1]. And if the old guard manages to retain its hold on power, it may downplay the importance of OO, regardless of its technical merits. The result is likely to be a mixture of OO projects and old-fashioned projects for a period of several years.

Aside from these larger political issues, it is safe to predict that in most large DP shops, OO will take the evolutionary route—simply because that is the way that almost all technological innovations are introduced into society. True revolutions are few and far between; even those innovations announced as revolutions usually have a long evolutionary history.[2] And the history of our own field has been one of evolution. Technologies like structured programming, relational databases, virtual memory, etc., have typically spread slowly through the industry over a period of 14-20 years.

Obtain Initial Consulting Advice

A small IT organization, with a staff of only a dozen software engineers, might decide to jump on the OO bandwagon with no outside help. After all, there are lots of books and magazines offering information about object technology; and there are numerous seminars and computer conferences where one can obtain information. But a large IT organization, with a staff of hundreds or even thousands of people, has a different situation altogether. Because of its size and resources, it has more choices; but for the same reasons, the consequences of a mistake can be far more serious. The consequences of choosing this CASE tool or that one, and this version of OO analysis methodology or that one, can be far-reaching and subtle. Doing this without any previous experience with OO is highly risky. The first step should be to obtain advice and guidance from an experienced, objective outsider.

In many cases, this initial step will include a brief training session to acquaint management and application developers with the benefits of OO, as well as an overview of the technology itself. But more important is the planning activity that follows. An experienced consultant should have a battle plan similar to the one discussed in this chapter, which shows the key decision-makers in the organization what steps are involved, how long it will take, how much it will cost, what benefits are likely to accrue, and what risks must be accepted.

Sometimes this advice is provided by individuals or companies that have a hidden agenda—e.g., to put dozens of their own consultants on the client site to begin building an application with the latest high-tech object technology. Ideally, the initial consulting effort should be a "one-shot" engagement, in order to ensure objectivity, with no commitment of ongoing training, consulting,

---

[1] Aside from the politics, there is a natural reason for this marriage: as mentioned elsewhere in this book, OO methods are typically a better "metaphor" for modeling a client-server, GUI-based system. So if the organization is prepared to endure the revolution of GUIs and client-server, it should also be prepared to embrace the revolution of objects. Indeed, to do otherwise may doom it to failure.

[2] For an excellent discussion of this point, with examples going back to the steam engine, the cotton gin, and other major innovations of the Industrial Age, see George Basalla's *The Evolution of Technology* (Cambridge, England: Cambridge University Press, 1990).

or software tools from the vendor. Depending on the size of the client organization, the initial engagement should take somewhere between a few days and a few weeks, and the cost should be a negligible percentage of the organization's overall investment in object technology.

Obtain Management Commitment

There is no point beginning an OO implementation plan if the organization cannot obtain at least a "gut-level" management commitment that the technology is worth considering. It must be remembered that, for many senior executives, OO is just another buzzword—like structured methods, client-server, CASE, downsizing, expert systems, reengineering, and a dozen other buzzwords. If it provides quantifiable business benefits, they *may* be interested. However, even with the prospect of improved productivity and quality, they may perceive political risks that they would prefer to avoid, and they may suffer from the pervasive problem that software people normally associate only with end-users: resistance to change. Even if senior management does support object technology, they may not be *excited* by it. It's just one more decision to make.

This is a crucial issue, and it is often more important for the success of object orientation in an organization than the technical features of the methodology and CASE tools, or the choice of C++ or Natural OO over Smalltalk. If management is opposed or blasé about object technology, then it probably won't work. A grass-roots revolution may lead to some low-level OOPL usage, and a few renegade OO projects, but it will fade away after two or three years, and the organization may return to business as usual. To make OO really work well, for example, usually requires a commitment to reusable components, and that requires a rather substantial change in management practices and policies. And on a larger scale, to make OO work requires a commitment of *time*. It will probably be 2-3 years before the investment begins to pay off.

The willingness to make such a commitment—even though it is a tentative commitment at this early stage—is usually based on a strong feeling by management that things are not going well, or that they should be going much better; and it requires an act of faith that object technology can be one of the major solutions to the existing problems. In the chaotic world of the 1990s, it's hard to imagine that any IT organization could conclude that it has no problems—but it must be remembered that the perspective of the application developers is not always the same as that of senior management. Management may have become cynical over the years, and may be resigned to the fact that things will be screwed up no matter what they do. This is sometimes expressed with phrases like, "This is the best of all possible worlds; anything else that we might consider doing would just lead to worse results."

Also, note that management may have decided to invest its time, money, and energy in alternative approaches to improving software productivity and quality. For example, tremendous improvements can be achieved by focusing on peopleware issues, CASE tools, reusability, and a variety of technologies that are compatible with OO, but do not *require* OO. And some organizations are so thoroughly involved with downsizing strategies involving client-server systems, networks, distributed databases, and other technologies that they have no time for OO. This can be frustrating for the application developers in the organization who are passionately committed to OO, but it may make good business sense.

Ultimately, a passionate commitment is crucial for OO to survive the ongoing political crises that the organization faces, as well as the more deadly problem of inertia. And while it is unrealistic to assume that all of the organization's management hierarchy will exhibit any degree of excitement toward OO, it is important to find at least one such person. That manager, often dubbed the champion, is the one willing to continue popularizing OO in the face of boredom, passive resistance, or outright hostility. In many cases, that manager is willing to risk some of his/her political career by using OO on a pilot project, so that the results can be demonstrated to the rest of the organization.

Conduct Pilot Projects

Like all new technologies, OO needs to be validated and demonstrated to the organization. This is usually done through the mechanism of a pilot project. An organization that has used pilot projects to introduce CASE, or structured methods, or various other new technologies will be familiar with this concept. It has been discussed in various other books,[1] and is summarized briefly here.

A key characteristic of a pilot project is that it should be medium-sized, within the context of the organization. For most organizations, this typically means a project that will involve half a dozen technical staff members, and last about six months. The danger with a pilot project that is too small is that it won't impress anyone—after all, who needs fancy technology to build a system that your 10 year old kid could do over the weekend? And the danger of a pilot project that is too big is that (a) it may take years before anyone will see the results, and (b) its size and scope may create problems that will be unfairly blamed on object technology—indeed, OO may turn out to be the straw that breaks the camel's back.

A good pilot project is important and visible, but not so critical that its failure will bankrupt the organization; another reason for avoiding the overly-large pilot project. On the other hand, a pilot project that is buried in the back room of the research labs won't get the attention of the key decision-makers in the organization. And a pilot project judged to be a frivolous toy won't get the respect of the managers who risk their careers on mission-critical projects.

A good pilot project should be staffed by enthusiastic volunteers who are well-trained, and well-supported by expert consulting assistance. There is no point holding a gun to someone's head and insisting that they participate in a pilot project. There are likely to be enough problems without worrying about sabotage and sullen resistance. Training of the pilot project team is essential. Even if management needs to pinch pennies when it considers the full-scale training plan, it should avoid scrimping on this initial training effort. A full week of training in OO analysis and OO design is an absolute minimum, and 3-4 weeks is preferred. Outside mentor consulting is also highly recommended. In this case, it may be wise to choose a consultant associated with the

---

[1]   See, for example, Ed Yourdon's *Managing the Structured Techniques*, 4th edition (Englewood Cliffs, NJ: Prentice-Hall, 1989).

CASE tool used by the project team, or a consultant who carried out the initial training for the pilot team staff.

Another important component of a good pilot project is metrics. The team should have additional resources who can devote time to measuring key aspects of the analysis, design, coding, and testing activities—especially the basic metrics of cost, effort (in person-days), schedule duration, and quality (e.g., defects per thousand lines of code). This may turn out to be a part-time job, but it should be carried out by someone who is independent of the technical work itself. At the same time, the schedule should allow for the project team members to record their own observations throughout the project—in the form of logs, diaries, or informal notes. This information can be invaluable for the rest of the organization, if OO is eventually adopted on a full-scale basis.

Obviously, the successes and failures of the pilot project should be publicized. There is a natural political tendency to over-emphasize the successes and hide the failures, but this is unfortunate. A great deal can be learned from things that went wrong, and it does not require that the fundamental technology used in the pilot project has to be thrown out. Indeed, for large organizations, it's a good idea to try two or three pilot projects before a final conclusion is reached about the viability of the proposed new technology.

Develop a Risk Management Plan

One of the key benefits of a pilot project is that it provides valuable data for a risk-management plan, which should be part of the planning process for implementing any new technology. It would be foolish, of course, to suggest that object technology is risk-free. One of the first risk-oriented questions that management will ask is, "What if this stuff doesn't provide the benefits that we keep hearing about?" What if we try this on a large, risky, mission-critical project and it fails? What if it takes longer to implement OO in the organization than originally planned? What if it costs much more than planned? And so forth...[1]

In addition to the management-oriented risks, the application developers can usually identify additional risks. What if we can't find decent CASE tools? What if we can't find a compiler for C++ on the machine we use? What if OO leads to performance problems, hampering the run-time efficiency of high-volume on-line systems? What if we choose the wrong OOAD methodology, and find three years from now that it's not supported by any of the major CASE or OO vendors? And so forth...

---

[1] On the other hand, there are presumably some risks associated with continuing with the current methods, techniques, tools, and technologies. The risks of the old way have to be compared with the risks of the new way.

The defenders of object technology will be tempted to put their blinders on and ignore many of these risks. They may also become emotionally involved in their defense of OO, making it difficult to carry on an objective evaluation. Conversely, the skeptics and cynics will revel in this activity, for they can conjure up all manner of risks ("What if the sky collapses? What if object-orientation causes cancer?") Clearly, objectivity and experience are crucial in this area of planning for OO. Fortunately, there are now a number of excellent references to help managers assess software risks.[1]

Identifying and quantifying risks is just the beginning. Managing the risks is an ongoing activity, and it requires a conscious management effort and plan. For example, the risk associated with OO CASE tools is not one that can be evaluated once and then forgotten. The old-guard CASE vendors are going through an evolutionary process of deciding when and how to introduce OO support in their products; meanwhile, the young Turks are introducing brand-new CASE tools, but there is no guarantee that their products (or their companies) will survive in a highly competitive marketplace. This is especially problematic because neither the CASE vendors, nor the users of CASE tools, can be certain which of the commercial brands of OOA/OOD methodology will survive and prosper over the next few years.

Thus, a careful OO implementation plan will follow a standard risk-management approach of identifying the top-ten risk items and then tracking them on a regular basis. In monthly status meetings, for example, management should be apprised of the changes in the top-ten list, and should review the plans for mitigating and minimizing those risks.

Develop a Training Plan

Training and education is as important for successful implementation of object technology as it is for any other new technology introduced into a DP organization. Whenever an organization has considered the introduction of CASE, structured methods, relational database technology, client-server systems, or pen-based computing, it has typically acknowledged the need to provide the software engineers and the project managers with appropriate training. However, the need for education may be greater with OO than with previous methodologies because it requires a substantial shift in the mind set of the software engineer. Structured analysis and design, for example, involves a number of specific terms, graphical notations, and techniques. However, it employs the fundamental principle of top-down functional decomposition, which is likely to already be familiar to most software engineers.

A key factor in implementing OO is providing the right training at the right time. This is no simple feat. In addition, formal training is rarely sufficient for complete mastery of complex technical subjects like OO, and it is often poorly timed within the organization (e.g., the training takes place the week *after* the analysis and design phase of the project has formally ended, when everyone is told that they are supposed to be busy coding). If your training program consists only

---

[1]   See, for example, Robert Charette's *Application Strategies for Risk Analysis* (New York: McGraw-Hill, 1990) and *Software Engineering Risk Analysis and Management* (New York: McGraw-Hill, 1989).

of formal training options of classroom, CBT, books, etc., then you are bound to fail in your effort to implement OO. This type of training also will not overcome most of the resistance you are going to face to this new way of doing things. You should assume that everyone is a skeptic and will need to not only have the rightness of OO proved through formal training but also through their accomplishment of successful projects using OO.

For these reasons, you need to have a complete training program set up, implemented and managed. This training program should encompass the following components:

- A plan or career path for developing the OO skills in each of your staff. You may not want to, or need to, train all of your staff members this year; but if any of your staff members are left out of the plan, they may well conclude that they have been sentenced to technological obsolescence.

- A standard business process (methodology) for the use of OO in your organization, that is set up to meet your needs.

- Formal training options,

- Special guided training experience, or mentoring,

- Practice sessions,

- Internal conferences where staff present their work and their results

- Measurement of progress and success

The success you achieve in training your staff depends on how complete your program is. If you leave out any of the components then you run the risk of your staff falling back into previous patterns.

For most application developers, a one-day lecture is sufficient to introduce the concepts of OOA, and a 5-day workshop is sufficient to explain the concepts, discuss them, and practice their application on small classroom exercises. The same is true for OOD and OOP, as well as OO-related project management. The training requirements for a full exposure to object technology range from a minimum of four days to a maximum of four weeks. In addition, a half-day or full-day executive briefing for senior management is important in order to enable the culture-change required for OO. And a one-day or two-day course is usually necessary for project managers and middle-level managers to discuss the key differences between managing conventional projects versus OO projects.

That's enough to get started, with some reasonable chance of applying the technology successfully on a real system. The length of time required to practice the technologies to the point where the application developer feels comfortable and competent ranges from an absolute minimum of one month to a maximum of three years. For most veteran software developers with some prior exposure to programming and older methodologies, this competence-building period is likely to be 6-12 months. If it lasts longer than three years, it's unlikely that the techniques will ever be mastered. Obviously, these numbers can vary tremendously depending on the software engineer's age, intelligence, motivation, personality, attitude, aptitude, prior experience and habits, etc.—but the organization that expects overnight assimilation of object technology is in for a rude shock.

Not everyone in the organization will want or need management-related training. We might assume that the project managers and various levels of supervisory personnel would attend 1-day or 2-day sessions devoted to OO project management, while the software engineering technicians focus instead on OOA, OOD, and OOP. But this raises an interesting question: what comes first? Ironically, the same question arose 15 years ago, when structured analysis, design, and programming methodologies were first being introduced. The advice today is the same as it was then: begin with analysis, then move to design and programming, and conclude with testing.

The reasons are the same, too: brilliant programming may end up doing nothing more than helping the project team arrive at a disaster sooner than before. Admittedly, the introduction of prototyping in most OO methodologies makes this argument less persuasive; on the other hand, what many OO developers call prototyping is just hacking. For large, complex projects, it continues to be important to model the business requirements properly; and then to model the software architecture properly; and only then to worry about how the code will be written.

The political problems of beginning with OOP and then moving up to OOD and OOA are also the same as they were 15 years ago. There is a danger that the organization might run out of training money before the entire sequence of training courses is finished. And it would be a shame to have done nothing more than introduce a new programming language like Smalltalk without changing the mindset and the dialogue between the user and the analyst. On the other hand, politics may preclude the introduction of OOA at the outset. The user may simply *refuse* to discuss the requirements of his system from an OO perspective.

The special guided training experience is one of the key options in that it combines formal training and a pilot project into a major learning experience. In this type of program you set up an 8 - 12 week project that has 2 goals. The primary goal is the training of the team in the use and practice of OO. The secondary goal is the delivery of an application. The project plan takes into account all the formal training required and the work on the pilot project. All formal training is done in a just-in-time (JIT) fashion. That is, you concentrate each training event on those skills required to produce the next project milestone. Each training event should also include some orientation to what will come after this milestone, but should not place major emphasis on the transfer of those skills. When the training event is over the team sets about accomplishing the milestone. This is done under the guidance of an experienced project leader. During the work on the milestone periodic practice sessions should be led by the project leader. These practice sessions serve as formal reinforcers of what was taught during the training event and planning for how those skills will be utilized in the meeting of the milestone.

We have used these types of training experiences for over 7 years in helping our customers develop these types of skills. We call them Fasttracks. Many organizations have used similar types of experiences in carrying out an intern training program. The University of Texas, Austin, has just such a program that all new employees must go through. The difference between intern training programs and this concept is that Fasttracks do not use a case study. Instead they focus on an application needed by the business and include not only the IT staff but also the business professionals who will participate in the development of this and subsequent applications.

The practice session experience is one that we have found particularly useful for all staff, regardless of their experience. Its purpose is to make sure that everyone involved in a project is ready for what comes next. In other words that they have practiced or rehearsed exactly what they will be doing and know exactly how it will fit into achieving the next milestone of the project. No matter how much experience a person has, their skills will get rusty. These sessions help to reinforce good habits, sharpen up skills, diminish bad habits.

Organizations like NASA Ames Research have found that it is quite helpful to use their instructors as in-house consultants to OO pilot projects, making themselves available up to eight hours a week to assist in design workshops, model reviews, walkthroughs, etc. Indeed, this may evolve into the practice of mentors, where those more familiar with the object technology can act as leaders and guides to shepherd newcomers into the fold.

Most organizations are likely to introduce object technology the way they have introduced many technologies in the past: herd all the software engineers into a training room, subject them to an intense sheep dip form of training; and then herd them back to their desks with the instructions that their schedules have been cut in half because OO has doubled their productivity.

Whether this approach can ever work is debatable. However, it is particularly dangerous with the evolutionary approach to OO discussed earlier. If the training experience basically tells the application developers that "OO is really like that old stuff, except there are a few new buzzwords you have to learn, and you gotta start programming in C++," and if the CASE tools perpetuate that mental framework, then there is a strong likelihood they will continue doing whatever they were doing in the past—with a bit of window dressing to convince management that they really are doing up-to-date OO-stuff.

Instead of this, IT organizations should seriously consider a revolutionary training approach, *even if they intend to introduce the OO methodology in an evolutionary fashion*. Thus, don't teach OO concepts with C++ (or object-oriented COBOL); use Smalltalk instead, because it will *force* software engineers to look at the systems development process from an OO perspective. Don't use traditional CASE tools that have added a few OO bells and whistles; spend the extra money to buy one or two copies of a pure OO CASE tool that does *not* support dataflow diagrams, entity-relationship diagrams, and all the familiar icons from of methodologies of yore. Such an approach is roughly comparable to a total immersion form of learning a new language, or an Outward Bound experience of putting people into a strange environment where they have few familiar tools and comforts to work with.

Document Management Expectations

It is important to document management's expectations of the new object technology, in quantifiable terms, before everyone gets completely carried away with the new technology. Presumably, one of the expectations of object technology will be improved productivity. But how much improvement, and over what period of time? Will management be satisfied with a 10 percent improvement, or does success ultimately mean a tenfold quantum leap? Does it have to be accomplished over the next six months, or is this part of a five-year plan?

But, success with object technology also hinges on some other factors. For example, the productivity improvements from OO may turn out to be highly dependent on reusability. If so, how much reusability does management expect? Is this change supposed to happen overnight, or does management expect that it will be accomplished gradually, over a three-year period?

Some of the expectations will involve soft factors that may be hard to quantify. For example, OO may be seen as a necessary enabler technology to facilitate GUI interfaces for end-users—and while everyone is in favor of more user-friendly interfaces, how are we supposed to judge how good a job we've done? Sometimes it means simply that we have to try harder to find a legitimate quantifiable justification. For example, if we can document a reduction in training costs or data-entry errors with the new GUI interfaces, that can be used as part of the justification for OO. And sometimes the process may lead to passing the buck—e.g., object technology may turn out to be the necessary enabler for a soft benefit like GUI interfaces that the users insist on having, and that they are willing to pay for.

In any case, whatever the expectations are, they should be articulated, quantified, and documented in as much detail as possible. This is important in order to judge the success of the new technology later on—but it is also important in the early stages in order to find the hidden agendas that some technicians and managers may be holding close to their chest. Technicians, especially, may be clamoring for object technology simply because it is the latest and most interesting technology around; managers may be clamoring for OO to serve their own political purposes (e.g., to discredit a rival manager, etc.).

Develop an OO Development Life Cycle

The OO paradigm typically involves the concept of prototyping; however, it is possible—if one insists—to use OOA, OOD, and OOP within the most conservative waterfall life cycle imaginable. But since the introduction of OO is likely to challenge or threaten the existing life cycle culture within the organization, it is important that management address the issue carefully as part of the planning process.

Consultants and outside advisors are likely to recommend a prototyping or spiral life cycle model; the younger generation of application developers, who see OO as part of the new wave of computing, are likely to do the same. But if the organization has no previous experience with such life cycles, it may be hard to distinguish between prototyping and unadulterated hacking. An obvious way to experiment with the concept under reasonably well-controlled conditions is the pilot-project approach discussed above.

The change from a waterfall life cycle to a prototyping life cycle is a substantial change in itself, and one could reasonably argue that it should be investigated independently of OO. Indeed, there is no reason why one must follow an object-oriented approach in order to use prototyping (although the converse is easier to argue). With good CASE tools and/or a powerful 4GL and screen-painter, it's eminently practical to implement a prototyping life cycle using structured methods or information engineering.

But, as noted earlier, OO and prototyping tend to go hand in hand. If the organization decides to adopt OO, it is usually very hard to resist a prototyping mindset. Part of this is the result of another "hand-in-hand" phenomenon: OO systems are almost always associated with GUI interfaces, while older methodologies (which followed a waterfall life cycle) are associated with dumb-terminal, character-based interfaces. GUI interfaces demand prototyping; hence OO projects which use GUI interfaces inevitably find themselves operating in this fashion.

Choose OOA/OOD/OOP/OOT Methods

As noted in Appendix A, there are approximately half a dozen relatively popular, and another dozen or more less publicized, but equally meritorious, OO analysis and design methodologies in use throughout North America and Europe at the time this book was written. It is quite possible that some newcomers will join the list over the next few years, and it is also possible that some of those currently in vogue will quietly fade from the scene. But it is likely to be another 3-5 years before the field narrows to two or three dominant OO methodologies.

In the meantime, the typical application development organization has two choices: buy or build. The first choice involves choosing one of the commercially available methodologies—e.g., the OOA/OOD methodology of Booch, Rumbaugh, Jacobson, Firesmith, Coad/Yourdon, Shlaer/Mellor, Martin/Odell, or the approach described in this book—and adopting it essentially in its published form, with a minimal amount of customizing to adapt the methodology to its own needs. Such a choice must be made not only on the technical merits of the methodology itself, but on various other factors such as the availability of CASE tools, training courses, consultants, etc. And then one must cross one's collective organizational fingers and hope that the methodology prospers in the marketplace, and that one is not stuck with a fate akin to choosing PL/I as a programming language.[1]

The other alternative is to take the best of several different methodologies and merge them together. This has been the common practice of many large IT organizations when using older methodologies such as structured analysis and design. One could argue that it is unlikely that any single OO methodology will be universally applicable to all sizes, shapes, and types of applications in the full spectrum of IT shops around the world. Even if one could make such a claim, it is unlikely that it would be universally popular. For better or worse, people like to tinker and customize their methodology, just as they like to tinker with the human interface on their GUI-based workstations. A minimal amount of customizing is almost always necessary with any methodology.

In the past, an organization's decision to fiddle with a methodology had little impact on its ability to practice the methodology in a rigorous, consistent fashion. But this has begun to change dramatically with the proliferation of CASE-based methodologies. Of course, most CASE tools

---

[1] Our intention in this book has been to minimize the risk of introducing a stillborn methodology by synthesizing mainstream OO concepts; our aim in any future versions of the methodology is to remain in the mainstream.

allow for a certain amount of customization and flexibility—but only up to a point. Indeed, even relatively cosmetic features such as the shape or color of the icons in the diagrams may be frozen, with no facility for modification by users of the CASE tool. Thus, if the organization feels strongly that it wants to stray relatively far from the pure version of one commercial methodology, and especially if it decides to mix and match the features of several different methodologies, it will usually be forced to choose an expensive "meta-CASE" tool that permits a much broader, more powerful form of customization.

Of course, if the organization customizes too much, it will end up with an entirely unique methodology of its own. This has ramifications in terms of training, ability to recruit experienced software engineers, etc. There is an analogy with spoken languages. In a television-based society like the United States, for example, there is more of a tendency for people across the land to speak a neutral, unaccented "television-broadcaster" form of English. Local accents still exist, but they do not prove a hindrance to communication. Someone from Boston can communicate with someone from Texas, even though it may require a certain amount of tolerance on both parts. But in other countries, the accents are so different that they become known as dialects, and the dialects are sometimes so different that they might as well be different languages. The people from one region of China, for example, may be entirely unable to understand the people in another region. This is not a situation we want to create with OO methodologies.

Choose OOP Language and Compiler

Although this books focuses on the area of analysis and design, it is nevertheless obvious that a commitment to object technology eventually requires a commitment to a programming language. Though it is conceivable to adopt OOA and OOD within a non-OOPL environment, very few organizations are likely to do so. At the time this book was written, most organizations tended to equate a commitment to object technology with a commitment to C++. But of course, there are other choices: Smalltalk, Eiffel, Ada9X, and object-oriented COBOL. There are higher-level OO-based languages such as Software AG's OO-Natural, PowerBuilder, Visual Basic, VisualAge, etc.

As with the choice of OOA/OOD methodologies, the choice of an object-oriented programming language is based on many factors—only one of which is the list of technical features for supporting OO concepts. The organization typically must decide, first, whether it wants to make a revolutionary change (e.g., from COBOL to Smalltalk) or an evolutionary change (e.g., from C to C++). It must take into account the availability of trained programmers, ease of training, performance issues, ability to interface with the existing database and telecommunications environment etc. It must also take into account the suitability of the language for the application domain—which is probably the most important reason application developers have been slow to adopt a language like C++ for business applications.

And, of course, it must take into account the availability of compilers for the language. There are numerous compilers for languages like C++ and Ada, and one can be reasonably sure of finding one or two for almost any hardware platform and operating system environment. With Smalltalk, the choice is essentially limited to four vendors: Digitalk, ParcPlace Systems, IBM, and Easel. With other languages, such as Visual Basic, the choice may even be limited to a single vendor.

We believe that in the next few years, the language issue is likely to become less important—simply because more and more CASE tools will come with robust code-generators. But this may simply shift the emphasis to the CASE tools, as discussed below.

Choose OO CASE Tools and Repository

A serious investment in object technology is not recommended unless the organization acquires adequate tools for its software engineers. This does not mean that every application developer must have a CASE tool on his or her desk the very instant the organization makes the commitment to object technology—but CASE tools must definitely be part of the planning process.

The key issues for OO CASE tools are these:

- ability to support appropriate diagramming notation for the basic OO concepts of classes, objects, inheritance hierarchies, aggregations, etc.,

- ability to hide and reveal portions of the model,

- browsing capabilities,

- consistency-checks and error-checking capabilities,

- code generation, and

- integration with other tools, repositories, etc.

Each of these criteria is discussed in more detail below.

Support for diagramming notations

While one could carry out object-oriented programming with nothing more than a C++ compiler, it's difficult to imagine a serious form of OOA or OOD without a CASE tool that supports the various diagrams that have appeared in this book. The issue of graphical support is a familiar one to CASE users, and is discussed in great detail in standard CASE textbooks.

Hiding and revealing portions of the model

OO models can become incredibly complex. An important feature of an OO CASE tool is its ability to hide or reveal portions of the model, so that the systems analyst and/or user only has to see the relevant portion. Examples of this capability include the following:

- Hiding or revealing the relationships between object classes.

- Hiding or revealing the attributes in an object class.

- Hiding or revealing the operations/methods in an object class.

- Hiding or revealing messages between object classes.

- *Selective* hiding of messages or operations—e.g., hiding all messages between implicit operations in the object classes (e.g., the operations to read and update attribute values, create new instances of classes, etc.).

- Highlighting sequences of messages (sometimes known as threads) between a specified group of collaborating object classes.

- Hiding or revealing the parameters associated with a message.

Browsing capabilities

Since OO methodologies place such great emphasis on reusability, it is important for the analyst to have powerful tools to help find potentially reusable object-classes. At a bare minimum, this means that the CASE tool must have an adequate find or search capability; but it also means that the tool should allow the user to open one or more windows in a GUI environment, so that a search can be conducted in the midst of various other activities.

A great deal of browsing takes place in a manner quite different from the straightforward searching by keyword. Analysts may wish to browse through the levels of a class hierarchy; they may wish to quickly determine all of the classes which a given class uses, or is used by; etc.

Consistency checking and error checking

Error-checking of a large, complex systems analysis model has always been one of the major justifications for CASE technology. This issue existed long before OOA and OOD methodologies became popular. Every application; developer and project manager knows that it is far more cost-effective to detect a systems analysis error *during* the analysis phase, rather than letting it remain undetected until the programming, testing, or operational phase of the project.

The details of error-checking depend, of course, on the particular OO methodology chosen. But it's appropriate to ask questions like: does the CASE tool support encapsulation, inheritance, message-passing and the other characteristic features of OO? Does it really support the *details*, including all of the error-checking features, of your favorite OO guru? Amazingly, some CASE vendors are now promoting their tools as object-oriented in nature, and yet users have no way of *seeing* an object on the CASE tool display screen. All they can do is view the data relationships (via ERDs), the object behavior (via state transition diagrams) and the object communication (via a recently renamed diagram heretofore known as a DFD). With such tools, beware: you may not get any OO-based error-checking capabilities at all!

Code generation

Without code-generation capabilities, an OOA/OOD CASE tool becomes little more than an electronic Etch-a-Sketch. We learned this lesson with traditional CASE tools by the end of the 1980s. Sadly, we seem to be learning it all over again with OO CASE tools. One reason this is a problem is that a substantial number of the early OO CASE tools have been developed by small vendors who lack the resources to provide code generating capabilities in their product. Some of them evolved from earlier tools to support structured analysis and data modeling—and they had no code generation capabilities for those tools, either!

Fortunately, this situation is beginning to change: there are now a respectable number of OO CASE tools which generate C++, Ada, Smalltalk, or other OOPL code. This is particularly important for the OO field, since many of the current "true believers" of OO methodology are actually OO programmers. If someone recommends that they use an upper-CASE tool which does *not* generate code, they are likely to ignore it and return to their hand-coded OOPL world.[1]

Even if the CASE tool does generate code, there is a danger of anarchy and chaos. If the programmer makes changes to the generated code rather than to the analysis-level or design-level models, then (by definition) the models and the code will begin to drift apart. Sooner or later, the CASE-level analysis/design models will be seen as obsolete or irrelevant, and will be thrown away. As a result, another important feature of an OO CASE tool is its ability to maintain bidirectional synchronization between the graphical models and the generated code. Thus, the real key is that the code (whether automatically generated, or manually written by the programmer) should be integrated with the CASE tool.

Integration with other CASE tools

Even though OO is a brave new world for many software engineers, OO CASE tools will not live entirely in their own world. There are already a number of extremely important and useful CASE tools which should continue to be useful even if the organization changes its software development methodology. These include tools for metrics, software quality assurance, documentation, testing, etc. OO CASE tools should be constructed to take advantage of these existing capabilities, and should interface smoothly with them wherever possible. Ultimately, this means that the OO CASE tools will have to be aware of the CASE industry standards such as PCTE, SGML, CDIF, etc.

Identify OO-based metrics

Researchers like Chidamber and Kemerer have begun proposing specific software metrics to evaluate the goodness of an OO-based design. Similarly, organizations like the International Function Point User's Group (IFPUG) have begun developing an object-oriented version of the "function point" metric, while other researchers like Tom McCabe have begun developing object-oriented extensions of the cyclomatic complexity metric.

In addition to metrics like these, the organization will need to decide what metrics need to be captured to help manage the process of OO-based software development. What kind of units of work need to be measured, and what activities of what kind of project personnel need to be measured? If reusability is a major component of the OO paradigm, it is likely, for example, that more attention will be focused on the reusable class library (how many components are in the library? how often are they used? how many people are involved in maintaining and testing the library components?) Similarly, there will be more people involved in user-interface issues, and various other differences in the mix of people and activities during the project.

---

[1] Sometimes the opposite problem exists: an OO code-hacker may not trust the code generated by the CASE tool, and they may resist using an OOA/OOD CASE tool if it *does* generate code!

The pilot projects, once again, should be seen as an opportunity to experiment with metrics. Indeed, the organization is likely to be utterly unaware of *what* metrics it wants to capture until it sees how the pilot projects unfold. And, as is true of any software metrics initiative, *no* metrics should be considered permanent. As the organization evolves, and as it becomes more mature in its use of object technology, the metrics should change, too.

Software metrics have become a hot technology in the past few years. There are several excellent textbooks on the subject, including those of Capers Jones[1], Larry Putnam[2], Tom DeMarco[3], and Bob Grady.[4] Thus far, the standard treatises on software metrics do not have an object-oriented perspective, but this is likely to change over the next years.

Revise Software Development Plan

All of the activities discussed previously are part of an overall software process that the organization uses. The new OO practices and procedures should be consolidated into a single reference document. Note that a complete software development plan will typically include descriptions of standards for analysis, design, coding, and other activities in the project; reviews of the various work-products produced during the project; and documentation of those work-products. All of these need to be adapted for the new OO world.

Of course, the organization is unlikely to have enough experience to develop an adequate process manual at the beginning of its adventure in OO-land. Based on the experiences of the initial pilot projects, a condensed version of such a document can be drafted—perhaps in as little as 10-20 pages. Even if it ends up being a document as big as this book, it should be done quickly by a small group that recognizes it is involved in a prototyping effort, too. The document they write should be considered a first draft of an evolving set of process standards.

Modify software development organization

When all of the steps described in this chapter have been carried out, it is inevitable that the software development organization itself will change. The introduction of object technology becomes a catalyst for reengineering of the development organization itself. The political structure and organizational culture changes; job titles may change; responsibilities will have to be redefined; and—though it is certainly not our intention with our methodology—downsizing may occur.

---

[1] Capers Jones, *Applied Software Measurement* (New York: McGraw-Hill, 1991)

[2] Larry Putnam and Ware Myers, *Measures for Excellence: Reliable Software on Time, Within Budget* (Englewood Cliffs, NJ: Yourdon Press/Prentice Hall, 1992)

[3] Tom DeMarco, Controlling Software Projects (Englewood Cliffs, NJ: Yourdon Press/Prentice Hall, 1982)

[4] Robert Grady, Practical *Software Metrics for Project Management and Process Improvement* (Englewood Cliffs, NJ: Prentice Hall, 1992). See also Robert Grady and Deborah Caswell's earlier book, *Software Metrics: Implementing a Company-Wide Program* (Englewood Cliffs, NJ: Prentice Hall, 1987)

The most common aspect of organizational change caused by object technology involves reuse. While it is certainly possible for each application developer and each project team to act as a producer and consumer of reusable object-oriented components, this kind of laissez-faire approach has severe organizational obstacles. In most cases, the manager of an application development project has a fixed schedule and budget that does not permit any investment of resources for creation of a general-purpose component that might be useful in other projects. Even if a project team does create a potentially reusable component, the resources usually don't exist within a single project budget to provide for the additional testing, quality assurance, and documentation that would be required to make it a truly robust component that could be used safely across the organization. And even if such a robust component *was* developed, there would be problems during the ongoing use of the component. If the author of the component decided to change it for the benefit of the application for which it was originally developed (a common occurrence during the maintenance phase of a system), then who will worry about the potential impact of the change on the other users of the component? How will version control and configuration management be carried out?

The answer to these questions, in many cases, is to create a new organizational group whose only task is the creation, management, and support of the organization's reusable components. This Software Parts department has its own budget, reflecting the organization's understanding that the components are capital assets, rather than something to be funded by the normal operating budget. Such a department can have its own testing, quality assurance, documentation, and development personnel. And it might have its own consultants or hot-line help desk, to provide information to other potential users of the components throughout the organization.

The rest of the organization then becomes consumers of these components, though they would probably be encouraged to submit candidate components to the Software Parts department for inclusion in the library. To make this work properly (i.e., to avoid the dismal fate of having the entire thing ignored by the application developers), the organization may also wish to change its compensation and reward structure. Some US organizations, for example, offer cash rewards to their application developers when a reusable component is accepted, and ongoing royalties when those components are used by other members of the organization.

All of this has a feedback effect on the development process. For example, one software factory in Manila has devoted 25 percent of its application developers to the Software Parts department. Meanwhile, the remaining developers are instructed that they may not create a component of their own, during an application development project, unless they can convince their project manager that the required component does not already exist in the library.

Chapter 10

Overview of Object-Oriented Project Life Cycles

Once object technology has been introduced into an organization, it needs to be applied to individual application development projects. We realize, of course, that the organization may not be able to apply object technology to every project at the outset, and that some projects may involve only limited activities (e.g., minor maintenance enhancements of an ancient legacy system). But the typical case, which we will explore in detail in this book, is the development of a *new* application, which will be specified, designed, coded, tested, and delivered to the user.

In Part II of this book, we explored the various models which comprise our OOAD approach. In this section of the book, we examine the *process* of object-oriented development: what activities should be carried out, what tasks are performed, and what deliverables should be produced? We provide an overview in this chapter; Chapters 11-17 discuss each of the development process activities in more detail.

The Phases of Development

Our approach follows a traditional definition of the life cycle phases of an application development project:

- ***Project definition and planning***—this is where the scope and boundary of the project are defined; thus, for example, the project sponsors may determine that the project will encompass payroll but not all of human resource management within the organization. Feasibility studies and cost/benefit calculations are normally carried out at this stage (subject, of course, to revision based on more detailed information provided in the subsequent phases); project personnel are assigned, and tentative budgets and schedules are estimated (or negotiated). These activities are not discussed in this book, though they can be significantly affected by the use of object technology; the existence of reusable components, for example, can have a significant impact on the schedule and budget -- and thus the fundamental feasibility -- of the project. Similarly, the benefits that are expected from the new system may depend on the use of object technology in order to provide, for example, GUI interfaces or client-server features of the system that would otherwise be impractical.

- *Analysis*

    - *Business analysis*—this is where we model all or part of the business, in order to understand the nature of the business, how it is carried out today, and/or how the user wishes to carry it out in the future. Business analysis provides a preliminary understanding of specific business areas for which computer technology is presumed to be needed to implement significant changes or improvements in the way the business is carried out. We recommend that business analysis should be time-boxed to ensure that it does not absorb an unnecessary amount of effort or a prolonged period of time.

- *System requirements analysis*—this is where we develop a clear understanding of the required capabilities of the system to be developed, based on business use. These capabilities are documented in such a way that the application developers have a clear statement to work from, and also so that the system that is produced can be validated to ensure that the requirements have indeed been met. This analysis activity should not involve unnecessary detail; in particular, it should avoid imposing arbitrary or accidental design decisions upon the developers in the subsequent phases of the life cycle.

- *Design*

  - *Logical design*—this is where the system developers identify the hardware/software components that satisfy the requirements, as well as specifying the architecture (e.g., layers, interfaces, etc.) between those components. The logical design should avoid specific technical details that are required to map the design onto a specific implementation environment. On the other hand, it should be carefully organized so that when the system is implemented, it can accommodate changes easily— changes will be localized and easy to carry out.

  - *Physical design*—this is where technical decisions are made regarding specific hardware architecture, DBMS packages, programming languages, use of middleware or GUI packages, etc. This is also where the "physical" decisions will be made regarding client-server implementation, distribution of objects in a networked environment, etc. Modifications are typically made to the logical design to accomplish this, though they should be minimized wherever possible.

- *Construction*

  - *Development*—this is where the physical design is implemented in a programming language or application development environment, e.g., NATURAL OO. In this book, we cover physical design and construction together, as they are often carried out together in application development organizations today, without being formally separated into separate phases.

  - *Testing*—despite rumors to the contrary, object-oriented systems still have to be tested. We discuss the issues involved in object-oriented testing in Chapter 17.

  - *Documentation*—documentation requirements vary considerably from one project to another. It's typical to see various forms of user manuals and technical documentation of the software. User manuals are typically independent of the methodology used to build the software, though overview descriptions of the system can take advantage of the same object-oriented paradigm used to describe business requirements in the earlier phases of the project. The technical documentation usually consists of the various models described in this book, with additional supporting detail as necessary.

- *Acceptance and cutover* —this activity is carried out without any special regard for the object-oriented nature of the development process. We discuss it briefly in Chapter 17.

- *Operation and maintenance*—this activity is carried out without any special emphasis for the object-oriented nature of the development process. We discuss it briefly in Chapter 17.

Note that this discussion of life cycle phases is not intended to impose a waterfall approach to application development, nor is it intended to require prototyping or iterative development, etc. There is a common tendency today to promote prototyping and iterative approaches because of the benefits of early visibility, etc. — but this is a decision that should be made independently of the choice of modeling techniques for business analysis, etc.

Model Usage in the Various Development Phases

The usage of the various models described in Part II of this book within the life cycle phases is summarized in Figure 10-1.

Business Analysis

During the business analysis phase, the three primary OO models are used in the following way:

- The *object structure model* is used to identify and model business-related objects. This will help address questions like, "What objects do we need in order to carry out the business we have identified? What do those objects know, and what are they capable of doing? How do they interact with one another?"

- The *business process and transaction sequence model* can be used to describe business processes in a form which is compatible with the description of transaction sequences in the subsequent phase of systems requirements analysis. At this stage, though, we are trying to achieve a high-level understanding of the business processes; the system requirements that we will eventually specify for a business process will be described in one or more transaction sequences.

- *Object life cycle diagrams* can provide further understanding of the dynamic behavior of business objects over time. The utility of such a model depends on the nature of the project, and often depends also on the level of business analysis (or business reengineering) that is taking place. Some projects may find it unnecessary to create life cycle models during business analysis. Other projects will find that they provide an enormously important perspective for the users to better understand their business.

	Analysis		Design	
	Business Analysis	System Requirements Analysis	Logical Design	Physical Design
Object Structure Model				
entity objects	✓	✓	✓	✓
interface objects			✓	✓
control objects			✓	✓
operations	✓	✓	✓	✓
attributes	✓	✓	✓	✓
constraints	✓	✓	✓	✓
relationships	✓	✓	✓	✓
inheritance		✓	✓	✓
aggregation		✓	✓	✓
communication			✓	✓
visibility			✓	✓
data types				✓
pointers				✓
Business Process & Transaction Sequence Model				
business processes	✓			
transaction sequences		✓	✓	
activity flow diagram	✓	✓	✓	
Object Behavior Model				
object interaction diagram	✓		✓	
object life cycle diagram	✓	✓	✓	
System-Wide Model				
context diagram	✓			
system overview diagram		✓	✓	
physical design components				✓

Figure 10-1: Model usage during the application development life cycle

System Requirements Analysis

When systems analysts document the requirements for a system, they normally have available a number of sources of information. For example, it's common to conduct interviews or JAD sessions with future users of the system, as well as customers, auditors, regulators, and various other interested parties. The analysts may also have access to various documents and manuals describing the application domain, as well as narrative descriptions of system requirements and various other requirements documents whose format is not controlled by the analysts themselves. And, of course, we would expect that the analyst has access to a business analysis model produced in the previous phase, which includes a description of the relevant part of the business.

For the methodology described in this book, the product of the system requirements analysis life cycle phase would be documented as follows:

- an *object structure model*, which contains entity objects only and which may be derived in parallel with the transaction sequences, as the analyst identifies detailed requirements for individual objects. The object structure model produced here is likely to be more detailed than the one produced in the business analysis life cycle phase, for it will include objects, relationships, inheritance, attributes, and constraints.

- *transaction sequences*, which are used to describe required system functionality.

- *object life cycle diagram* for objects whose life cycles are complex enough to need such clarification. In the business analysis life cycle phase, the decision to include or exclude object life cycle diagrams is likely to be controlled primarily by the level of interest in key objects, on the part of the business user. But in the system requirements analysis phase, the analyst often finds it important to document the dynamic behavior of objects in detail to ensure that the requirements are correctly understood. However, this depends on the nature of the application. In some cases, the life cycle behavior of the objects is so obvious and straightforward that there is no need for this level of documentation.

For large systems, it may be necessary to identify subsystems — even at the requirements analysis stage — to allow work to be partitioned between teams, and to allow the requirements to be discussed and negotiated with different groups of users in a manageable fashion. Subsystems are identified and documented, where necessary, with system overview diagrams.

Logical Design

During the logical design life cycle phase, the following activities take place:

- transaction sequences are examined and used to extend and change the object structure model that was produced during the analysis phase, by adding interface objects and control objects, where appropriate.

- object interaction diagrams are drawn for each transaction sequence which is complex enough to require it, showing the events and interactions between objects which are needed to support the transaction sequence.

- operations are defined, with informal descriptions of their required behavior.

- object life cycle diagrams are created where appropriate, or updated and extended as necessary.

- subsystems are defined and system overview diagrams are drawn, as required, for organizational, complexity-management, and/or presentation purposes.

Physical Design/Construction

During the physical design and construction life cycle phases, the following activities take place:

- The environment for the system must be determined, and/or initial choices must be finalized. This includes the choice of programming language, operating system environment, DBMS, network, hardware (e.g., PC versus Mac versus Sun workstation versus mainframe) and user-interface environment, as well as the use of class libraries, frameworks, and patterns.

- Task management and distribution of objects/functions decisions must be finalized.

- Attribute types must be finalized, depending on the environment — e.g., whether attributes will be implemented as objects, as in the case of a Smalltalk implementation.

- Relationships will be implemented (e.g., in the form of pointers or links from one object to another).

- Decisions relating to the implementation of constraints must be finalized, depending on the programming language, GUI-builder, and/or DBMS environment used.

- The user interface must be finalized.

- Decisions regarding the handling of persistent objects must be made, potentially involving a mapping between objects and a relational database. This may require implementing an "access layer" of application software, or it may be handled by a vendor package.

- Object wrappers will be developed for any non-object-oriented components which will be used in the application.

- Coding of the methods for all operations will be carried out.

The Role of Versions in an Additive Development Process

The OO analysis and design methodology described in this book is *additive*, which means that the results of each phase are used as input to the next phase, and updated/extended as appropriate. This is in sharp contrast to methodologies which are *transformational*, such as the structured methods approach which transforms analysis-level dataflow diagrams into a design-level structure chart.

Because of the additive nature of our methodology, it is technically unnecessary to retain versions of the results of earlier phases of the project. However, there may be contractual or organizational reasons for retaining a copy of the systems requirements analysis model. Often, this model represents a contract between the users (or requesters of the system) and the developers. The model is kept in order to provide a mechanism to check that the delivered system does indeed fulfill the agreed-upon requirements. However, it does not need to be kept in step with the version of the specification used for design and construction, except where changes to the requirements are negotiated and agreed.

Once the implementation has been accepted and the system is operational, the requirements model is no longer needed. The specification of the system as actually implemented should be adequate for communication and documentation purposes, and for subsequent maintenance purposes.[1] However, it may be necessary to maintain multiple versions of the object model to document before and after.

The Six Component Architecture

As noted above, it is common to divide a large, complex system into appropriate subsystems. But it is also useful to divide a system of any size into subsystems based upon architectural considerations that are especially relevant during the physical design phase of the project. The six recommended architectural subsystems are shown in Figure 10-2.

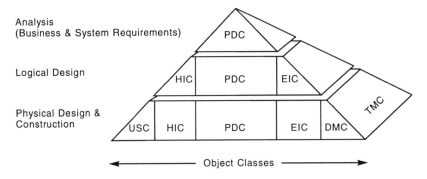

Figure 10-2: The Architectural Subsystems of an Object-Oriented Application

---

[1]   Ideally, the development team has a CASE tool that allows bidirectional synchronization of the source code and the object models described in this book. In most organizations today, it's almost impossible to imagine maintenance activities being performed upon the object models. Maintenance programmers want to get their hands on the *code* in order to fix bugs, add new enhancements, etc. But to keep the original object models current and up-to-date, requires a CASE environment that automatically updates the diagrams if the code is changed. Updates in the other direction are useful too. If the diagrams or details of the object model are changed, then it is nice to have revised code generated automatically.

The six components, and the life cycle phases where they are likely to be relevant, are summarized here and discussed in more detail in Chapters 14 and 15:

- The *problem domain component* (PDC) represents the application or real-world part of the system and consists of all entity and control objects identified during the phases preceding physical design. The entire object structure model developed during analysis and logical design becomes the starting point for the PDC. It is then modified and extended, as necessary, to deal with performance and implementation issues (e.g., limited support for inheritance mechanisms in the programming language).

- The *human interaction component* (HIC) consists of all objects and object classes required for the user interface implementation. The HIC consists of the interface objects used to define the interface with human actors during logical design, plus any additional objects required to fully define and implement the user interface during physical design and construction.

- The *external interface component* (EIC) consists of all interface objects used to define the interface with non-human actors, like external systems or printers. The EIC consists of the interface objects used to define the interface with non-human actors during logical design, plus any additional objects required to fully define and implement external interfaces during physical design and construction.

- The *data management component* (DMC) provides the infrastructure for the storage and retrieval of objects in some data management system. This component is added during the physical design stage of the project, because it involves issues of implementation technology rather than logical design.

- The *task management component* (TMC) handles concurrency, where necessary, within a system. In theory, this could be relevant in the system requirements phase or logical design phase of the project, if the user's business requirements include explicit timing or concurrency constraints. However, it is relatively rare to see this except in real-time systems. For business applications, the TMC is usually created during the physical design stage, when the developers are aware of the concurrency issues they must face, and also the capabilities provided by the operating system or run-time features of the programming environment. However, there may be situations where the TMC will be developed at an earlier stage to help model issues of coordination and synchronization of multiple entity objects within a business data processing application.

- The *utility services component* (USC) provides general utility services which can be requested by all other components, such as for common handling of implementation data types, etc. Again, this typically becomes relevant in the physical design stage of the project, when the development team has a complete definition of the logical design as well as a complete inventory of available libraries, packages, and utility services provided by the hardware/software environment

Chapter 11

Planning an Object-Oriented Project

Successful projects need more than object-oriented analysis methods, modeling techniques, and clever programmers. There is still a need for traditional project planning and management skills. A full treatment of project management is beyond the scope of this book. However, this chapter summarizes some of the relevant issues concerning managing application development projects in an object-oriented environment.

Project Definition

One of the first things that project managers need to do is obtain a realistic scope of the projects they are working on. It's impossible to develop estimates, schedules, and staffing requirements if you don't know the boundary that separates your system from the rest of the world.

With traditional structured methods, a context diagram was typically used for this purpose. In an object-oriented environment, a system overview diagram, of the sort discussed in Chapters 3 and 8, is quite adequate. As illustrated in Figure 11-1, a system overview diagram shows the entire application project as a single subsystem, and it shows the actors (typically individual customers or organizations external to the system) who initiate events within the subject area and/or receive results from the business processes within the subject area.

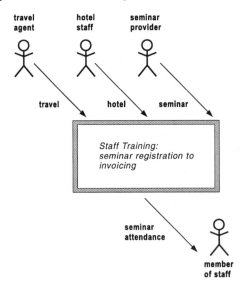

Figure 11-1: An example of a context diagram (system overview diagram)

The part of the business which lies within the scope of the project is called the problem domain. This is the area of the business where the analysts, designers, programmers, and testers are seeking to bring about change in the form of automation and new processes. By definition, everything else is outside the domain of change; portions of the remainder of the business might be included in the diagram if (through the mechanism of actors) they have interactions with the problem domain. But vast portions of the business may not appear on the diagram at all if they are completely independent of the problem domain represented by the project.

The primary purpose of a context diagram like Figure 11-1 is to ensure that the project manager and the user/customers have the same understanding of the scope of the project. For example, when we look at Figure 11-1, it becomes evident that the system is not carrying out payroll or inventory control functions. It is not concerned with career planning for members of our staff, nor is it concerned with planning or forecasting of training needs for the staff. It does not provide data for a "skills database" in a human resource system, nor does it provide management reports on the number of seminars attended by various staff members. It doesn't provide tax information to the IRS about potential deductions associated with training; it doesn't control the NASA Space Shuttle; it doesn't .... indeed, there are many, many things that the system portrayed in Figure 11-1 does not do. By having a fundamental understanding of what the system is and isn't required to do, the project manager is in a better position to carry out planning activities.

Of course, it's possible to imagine many other diagrams which would also adequately represent the scope of a business analysis of the organization of external training; but it's convenient to use a diagram that fits into the other components of our object-oriented approach. A system overview diagram can also be used to show the relationship between the problem domain and other business areas or subsystem, or to break a large analysis area into sub-areas. Chapter 8 has a more detailed discussion of the use of system overview diagrams for these purposes.

Selecting a Development Life Cycle

As discussed in Chapter 10, the choice of a development life cycle is independent of the definition of the phases in the project. Nevertheless, it is rare to see OO projects following a traditional waterfall approach. An evolutionary, rapid prototyping, or incremental development approach is particularly appropriate.[1]

We recommend delivering a system in stages based on transaction sequences. Transaction sequences describe how users interact with the system. They are often easy to explain to the user in terms of features they will be able to use. The first release of a system may be restricted to particular functional areas, and may cover only the most important features in those areas, with each subsequent release adding functionality. Subsequent releases will also typically refine and extend the human interface portion of the system, which may initially be delivered in a rather unglamorous fashion.

---

[1] For a good discussion of rapid prototyping in an object-oriented environment, see John Connell and Linda Shafer, *Object-Oriented Rapid Prototyping* (Englewood Cliffs, NJ: Prentice Hall, 1994)

Even within the development of major releases, an incremental approach to development of the release is often useful. With an incremental approach, a 90-day cycle can be used. This corresponds to the short-term planning period in many organizations.

It is easier to manage an evolutionary approach with object-oriented techniques than with traditional techniques because the OO development process is additive, using the same techniques and models through all the development phases. These models are easier to change and extend than those typically used in a non-OO development method, where separate models are used for each development phase, with transformations at the beginning of each phase. In such an environment, the enhancements and modifications that occur in successive releases make it necessary to change a number of different models, which exacerbates the problem of configuration management and control.

An evolutionary approach has the advantage that users acquire something which is of value to them as soon as possible. It reduces risk, both because user feedback comes sooner (allowing development effort to be redirected if necessary), and because architectural decisions and system performance are tested sooner than they would be if the first release provided the entire planned functionality of the system.

Another key point for the project manager: if the development team is relatively unfamiliar with OO technologies, an evolutionary approach allows the team to move forward through all of the phases—analysis, design, construction, and testing—as quickly as possible, in order to implement a portion of the system. Learning an object-oriented approach is also iterative and feedback from completing implementation of a part of the system is an essential part of the learning process.

Defining Project Phases, Checkpoints, and Reviews

The project phases described in Chapter 10 are the ones we expect project managers to follow. A typical scenario for a project might include the following:

- *business analysis*—this will usually be completed and approved before the next phase begins, because (a) costs and benefits have to be identified in detail in order to justify the project, and (b) if the project involves significant business reengineering, the implementation of the system will typically require political and organizational changes that need to be planned and initiated while the system development effort is taking place. On the other hand, with a large project whose business analysis is predicated upon the success of new, untested computer technology (e.g., a combination of client-server, voice-recognition, mobile computing, and pen-based handwriting recognition), we strongly recommend that the business analysis be carried out in an evolutionary fashion that is consistent with the remaining development phases.

- *system requirements analysis*—except on tiny projects, we recommend that this phase be carried out in an iterative fashion. The business processes identified in the previous phase (which may or may not have been completed, depending on whether business analysis is being carried out in an evolutionary fashion, too) become transaction sequences. The object structure diagram should be developed at least to the point where the object classes have been identified, and a provisional inheritance hierarchy has been established. Detailed information about attributes and operations and object life cycles may be identified for those objects which participate in the transaction sequences of an evolutionary release of the system, but the remaining object classes may be left in a skeleton form. A system overview diagram is typically useful to help indicate which objects are involved in the development of the current release.

- *logical design*—interface and control objects will be added to the objects participating in the evolutionary release that the development team is working on. Object interactions, object life cycles, and operations will be filled in for those collaborating objects, and the system overview diagram will be updated as necessary.

- *physical design*—adjustments to the model will be made to accommodate the hardware, operating system, DBMS, and other technology issues. For the first few evolutionary releases, the development team's understanding of these technology components may be somewhat limited; consequently, it may be necessary to continue making substantial changes to eliminate defects and fix various implementation problems. Gradually, though, the transition from the logical design to physical design should become smoother and smoother, since the technology will be well understood.

- *construction, testing*—obviously, this is where the development team codes and tests the evolutionary release that they are working on. However, two caveats should be kept in mind: first, regression testing is quite important, so that the development team can be assured that the next evolutionary release doesn't break some functionality in the current release (this should be minimized because of the encapsulation properties of object-orientation). Second, the development team should consider adding some instrumentation code to the evolutionary releases, because it will provide feedback on *how* the evolutionary release is being used by the customers. This is especially important in the area of the human interface, because it may turn out that interface features (scroll-bars, windows, pop-up menus, and various options) that the development team invested significant energy and time to develop are not being used—or vice versa.

Throughout the development of these evolutionary releases, it is appropriate for the project manager to conduct reviews of the work being performed in the various phases. The models produced in business analysis, system requirements analysis, and logical/physical design phases are the intermediate products of the evolutionary release of the system; they should be reviewed for completeness, correctness, consistency, and quality. Some of the review can be performed automatically by a CASE tool or by the technical developers. However, the models produced in the early phases of the project should also be reviewed by the customer/user to ensure that they are satisfied with its progress. Ultimately, of course, the code and the documentation produced at the end of each evolutionary release of the system becomes an item for formal review.

Estimating and Monitoring Progress

Aside from planning the life cycle activities, the other critical requirements for project managers are estimating, scheduling, and monitoring the progress of projects. It might well be argued that the software industry never did this very well for traditional methodologies; why should we expect any better results with object-oriented methods? In any case, veteran project managers will argue that they know how to estimate and schedule and monitor the progress of a project using traditional methods and techniques; what they want to know is how it should be performed in an object-oriented environment.

In very gross terms, the delivered functionality of an application is the same, regardless of what methodology is used to develop it. From an external perspective, a payroll system is a payroll system, regardless of whether it is developed using a structured analysis approach or an object-oriented approach. So if the application development organization has a successful technique for estimating the delivered functionality of a system and expressing it in language-independent units such as function points, this should remain the same for an object-oriented project. If we were using a waterfall life cycle approach, with conventional hardware/software technology, we might be tempted to use approximately the same schedule, budget, and resource (manpower) estimates for OO projects as for non-OO projects.

But life is not so simple. An immediate difference between most OO projects and typical non-OO projects is the presence of a significant GUI interface. In the best case, the GUI interface will be developed with power screen-painters and GUI-builder tools, and will require no more effort than used to be required for dumb-terminal character-based user interfaces. But in the worst case, the project manager may find that as much as 50-75 percent of the effort and resources are devoted to the human interface—either because the GUI-building technology is inadequate, or because the users insist on endless changes to the user interface, or a combination of similar factors.

GUIs are only one example of new technology typically associated with object-orientation. Client-server technology is another; and the project manager's first few OO projects may also involve the introduction of new languages (C++, Smalltalk, etc.), new DBMS packages, new CASE tools, and even new operating systems. All of this inevitably requires investments in training for the project personnel, and the project manager has to estimate the impact of the learning curve on the productivity of the team over the duration of the project.

One more significant factor needs to be taken into account: reuse. As we have stressed repeatedly, one of the benefits of object technology is the potential for reuse of existing objects and classes. The extent to which this can be accomplished depends on the organizational steps that have been taken to implement a reuse culture in the organization, and also the robustness of the class library available to the application developers. Of course, the application developers are likely to use a language or CASE tool that provides a robust library of low-level objects, but when OO is first introduced into the organization, there are probably few business objects that support the application domain of interest to the organization. As time goes on, the organization will gradually build and refine its own application-oriented class library, which will enhance the level of reuse—and thus the productivity of the developers. Many organizations find they have to go through three iterations of a class library before they have one that is solid. The first one is usually mediocre, because the developers are not very familiar with the OO concept, and the initial effort to classify and partition the application-domain objects is difficult. As a result, the organization eventually becomes disgusted with its work, scraps the class library, and completely rebuilds it. The second version is usually much better—but still not perfect. It's usually only when the third version appears that everyone nods their head and says, "Yeah, that's it! Now we've got a *solid* library."

In any case, the project manager has to take into account the anticipated level of reuse in the project in order to derive an accurate estimate of costs, schedule, and resources. In a few cases, the situation may be more difficult. The project manager has to estimate how much time, effort, and resources the project has to invest in *creating* reusable objects. This usually occurs when the development team creates a project-specific object and then recognizes the opportunity to make it more broadly useful. But it takes additional time to modify the object, as well as additional time for testing, quality assurance, and documentation effort beyond what would be required for the project-specific version.

The reality is that estimates and schedules and budgets for OO projects are likely to be relatively inaccurate for the first few projects. This is a phenomenon that the entire industry is dealing with: we have reasonably accurate estimating models for non-OO projects, but only because we have metrics from tens of thousands of projects over the past three decades. There are now some preliminary proposals for object-oriented estimating algorithms,[1] but it will probably be another few years before they reach the level of commercially-available estimating tools.[2]

In the meantime, the incremental delivery approach is the practical compromise for most project managers. This is often carried out in a timebox fashion, where the project manager says to the customer, "I guarantee I'll deliver a working version of your system 90 days from now, and an enhanced version every 90 days thereafter. Let's negotiate how much functionality I'll deliver in the first 90 days, and we'll renegotiate the details of additional functionality at each 90-day checkpoint."

---

[1] See, for example, Brian Henderson-Sellers and Julian M. Edwards, *BOOK TWO of Object-Oriented Knowledge: The Working Object* (Sydney, Australia: Prentice Hall of Australia, 1994)

[2] Developers of estimating tools as ESTIMACS (developed by Howard Rubin, and now supported by Computer Associates) and CHECKPOINT (from Capers Jones's Software Productivity Research, Inc.) and SLIM (from Larry Putnam's QSM, Inc.) are already incorporating metrics relating to object technology.

Chapter 12

Business Analysis

Business analysis is used to model a part of the business, or the business as a whole, in order to understand the current nature of that business and how it is carried out. [1]

A clear understanding of the business is desirable before starting application development. This helps ensure that all staff involved in a development project are speaking a common language and have an understanding of the business processes involved. It helps to avoid problems which can arise as a result of focusing immediately on system requirements without first checking that the business itself is adequately understood.

Once the business is understood in high-level terms, it may also be possible to narrow the focus of any subsequent application development project. Business analysis should make it possible to define more precisely the scope of any application which is to be developed.

Business analysis concentrates on two aspects:

- modeling of the objects used to support the business (i.e., business objects), and
- modeling of business processes.

The first aspect, modeling the objects used to support the business, is central in the development of an object-oriented view of the business. The development of an object-oriented view of the business is the first step in the additive process of building an object-oriented application for that business. Modeling business objects also aids in gaining an understanding of the business.

The second aspect, the modeling of business processes, facilitates communication between business professionals and system developers. For object-oriented application development, analysis of business processes is important in order to ensure that the object-oriented system supports the users' business requirements. It is also important when considering opportunities for business process re-engineering (BPR), although this potential use is not our main concern in this book.

Business professionals often think in terms of the sequences of actions they undertake in order to achieve business objectives. Analysis of business processes provides a good medium for the communication between a business professional and a system developer.

---

[1] While the main purpose of business analysis is to model a part of the business which is the subject of an application development proposal, it can be used to gain a picture of the business processes involved in a business as a whole (particularly relevant for business process re-engineering) or to develop a company wide object model. This object model would be used as the basis for systems subsequently implemented by the company and to assist in obtaining a unified view of data managed by existing systems.

How Business Analysis Fits into the Development Life Cycle

Business analysis is not an end in itself. Its purpose is to facilitate a good understanding of the business so that there is a sound basic understanding of the business that can be built on when carrying out system requirements analysis.

This means that a few hours' effort could be sufficient where the nature of the business is already well understood. Indeed the amount of effort allocated to business analysis should always be strictly limited. It is rarely necessary to invest more than a few weeks in business analysis. The most important objective is that the question 'Do we understand the business?' is posed separately and independently from the question 'And what are the requirements for the application?'. Diving straight into an attempt to identify system requirements without at least a high-level understanding of the business can lead to problems at a later stage. It is useful to use timeboxing to limit the amount of effort spent on business analysis. Basically, the level of detail achieved is that which can be produced within the time allocated.

The results of business analysis do not normally need to be retained. Once business analysis, at an overview level, is complete, system requirements analysis often influences the way that business is conducted. Because the development process is additive, the versions of the analysis models developed during business analysis will become redundant and can be discarded.[1]

The object model and object life cycles are carried forward into system requirements analysis and will there be modified and updated as appropriate. The analysis of business processes results in the identification of transaction sequences supported by the application. The descriptions of transaction sequences effectively update parts of the description of the business processes. Often other aspects of the business process model will not change as a result of application development, particularly if the analysis is kept at a high level.

If the business process model does change, however, it is not essential to update the business process model. A fresh check should be made on how the business currently works when the next related system development project begins. Information as to how the business works at the time of the construction of the application is contained in the transaction sequences. Knowledge of how the business worked at a point in the past, as incorporated in past business process models, can be misleading. It is not worthwhile to invest effort in an attempt to keep a business process model constantly up-to-date.

Overview of Business Analysis Activities

The following activities are undertaken as part of business analysis:

---

[1] If the business analysis models are required again for use at a later stage, they can be extracted from the system requirements analysis models.

1. used in the business. Business objects are the most important type of entity object. They are defined in more detail later in this chapter. Additional entity objects may be added later during system requirements analysis and logical design.

2. Drawing of object life cycle diagrams for any business object which has an interesting life cycle that is relevant for the problem at hand. These diagrams document significant states in the life cycle of objects of an object class and the events which cause them to make a transition from one state to another.

3. Modeling of business processes. This involves identifying business processes and obtaining a high-level understanding of the workflows (sequences of activities and events) involved in these business processes and the agents (human or machine) who interact to achieve the required results.

4. Checking of consistency and completeness. Among other checks, this includes checking that object life cycles have been considered for each object class and that the business processes which trigger each state change can be identified.

Setting the context for business analysis

The scope of a business analysis project (also referred to as the project's *business domain*) will normally be defined during the project definition phase. Figure 12-1 illustrates a context diagram for the seminar registration system example.

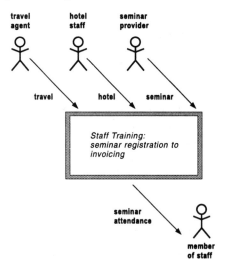

Figure 12-1: Seminar registration system context diagram

The scope of this particular business analysis project is restricted in fact to a business process. We have chosen to show the product of the business process (seminar attendance) and the major external contributors to the production of this product (travel, hotel and seminar).

Additional business processes would be indicated by more than one major output being produced by the business domain in the context diagram. When more than one business process is involved, then a descriptive name for the business domain would be used instead of the name of the business process as in this diagram.

Modeling Business Objects

Modeling business objects is the first definition of the object structure model for the application. When this phase is complete, it will contain all the business objects relevant to the project's context. Building the object structure model and the business process model is ideally a simultaneous task.[1] It is not always practical to do both at the same time. When that is the case, then we recommend starting with the object structure model in business analysis. Modeling objects is the primary focus of object-orientation. The key argument in favor of this primary focus is that the objects involved in the business remain relatively constant while the business activities which use these objects are more liable to change. Ultimately this is the model which will represent the full design of the application.

Overview of business object modeling

The object structure model developed in this phase will be added to throughout the development process. But the resulting models expected from this phase and the system requirements analysis phase are very similar. The main differences are:

- The scope of the business object model may be larger. It may include objects which are relevant only for manual systems and are not to be represented in any computer system.

- The business object model may be less detailed as usually only real-world objects are modeled. In system requirements analysis less obvious objects (e.g., object classes to represent events) are also identified.

- In business analysis, the model contains the business objects, their main attributes and the relevant static relationships. In system requirements analysis, additional entity objects may be added, along with a more complete set of attributes and the basic operations for each of the objects in the model.

- Definition of inheritance hierarchies and aggregation structures is usually left until the system requirements phase. It is undesirable to fix such structures before a good level of understanding has been reached. Sometimes it may be useful to begin their definition in business analysis as a way of obtaining a better understanding of the business objects involved.

---

[1] The same is true in system requirements analysis, where work on the object structure model and the transaction sequences is also ideally a simultaneous process. See Chapter 13.

As previously noted, business objects are entity objects. They represent the business memory required for the business processes in the business domain. They may also represent key things that are used during each process, but are not required to be in the resulting application that will support the business processes. Figure 12-2 shows the relationship between business objects and the objects modeled during application development.

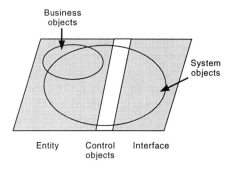

Figure 12-2: Business objects and system development objects

An object model developed during business analysis is usually brought into system requirements analysis and enhanced. For this reason, this chapter includes only aspects of object structure modeling particularly relevant to business analysis.[1]

Business object modeling can be carried out for the business as a whole or it can be limited to a specific area. Producing a business object model for the business as a whole provides a single unified description of the objects for a business enterprise. This single description can be used for creating a central information warehouse for building multiple applications and ad-hoc queries. This brings benefits in terms of consistency and reduces development effort for new systems by reusing existing components. A central business object model allows an evolutionary development strategy such that, as new systems are developed and old systems redeveloped, they can be based more and more on a common business object model.

Steps in business object modeling

Business object modeling includes the following basic steps:

1. Determine the candidate business objects.

2. Abstract the candidate objects into classes and define the purpose of each object class.

3. Determine the static relationships between the business objects.

4. Name and define the cardinalities for these relationships.

---

[1] For an introduction to object modeling, see Chapter 4. For details on refining the object model during system requirements analysis, see Chapter 13. Advanced discussions of various aspects of object structure modeling can also be found in Part IV.

The order in which these steps are carried out is not hard and fast. In most cases, after the first set of object classes is determined, succeeding object classes are found while trying to determine and define the static relationships. We recommend that you start by discovering and abstracting a first set of business objects and then adopt a flexible approach.

What to model

Model the objects required by the business to operate, avoiding redundancy. Objects can be identified by asking the question "What things (real or abstract) does the business care enough about to store data about them?" The emphasis is on identifying real-world objects, e.g., a person, place, thing or event, which lies within the scope of the analysis project and which a business person can also identify with.[1]

Try to think in terms of objects which have a meaning in relation to the business rather than in terms of any physical medium used to store information. For example, we would model an **Order** object rather than a **Filing Cabinet** object in which orders are stored. On the other hand, if the distinction between a telephone order and one received through the mail is significant for a business, we would model both.

Discovering business objects and defining the object classes

Sources of information that can be used in order to identify business objects include:

- existing documentation about the business or existing object models
- interviews with business professionals
- business process descriptions.

Candidate object classes are identified using these sources. A decision is then made as to which of the candidate object classes represent the best categorization of the business objects. Chapter 21 provides a more detailed description of how to identify objects and define object classes.

During business analysis, it is useful to record the following information about object classes:

- **Name**. Clear, business-oriented names for objects are important to ensure that objects can be found and reused. A standard vocabulary should be defined and used for the problem domain. We recommend that object class names be singular nouns or an adjective and a noun.
- **Attributes**. List the major attributes that describe the object.
- **Description**. A short description of the nature of the object and its use.

---

[1] An event is not always readily apparent to business professionals as an object. If they see an event as a relevant object, then it should be included in the model. But if they do not, then it is better to wait until system requirements analysis, where the transaction sequences should help determine its relevancy.

Discovering attributes

Here the objective is to identify attributes that are necessary in order to understand exactly what the object represents and to differentiate it from other objects. The objective is not to define the complete data structure for the object.

Discovering static relationships[1]

Relationships often correspond to verbs in business process descriptions. They are associations between objects which represent information which is necessary from a business point of view. For instance, for the two object classes **Order** and **Customer** there may be a relationship: *an Order is placed by a Customer*. They describe lasting associations where it is significant which object is associated with which other object, rather than transient connections. For instance, *Automated Teller Machine accepts cash card* is normally a transient connection, not a structural one. (Consider circumstances in which it would be relevant to model it as a relationship and you see that what should be modeled as a relationship depends on the planned scope of a system.)

Name relationships where this is necessary to make their purpose clear. Specify the cardinality of each relationship. For instance, if an **Order** can be placed by only one **Customer**, but one **Customer** can place many (or no) **Orders**, then the cardinality for the relationship is CN:1.

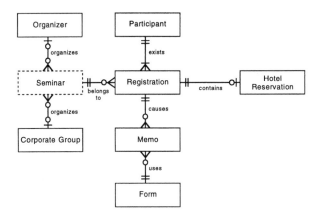

Figure 12-3: Object structure diagram for business analysis of seminar registration

---

[1] See Chapter 19 for more on the discovery and specification of relationships. Static relationships are more fully defined in Chapter 4.

Modeling Object Life Cycles

The main purpose of object life cycle modeling is to assist in the understanding of objects with complex life cycles. It is important to recognize any object behavior dependent on time and state because this can add significantly to the complexity of an application. Some of the key processing in a system, forming significant parts of business processes, is likely to relate to changes of state in the key business objects.

The use of object life cycle diagrams can enable the communication of knowledge about objects and business processes, which is sometimes difficult for users to verbalize without the assistance of a graphical representation.

Cross-checking of object life cycles with other information - business process descriptions, attribute definitions and operations - can also assist in ensuring that state-dependent behavior has been recognized.

When to model object life cycles

Draw life cycles only for objects which have behavior that varies depending on their objects' state. It is useful to take each object class in turn and consider whether any of its behavior is state-dependent. This question is answered by considering events which affect the object and considering whether the object's response to the event is always the same.

As an example of the type of behavior to look for, there are many object classes for which details of an object can be changed freely up to a point at which the details are approved or confirmed. After the object reaches this state, some changes may no longer be permissible, or the change process may mean that reapproval becomes necessary. This state thus affects how the object responds to a given event. Such states should be looked for and modeled.

How to model object life cycles

Object life cycle modeling includes the following steps:

1. Consider whether an object life cycle is required for this object class. Does it have behavior which is state-dependent? If it does not, then there is no need to draw an object life cycle diagram.

2. Identify the first state the object moves into when it enters the business.

3. Identify the event which causes the transition into the object's first state. This is used to label the arrow from the entry point (the point before the object exists) to the object's first state.

4. Consider what events can occur when the object is in its initial state and what states they cause the object to transition into. You can choose whether or not to show events which do not cause a state transition.Consider what happens to the object at the end of its life.

The final state symbol is normally used to identify the state in which the object no longer exists.

Figure 12-4 is an example of an object life cycle diagram from the seminar registration system example. Object life cycle diagrams are drawn using diagramming techniques based on state transition diagrams with the scope of the diagram being limited to the life cycle of objects belonging to a single object class.

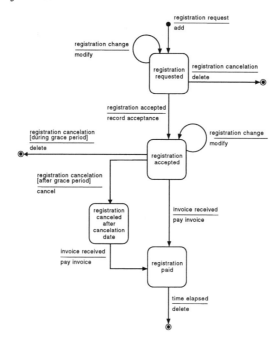

*Figure 12-4: Object life cycle diagram for the object class **Registration***

Basically the scope of object life cycle modeling is the same in business analysis and in system requirements analysis.

Modeling Business Processes

Business process modeling is used to understand and document the high-level activities performed by business professionals to accomplish the objectives of the business domain. This high-level understanding of how the business works is valuable as a preliminary step to ensure that the part of business affected by the application is understood before system requirements analysis is carried out.

Acquiring an understanding of business processes has gained added importance because a business process orientation as opposed to the more traditional business function or business area orientation is fundamental to attempts at BPR, as described for instance by Hammer and Champy. In BPR, there is a focus on looking at the complete course of whole business processes. It is often the case that a number of departments are involved in a single business process. Thus the sequence of activities required to complete the process often crosses existing organizational boundaries. A business function/business area approach tends to focus in on what happens within an existing organizational unit and thus defeats attempts at BPR because its scope is too narrow and because it is assumed that organizational structures will not be changed.

We have found the same problems in our previous application development work. The focus on business function/business area is just too narrow to ensure that the right application is developed. We need the broad view of a business process focus.

It is a common error to try to analyze a business process in agonizing detail instead of just trying to understand it. The temptation arises because it is easier to document than to understand. But full documentation only wastes time and tends to fix thought-patterns so that the new process reflects unnecessary aspects of the old process. The temptation to overstudy should be avoided.

What are business processes?

A business process is a collection of activities that takes one or more kinds of input and creates an output of value to the customer. In other words the output will be used by the customer and the customer should be willing to pay for it, if necessary.

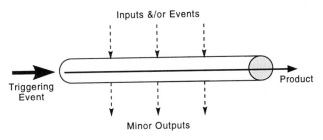

Figure 12-5: A conceptual view of a business process

Business processes produce results that are significant to the mission of the business not to the production of trivial interim results such as reports.

A second aspect is that a business process describes the sequence of activities that is required to produce this significant business result. It covers everything required to produce the product or deliver the service. A business process is significantly different from a business function. A business function usually describes an activity (e.g., accounting) that is required at some point in one or more business processes and is carried out within a given organizational unit.

The customer of a business process is not necessarily a customer of the company. The customer can also be inside the company, e.g., the customer of a purchasing process could be the company's manufacturing operation.

What is the scope of a business process?

It is important to focus on seeing a business process as a whole to counter the tendency to break the process up and see parts of it in isolation. As Hammer and Champy say, using the example of the order fulfillment process, "Under the influence of Adam Smith's notion of breaking work into its simplest tasks and assigning each of these to a specialist, modern companies and their managers focus on the individual tasks in this process - receiving the order form, picking the goods from the warehouse, and so forth - and tend to lose sight of the larger objective, which is to get the goods into the hands of the customer who ordered them".

For effective business process modeling, the focus should therefore be on each business process as a whole. There is a crucial distinction between a process and an organizational unit (e.g., accounting department). A process defines the sequence of steps involved in achieving some purpose (result) which is of practical use to the company. When the process is redefined (and it will be, if only in a minor way, by the development of the application), it may emerge that changes are required to organizational structures. Often such changes to the process and to the organizational structure reduce the number of handoffs between departments or people which are required to complete a process. Such handoffs are often a relic from the days of paper-based systems, when a piece of paper could only be in one person's hands at a time. (Photocopies alleviate but do not remove this problem.) These handoffs introduce unnecessary delays now that information can be made readily available to all who need it, using a computer.

The opportunities this gives us can only be seized if we return our focus to the business process as a whole rather than seeing isolated parts, the scope of which is often determined by the existing organizational structure. We differ here, though, from Business Process Re-engineering methods in that "business process" as used here does *not* necessarily refer to the whole of a "core business process" of an organization. It is unlikely that a whole core business process can be supported by a single application. Our focus is on building one of the supporting applications.

What initiates a business process?

A business process is initiated by the occurrence of one or more specific events that correspond to the availability of the required inputs. The event(s) cause the business professionals responsible for the business process to begin the activities that make up the process. These business professionals are called **actors**. Once the process has begun it continues until the result is produced.

How many business processes are likely to be required to define the business?

For any given business, there are very few core business processes. Hammer and Champy state that few organizations have more than 10 core business processes. However, we are not working with a core business process when we are working with a single application, but with one or more subprocesses of a core business process that the application will support. The actual number depends on the number of significant products or services.

Steps in business process modeling

Business process modeling includes the following steps:

1. Discovering business processes.

2. Subdividing business processes. The business process can be subdivided by identifying specializations or by partitioning it along the time axis into a sequence of subprocesses.

3. Describing business processes. The description of the business process describes the nature of the business process together with a description of its activities.

Discovering business processes

Business processes can be identified using one of two main techniques:

1. You can consider who the customers are and the products or services that they require. Check that these products or services are of value to the customer. If they are, then the production of these products or services will be the result of one or more business processes. The number of processes depends on whether the products or services really are part of a single whole or are different, and require different sets of activities to produce them.

2. You can consider what business events the business has to be capable of dealing with and what business processes these give rise to.

The use of business events requires further explanation. A business event is a stimulus that causes the business to take action. It is a trigger. It normally comes from outside the business or from outside the business domain being considered. A given type of business event gives rise to a given business process. The business process may need to respond to a number of business events before its complete output is achieved, where these business events may be internal to the company or may involve communication with the customer.

The same ultimate product or service (for instance, delivery of tickets by a ticket agency) may be achieved using alternative sequences of activities, depending on variations in the interaction with the customer (for instance, whether tickets were ordered over the telephone or whether the order was made in person at the ticket office).

A good way of naming business processes is to give them a name which includes both their beginning state (triggering event or major input) and their end state (the product or service). This ensures that a process is being focused on rather than an organizational unit. An example of this is: *Product Development: Concept to Prototype*. This is also the reason why, in the context diagram in Figure 12-1, we named the business process we wished to investigate *Staff Training: seminar registration to invoicing*.

How to describe business processes

The following main mechanisms can be used for describing business processes:

- an identification of the initiating event(s) and of the product(s) or service(s) of the business process.

- a text description of the activities involved in the business process.

- a description of the sequence of interactions between the agents (human or machine) which is required to produce the required products or services. Object interaction diagrams can be used for this description.

- a description of the variant paths involved in the process, showing points at which alternative paths start, potentially parallel activities and iteration. Activity flow diagrams can be used to document these paths through the process.

These mechanisms assist in understanding business processes. This does not mean that they have to be used in every case. It may often be adequate to identify initiating events and products or services, or additionally a text description may be used. Or you may wish to use both a text description and an object interaction diagram. Or you may wish to use all four mechanisms.

There are three different techniques that may be used to help gather the information required:

- Ask the business professionals to describe what needs to happen to produce the product or deliver the service. This is the most common technique and business professionals usually have no problem producing such descriptions.

- Model the object life cycles of the key business objects in the process. This technique is useful for certain business processes. In one insurance company, the process of certifying the sales agents is a very complex process. The manager of this process had a very difficult time explaining the process until we modeled the object life cycle of the object class **SalesAgent**. By following the states of this object class we were able to understand and document this process.

- Use direct observation. There are two different types of observations that can be used.

  - The first is to observe the business professionals doing the business process and document the activities and the products/services produced during the observation period. Be very careful not to get too detailed. Details may actually have to be removed after the observation period is over.

  - The second type is to observe the customers of the business process as they use the products or services. This will help understand the requirements for the product/service from the point of view of the customers.

Initiating events and products/services

You should identify the initiating events and products/services of the business process when you identify the business process. As previously stated, a business process should produce a product or deliver a service which is of value to the customer of the process. The initiating events and products or services form an important part of the description of the business process.

Text description

The most important part of the text description of a business process is a description of its standard path - what normally happens. Alternative paths, where relevant, should be noted separately. Separation of the standard path and alternative paths allows you to identify the most important part of the business process. You can then concentrate on ensuring that the bulk of normal transactions are processed efficiently.

It can be worth considering using a triage system. For instance: orders are received; standard, easy orders are processed using one route that enables them to be processed swiftly. Orders that have special complexity are separated and processed separately, perhaps by specialists.

Separation into a standard path and alternative paths can also alert you to cases where alternative paths contain processing which adds little value but takes a disproportionate amount of effort. A little thought may allow such processing to be simplified so that the cost of it bears a better relationship to the benefit it brings.

Object interaction diagrams

Object interaction diagrams are used in logical design to determine how object classes can be used to support the requirements described in transaction sequences. In business analysis, they are used to depict the sequence of interactions between the agents (human or machine) which are necessary to achieve the required products or services.

We show here two examples, admittedly for relatively trivial processes. The first example, Figure 12-6, shows the interaction sequence for the seminar registration system example:

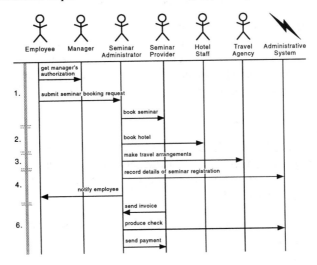

Figure 12-6: Example of object interaction diagram with several actors

Each vertical bar in the object interaction diagram represents the actor shown above the bar. Each arrow represents a request sent by one actor (represented by one bar) to another actor (represented by end of the arrow). The actor who receives the request processes the request and may need to send further requests to other actors in order to do so. The numbers shown on the left-hand side of the diagram represent links with an activity flow diagram and will be explained in the section on activity flow diagrams.

Figure 12-7 has fewer actors. This example shows an interaction sequence for a telephone booking request processed by a ticket agency.

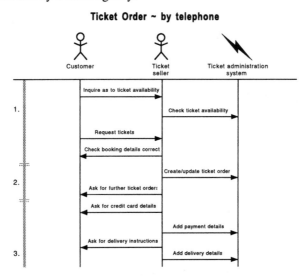

Figure 12-7: Example of object interaction diagram with few actors

These diagrams do not show decisions, iterations or the possibility that parts of the processing can take place in random sequences or in parallel. You can use text in the left-hand margin to record these aspects of the process. An alternative is to use an activity flow diagram in combination with object interaction diagrams, to provide another form of documentation of the business process. A discussion of activity flow diagrams follows.

Activity Flow Diagrams

Activity flow diagrams are used specifically to document decisions, iterations and parallel/random processing. An activity groups a sequence of interactions. Naturally, such diagrams could be used to document logic flow at a very detailed level. However, activity flow diagrams with too detailed a level of analysis should be avoided.

Figure 12-8 shows an example of an activity flow diagram for our *seminar registration to invoicing* business process.

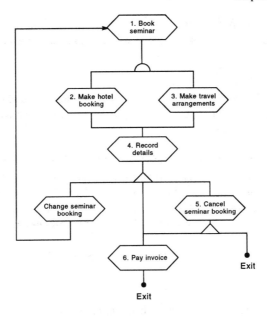

*Figure 12-8: Activity flow diagram for **seminar registration to invoicing** business process*

In Figure 12-8, the activities *Make hotel booking* and *Make travel arrangements* can occur in an undefined sequence, or in parallel. After details of the seminar registration have been recorded, there are three alternative paths. Normally the seminar will take place and the next activity will be *Pay invoice*. However, one of two alternative activities, *Change seminar booking* or *Cancel seminar booking*, may be the next activity to be required.

Figure 12-9 shows an activity flow diagram for a *telephone ticket order* business process.

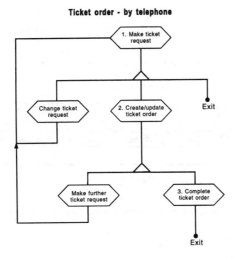

*Figure 12-9: Activity flow diagram for **telephone ticket order** business process*

Where a business process has been partitioned into a sequence of subprocesses, an activity flow diagram can also be used to show the sequence in which the subprocesses occur.

Subdividing business processes

Many business processes have a very large scope. If we consider one of Hammer and Champy's examples of business processes, for instance *order fulfillment*, it is obviously an example of a process that has a very large scope.

These processes can be divided into subprocesses, which can also have a very large scope. Hammer and Champy suggest, for instance, treating *manufacturing: procurement to shipment* as a subprocess of *order fulfillment*. Such a subprocess can hardly be described as trivial. When a business process has such a large scope it is necessary to divide the process up into manageable parts. Each manageable part (subprocess) should be a business process in its own right.

Two major ways of subdividing business processes are relevant: specializing and partitioning.

Specializing

Often a business process contains a number of different paths, such that it is not possible to identify one of them as the standard path. For instance, the processing of a telephone order may differ significantly from the processing of an order made in person. They both have exactly the same result; what is different is the activities that need to be carried out. It is undesirable to identify one as the standard path and the other as an alternative path. Therefore, each path should be described as a separate subprocess that is a *special* case of the parent business process. These subprocesses have the following characteristics:

- Each subprocess produces the same product or delivers the same service, but the activities involved are different.

- Each subprocess is in an 'exclusive or' relationship with the other affected subprocesses. Only one of the subprocesses is carried out in order to complete the parent business process.

Specializing the business process

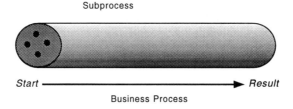

Figure 12-10: Specializations separate out strands within a business process

The specialization of a business process is indicated by the existence of one or more of the following:

- Different triggering events for the business process.

- Different environmental circumstances surrounding the triggering event.

- Similar, yet different products.

- Most uses of the process seem to be exceptions.

Partitioning

Sometimes a business process is very large and complex and can be divided along the time axis into a sequence of subprocesses that can stand alone as individual business processes. For instance, the *manufacturing* process mentioned above is treated as part of *order fulfillment*, and its scope is such that it makes sense to describe it separately. The same is also true for the other parts of *order fulfillment*. This method of subdividing a business process picks out activities which can occur in sequence, or in parallel with each other, and describes these as subprocesses. It is possible for these subprocesses to have multiple specializations. These subprocesses have the following characteristics:

- Each subprocess is a business process and has a tangible product or service.

- A particular subprocess may be reusable by one or more specializations.

- The subprocesses are in an 'and' relationship with one another. In other words, all the subprocesses must be carried out in order for the parent business process to complete.

Partitioning the business process along the time axis

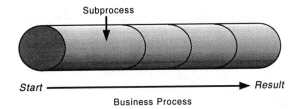

Figure 12-11: Partitioning into subprocesses divides the business along the time axis

Be careful when partitioning a process along the time axis, that each subprocess has a reasonable scope from beginning to end. Consider whether it delivers something of value to the customer. Otherwise there is a danger of falling back into a function-oriented breakdown of processes in which the emphasis on producing a product or service is lost and the internal functionality becomes the focus of attention rather than the business objective. It only wastes effort if you subdivide more than is absolutely necessary. Remember that in system requirements analysis, the transaction sequences which are described should still have a wide scope and should still aim to produce an output that is of value to the customer.

It is best to consider subdivision via specialization before you consider partitioning into a sequence of subprocesses, and only to use partitioning into a sequence when it is really necessary because of the large scope of the business process.

Discussing Object-Oriented Models with Business Professionals

We recommend that the business professionals be part of the application development process from the beginning. In many cases that means that one or two business professionals are members of the development team. Their involvement is needed not only during business analysis but in all phases as far as possible. We have found that in this phase, and to a certain degree in system requirements analysis, the business professionals in the team have been able to take the lead in certain parts of the process. In the insurance company mentioned previously, that is exactly what happened. The person responsible for the business process took the lead in the modeling effort.

In addition, it is very important that each of the models in this phase be contributed to, reviewed and validated by an extended set of the business professionals who are responsible for the business process. The Joint Application Design (JAD) technique is very useful as a way to facilitate the types of session necessary to do this.

This should not be overdone. Business analysis is not intended to be exhaustive, and as we recommended earlier, a timebox is very helpful in controlling this. Business professionals, who are not assigned to the project team, also have limited time available. Therefore, be very careful to use access to the business professionals in the most efficient way possible.

Checking the Business Analysis Model

Because the objective of business analysis is to obtain an overall understanding of the business, it is not as important to check the consistency and completeness of the business analysis results as during system requirements analysis. A level of informality is perfectly acceptable at the end of business analysis.

Business object model

The following points should be checked:

1. Are the object classes identified within the scope of the problem domain?

2. Are the object classes clearly named?

3. Are there object classes which duplicate each other or overlap?

4. Is there a short description of the nature of each object class?

5. Have all relationships been identified?

6. Are some relationships derivable from others and, if so, can these relationships be removed from the model or should they be kept for the sake of the information they provide and marked as derived?

7. Is the cardinality of each relationship correct?

8. Is the meaning of each relationship clear from its name and description (if any)?

9. Do any attributes represent information required from the business point of view?

Business object life cycles

The following points should be checked:

1. Has the life cycle of each object class which has an interesting life cycle been considered?

2. Does each state represent a significant state for the object class that causes it to respond differently to events from the way it responds when in other states?

3. Are all states for an object class mutually exclusive?

4. Is each state clearly named and described?

5. Is each state transition clearly labeled with either the event which causes the transition or the action which the affected object takes when the event occurs or with both?

6. For each state and event, has it been considered whether the object can receive each possible event when it is in each state?

7. For each state transition, is the resulting state correct?

Business processes

The following points should be checked:

1. Does each business process take one or more inputs and produce an output that is of value to the customer?

2. Has the sequence of events involved in the business process been described, at a level which is not over detailed, using text description, optionally supplemented by an object interaction diagram, optionally supplemented by an activity flow diagram?

3. If specializations of the business process have been defined, are the processing sequences described for the different specializations genuinely different?

4. If a business process has been divided into subprocesses, does each subprocess represent a coherent sub-sequence within the processing sequence described by the business process as a whole and does the subprocess produce an output which is of value to the customer?

5. Are the object state transitions identified in the object life cycle diagrams accounted for in the business process descriptions? Is it possible to identify at least one business process which causes each transition?

Summary of Deliverables

1. Key deliverables

    - Object structure diagrams

    - Object life cycle diagrams for object classes with complex life cycles

    - Business process descriptions.

2. Optional deliverables

    - Object class definitions including major attributes and a short description

    - Object interaction diagrams

    - Activity flow diagrams

Chapter 13

System Requirements Analysis

The system requirements analysis process should result in the production of a clear statement of the requirements for the new system that system developers can work from and against which the system can be validated. During business analysis a model is produced of the way the business currently operates. During system requirements analysis, we model how the business will operate using the new system.

The statement of requirements needs to be grounded in an understanding of the business point of view. It is not enough to know what the business professionals require from the application. In order to be sure that the new application supports the business properly, it is necessary to know the business purpose of each requirement.

A secondary objective of system requirements analysis is to provide the business professionals with the opportunity to change the way they are currently operating the business. With the new application as a stimulus, the techniques provided here allow them to consider and work out new ways to produce the products or services identified during business analysis.

How System Requirements Analysis Fits into the Development Life Cycle

The starting point for system requirements analysis depends on the context in which an application is developed. This context depends on how much business analysis was carried out.

Where the business domain for the application is small and well understood, then the business analysis phase is likely to be very short. System requirements analysis starts from business analysis models that contain very little detail. In this context, it is easier to treat the results from business analysis as part of the project's inputs and begin each of the models for this phase from scratch. Where an extensive business analysis has been done, or at least an enterprise level object model is available for use in business analysis, then the results of business analysis are used as the base models and this phase adds into them as appropriate.

Overview of system requirements analysis activities

The following activities are undertaken as part of system requirements analysis:

1. Defining transaction sequences based on the business processes.

2. Expanding or defining the object structure model for entity objects.

3. Drawing object life cycle diagrams for entity objects.

4. Partitioning the problem space.

The process of producing the specification of requirements is comprised of two main strands:

- The analysis of the required functionality of the system. This is documented using transaction sequences.

- The analysis of the entity object structure required to support this functionality. This is documented using the object model.

These two strands should run in parallel, with any new entity objects required being identified as functional requirements are identified. It is also possible to concentrate on the analysis of the entity object structure prior to starting the analysis of the functional requirements.

The main disadvantage of concentrating on the analysis of the object structure before considering the functional requirements of the system is that an object structure is produced which caters to too many possible enhancements that may never be required. Or areas are modeled which do not require computerization.

An object structure that is too narrowly based on current functional requirements may be difficult to enhance to meet new requirements as they arise. Depending on the scope of business analysis, you may already have a good draft of the required entity object structure. To complete this structure, input from the analysis of the functional requirements will be needed.

For a data-heavy system, modeling of object relationships and attributes is particularly important. For an 'algorithm-heavy' system or in business re-engineering projects, modeling of the functional side, represented by transaction sequences in combination with an object structure model, may be more important.

The requirements and starting point of each individual project should therefore be considered when determining whether transaction sequences and object structure are to be identified in parallel or whether the object structure model should be identified first.

The approach described in this book assumes that the functional requirements and the object structure to support these requirements are identified in parallel. Within this parallel process, the identification of functionality, using transaction sequences, drives the process of identifying object classes. As transaction sequences are identified, analysis of the required functionality is used as the basis for identifying what objects are required.

Defining Transaction Sequences

Steps in transaction sequence modeling

Transaction sequence modeling includes the following steps:

1. Identify the transaction sequences required.
2. Define the business context.
3. Describe the standard path.
4. Describe the alternative paths.

Identifying transaction sequences

The identification of transaction sequences begins with a decision as to which business processes or subprocesses the application is to support. Transaction sequences generally correspond to a business process or to significant subprocesses of business processes.

There are no firm guidelines as to the number of transaction sequences an application might include. Anecdotal evidence suggests a typical ratio of 10 transaction sequences per actor. Booch[1] suggests that:

> *Even the most complex production systems seem to embody only a few dozen scenarios, with many more variations on the theme of these central ones.*

(Booch seems to use the terms "scenario" and "use case" as synonyms, so that in the above quotation, "scenario" can be read as referring to a transaction sequence.)

Transaction sequences can be identified using one of the following two approaches. These approaches may of course be used in combination, and may be used iteratively.

Identifying transaction sequences using actors

Here, the first step is to identify the actors who will communicate with the system. Actors may represent human users of the system, or may represent interfaces with other systems. Each actor models a role which a human user or other system may play with respect to the system. Any individual user may play a number of roles.

If it is the system's objective to communicate with a human user, the human user should be modeled as an actor rather than any means the system uses to communicate with the user, e.g., an electronic mail system. Interfaces with other systems should be modeled as actors when the system's task is simply to give information to, or receive information from, another system, without responsibility for what the other system then does with information it receives or for how it acquires information it supplies.

For some systems, the process of identifying actors is a very trivial one, as there are very few distinct user roles involved. For other systems with more complex user structures, the process of identifying actors will be an iterative one.

For each actor identified, consider what the actor expects to be able to do with the system and describe this expected functionality using transaction sequences. It is useful to consider (as suggested by Jacobson):

- what are the main tasks of the actor
- what access (read or update) the actor requires to system information

---

[1] Grady Booch. The Booch Method: Measures of Goodness. *Report on Object Analysis and Design.* Vol. 1, No. 2, July-August 1994.

- whether the actor has to provide the system with information about changes in the world outside the system

- whether the actors should be informed about unexpected changes of which the system is aware.

A productive way of identifying transaction sequences can be for actors to describe their jobs, as a whole. Out of this discussion comes an understanding of system requirements which can then be described using transaction sequences.

It is also possible for transaction sequences to be initiated automatically by the application, as in the case of periodic or date-triggered processing. Often, though, periodic processing such as weekly reports can be traced back to the user who requests them, and it is worth considering whether they do in fact have an initiating actor.

Identifying transaction sequences using events

Another approach (which can be used in combination with the previous method, or to crosscheck the results derived from the previous method) is to consider what events occur in the outside world (external events occurring in the context of the business process) to which the system is expected to respond. The system's response to each event is then described using a transaction sequence. This approach is derived from the event partitioning approach of McMenamin and Palmer.

Since we are dealing with commercial systems, we are interested principally in business events. Not all business events need to be modeled. The only business events which should be modeled are those which the system is expected to handle.

External events are, to use examples from Yourdon, such things as:

1. Customer places order.

2. Customer cancels order.

3. Management requires sales report.

4. Book reprint order arrives at warehouse.

Temporal events or time signals may also be relevant. You could have events such as:

1. Daily report required at 9:00 a.m.

2. Invoices required at 3:00 p.m.

The first step involved in this approach to identifying transaction sequences is to produce an event list. Each stimulus from the outside world to which the system must respond is listed, including temporal events. External events may be associated with the presentation of data to the system or may have no associated data. Consider the nature of the business process in question to get an initial list of events and add in any others that are relevant.

Once events have been identified, the next step is to associate a transaction sequence with each external event. As a first cut, one transaction sequence is assigned to each external event. The transaction sequence represents the action that the system should take in response to the event.

There may be more than one response for a single event. In this case, one transaction sequence is required for each response. However, the responses must be genuinely independent of each other, requiring only the data associated with the event in order for them to occur.

It may also sometimes be the case that the same response (i.e., transaction sequence) is required for different events. In this case the response must genuinely be the same; the input supplied with the event is the same in all cases and the response delivered is the same.

Relationship between actors and external events

The event partitioning approach described in this section describes business events which often originate outside the company. The originator of the business event often does not communicate directly with the system. Instead, an actor who is an agent or intermediary within the company reacts to the event by initiating an interaction with the system. Thus the actor who initiates a transaction sequence is often responding to the initiating event rather than producing it.

Of course, the originator of the business event may sometimes also directly initiate the interaction with the system which is described using a transaction sequence. For instance, the user of an Automated Teller Machine originates business events and is also the actor who initiates the interaction with the system.

Transaction sequence diagrams

The actors and transaction sequences which are identified can be documented using transaction sequence diagrams. These diagrams show (among other things) the actor who initiates the interaction with the system. As discussed above, this actor is usually not the originator of the business event but a person who acts in response to it.

Transaction sequence diagrams are useful to document the transaction sequences which have been found. During the process of actually identifying transaction sequence, you may find transaction sequence diagrams useful, or you may prefer to use a list to record the transaction sequences you have identified.

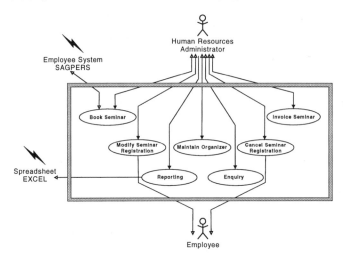

Figure 13-1: Transaction sequence diagram for seminar registration system

For a system of any size, a number of transaction sequence diagrams will be needed to represent all transaction sequences. Some possible ways of dividing transaction sequences between diagrams are:

- Use a separate diagram for each different initiating actor.

- Use separate diagrams for different areas of the system, i.e., areas covered by different groups of object classes (see Chapter 8 on System-Wide Modeling).

- Omit common sequences or include them only on more detailed diagrams.

Scope of a transaction sequence

A transaction sequence should cover a logical, cohesive sequence of events. It may legitimately cover a flow of events which lasts several days.

To decide the scope of a transaction sequence, two criteria can be used:

1. The transaction sequence should have as large a scope as is manageable (in order to be sure the whole processing sequence is handled in a satisfactory way). The business process as a whole is the default scope for a transaction sequence.

2. Where the sequence is broken down, (which is legitimate since we need units that have a reasonable scope and do not exceed our ability to handle complexity), we choose units the user accepts and perceives as accomplishing an objective which is of interest from the business point of view. Often such a unit starts with a stimulus from the customer. The unit may also correspond to a major menu option or system command.

The scope of a transaction sequence should achieve a task which the business professional recognizes as a cohesive unit. This is different from a system-oriented perspective. Taking a system-oriented perspective, actions can be packaged together into a system command, e.g., a menu option, without reference to whether a business professional uses these actions in sequence or not. A transaction sequence describes actions in the sequence in which they are used, and makes no statement about whether these actions are packaged together into a single system function or not. We adopt the business professional's perspective on what is wanted from the system, rather than using a system builder's perspective.

As one example, the business professional's objective could be to open a bank account on behalf of a customer. This would be described as a transaction sequence. In this case, the transaction sequence will normally only involve a user sitting down at a terminal on one occasion assuming no separate authorization process is required.

A transaction sequence can however involve the user (or more than one user) in sitting down at a computer terminal on more than one occasion. As an example of this, another unit of work meaningful from a business user's point of view is the computer-controlled moving of an item of stock from a warehouse for delivery to a production unit. This might involve the warehousing system in communications with the computer system which orders the stock, with the foreman, and also with the warehouseman who moves the stock, over a period of time which could exceed a day. This example is shown in Figure 13-2.

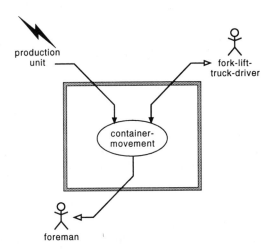

Figure 13-2: Transaction sequence diagram for a container movement

The point is that the definition of the product or service that is required from the application is user-oriented and not limited in scope to a single computer function.

The main criterion for determining whether the scope of a transaction sequence is correct is that the transaction sequence should be something, with a beginning, middle and an end, with which business professionals can identify and can use as a basis for verifying that what they require from the system is understood.

Sometimes, if a sequence of events is very complex, it is better described as a series of transaction sequences. The use of specialization and partitioning as described in Chapter 12 may help in defining the series of transaction sequences. Bear in mind that:

- ideally, a transaction sequence will represent a flow of events which the initiating actor would consider as a single unit, since it is the purpose of transaction sequences to describe the functionality the business professional requires from the system, not to describe units which only have meaning to a system developer.
- a cohesive flow of events is likely to be easier to test.
- where a transaction sequence is extremely complicated, with multiple alternative paths, it may be better to split it into a sequence of transaction sequences, in order to make the complexity manageable.

Variant courses of events can be handled within a single transaction sequence or as separate transaction sequences. If the differences between the variants are small and there is a strong logical connection between the variants, they should be described within one transaction sequence. If the differences are large, separate transaction sequences should be used.

The most ubiquitous example of a case where issues arise as to what the scope of a transaction sequence should be is the question as to whether the first introduction of an order and its subsequent maintenance (changes to details of the order) belong in the same transaction sequence. This is a matter of perception and will often depend on how critical the functionality is to the user of the system and how different the actions required are. Where changes are critical, or the processing of changes is very distinct from the process of entry, the user will tend to separate the actions. Otherwise, the user will tend to see maintenance as a minor detail which belongs with the input of the object.

Each transaction sequence should be independent of other transaction sequences. If it is not, then consider merging the transaction sequences in question.

Trivial transaction sequences

Trivial data entry transactions for static data in a system, e.g., currency codes, do not normally require transaction sequences, or, if these are included in order to have a complete list of transaction sequences, no detailed description is required.

Standard and Alternative Paths

Describing the standard path of a transaction sequence

The standard path of each transaction sequence is described using a text description. A restricted vocabulary and short, concise sentences should be used. (Alternatively, pseudocode may be used, but users may prefer standard text.)

The standard course of events should be meaningful in itself, without requiring that any functionality contained in alternative paths be executed.

In the transaction sequence, what the system should do, how it should interact with the actors and the business context for this interaction is described. The transaction sequence does not describe how this is achieved. This is described in the object structure model.

Where the transaction sequence describes interactions with the business professional, the description must be concrete enough to be clear as a specification of requirements, but it should attempt to avoid technical detail which is specific to a given user interface. For instance, it may be useful to say that the user is able to perform a certain action, e.g., modify customer details, but it is not desirable to refer explicitly to a button the user can use to invoke this action. Inclusion of such detail is unnecessary and creates an unnecessary maintenance overhead to keep transaction sequence descriptions consistent with the physical implementation. A balance must be found between the need for a concrete description and the avoidance of too much detail.

Describing alternative paths

Alternative paths are specified separately from the standard path for a number of reasons. One reason is that this makes it possible to read the standard path without being distracted by details of unusual cases and exception handling. A further reason is that the separation of the normal case from unusual cases helps to remind the developer to direct effort towards ensuring that the bulk of normal transactions are handled correctly and to avoid spending disproportionate effort on cases which are uncommon.

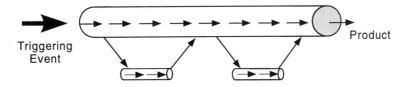

Figure 13-3: The relationship of standard and alternative paths

The description of alternative paths includes extensions to the functionality described in the standard course of events. Such extensions should be independent of the standard course of events so that when extensions are described, no change to the description of the standard course of events is required.

Examples of functionality which can be described under the heading *Alternative Paths* are:

- optional parts of a transaction sequence,
- alternative courses of events which seldom occur,
- separate subcourses which are only executed in certain cases,
- error handling.

The point at which the alternative path is to be inserted in the standard path should be stated at the start of the description of the alternative path. This is not included in the standard path as doing so simply makes the standard path more difficult to understand.

Other ways of documenting subcourses are:

- documenting it as a common sequence (see below), if it occurs in more than one transaction sequence.

- documented it within the standard flow of events, as an integral part of the description of the standard flow of events. This option should only be used when the deviations from the standard path are minor; otherwise there is a danger of undue complexity for the standard path.

Describing the business context of a transaction sequence

It is useful to understand the context in which the transaction sequence is initiated. The following types of information can be documented to help define this context:

- A brief note, i.e., a brief explanation of the circumstances in which the transaction sequence is used and of any preconditions which determine when or whether the business professional will use the transaction sequence.

- The frequency with which transaction sequences of a given type are initiated, as a number per day, week, month, quarter or year.

- A required response time.

Identifying and defining common sequences

Sequences which are common to a number of transaction sequences can be identified and described as a separate transaction sequence, called a common sequence. Both transaction sequences and common sequences can use common sequences and common sequences can be used to describe both standard and alternative paths. Where transaction sequences are initiated by an actor and describe a complete flow of events in the system, a common sequence is not complete and is not initiated as a separate transaction sequence.

Common sequences are often associated with inheritance, both with respect to object classes and to actors. Often the individual transaction sequences describe logic which applies to object subclasses while the common sequence describes logic which applies at the object superclass level and is therefore common to all the subclasses. For comments on inheritance for actors using actor hierarchies, see the next section.

Common sequences are for modeling common business-related functionality. Much technical common functionality can be specified once, e.g., in user interface standards, and then left implicit in transaction sequences. There is no great benefit to be derived, for instance, from spelling out in every transaction sequence that a query on possible values of each field is to be allowed.

Hierarchies of actors

Actors represent user roles. In cases where different types of actors share common capabilities, it can be useful to define a hierarchy of actors. For instance, an administrator and a normal system user may have some common capabilities which can be modeled using a superclass actor. Each actor can then be said to *inherit* from the superclass actor.

Hierarchies of actors become necessary when common logic is found in two transaction sequences which communicate with two different actors. When you separate this common logic out into a common sequence, the common sequence may need to communicate with these two different actors depending on which transaction sequence is calling it. The different actors play an identical role with respect to the common sequence, i.e., can be regarded as a single actor within this common sequence, but there may be reasons for distinguishing them in the two source transaction sequences taken in their entirety. In this case, it is convenient to define a superclass actor from which the two original actors inherit and with whom the common sequence can communicate.

Note that in many systems the number of different user roles which are modeled as actors is fairly small, say two or three. Deep actor hierarchies are unlikely to be required.

Modeling user interfaces and external interfaces

At the points where actors initiate or communicate with transaction sequences, there is often a data interchange. Either the actor presents the system with data or the system presents the actor with data.

It is useful to identify what data is passed. This data can be described using interface object classes (which will correspond to windows or reports or interfaces with other systems). It is necessary to identify the object classes from which data included in these interfaces is taken, or which receive data from these interfaces.

The process of identifying user requirements and describing transaction sequences can usefully be assisted by producing prototypes of user interfaces. This allows a sort of *storyboarding*. This use of early user interface prototypes is recommended because it is generally easier to grasp the implications of something concrete than of something which is seen only in an abstract form.

However, there is a risk when user interfaces are specified very early that the developer will get caught up in the detail of specifying the user interface at a point where requirements are still unclear, and forget the issue of identifying and clarifying requirements. For this reason, we advise leaving finalization of the user interface until logical design. The definition of interface layouts is discussed under logical design.

Expanding/Defining the Object Structure Model

The main objective of object structure modeling in this phase is to produce the complete model for the entity objects. Depending on how detailed a business analysis was done, it may only be necessary to expand and refine the existing object structure model.

Steps in object structure modeling for system requirements analysis

1. Determine the candidate entity objects or any missing entity objects and add them to the model.
2. Add static relationships between the entity objects.
3. Complete the basic definition of each entity object by:
   - defining the basic set of attributes,
   - defining identifying attributes,
   - defining constraints,
   - identifying operations, where required.
4. Add in the appropriate inheritance structures for the entity objects.
5. Add in any aggregation structures for the entity objects.
6. Refine relationships to take into account the inheritance and aggregation structures.

Building the basic model

What to add to the model

During system requirements analysis, as in business analysis, the emphasis is on adding real-world objects to the model which a user of the system can identify with. An event is one kind of real-world object which is often forgotten but which it can be very important to model. The objects identified should also be relevant to the requirements of the system. This can usually be determined by considering whether the system needs to retain information about the object.

The object model which is developed should be independent of implementation constraints, e.g., what database is used or the control architecture of the system, and of such system implementation concepts as linked lists. There may however be objects which are identified during system requirements analysis which are required specifically because a computer system is being developed. These objects model system requirements which are directly relevant to the user, e.g., the user interface, or archive or audit requirements. It is recommended that these *application* objects are considered in a second pass, after the problem domain objects have been identified.

Sources of information about objects

The starting point is usually the business object structure model produced during business analysis. From this model, the objects that are not relevant to the system should be identified and removed. This model is then checked for completeness and additional object classes added where necessary.

Information on the system requirements should be used to find additional objects and to check what objects are relevant to the requirements of this application. Sources of this information include:

- transaction sequence and business process descriptions,
- interviews with users and business professionals, and
- other existing documentation about the business or about existing systems.

Other sources for potential objects include:

- an existing non-object oriented data model which can be converted to an object model,
- object classes which have already been identified for the existing problem domains, and
- a class library from an external supplier which covers a part of the problem domain.

Discovering objects and abstracting objects into object classes

The above sources need to be analyzed for candidate objects. These candidate objects are then considered for relevance to the problem domain by checking them against the system requirements. Relevant objects should be included in the object structure model. Where an existing, implemented object class is relevant but modifications or extensions will be required for the purposes of the new system, a new version of the object class will be required. Chapter 18 provides a detailed discussion of how to discover candidate objects and abstract them into object classes.

Discovering static relationships

Whenever an object class is added to the model, its associations to the other object classes in the model must be discovered and added. The static relationship is usually the first type of association[1] that is looked for when entity objects are involved. Chapter 19 provides a detailed discussion of how to discover static relationships.

Discovering and specifying attributes

Both attributes and relationships are used to model information which is relevant in the context of the problem domain and of the planned system's responsibilities. Both are generally persistent and form part of the description of an object's data structure. While an attribute links an object class with a literal value, a relationship links two object classes.

In business analysis only those attributes that are necessary to understand an object as an object and differentiate it from other objects are identified. By the time logical design is completed, the complete data structure for each object class in the object structure model will have been defined. During system requirements analysis, transaction sequences provide much of the information needed for this definition process.

As soon as an attribute is discovered in this phase, information about it can be recorded. Further details of all attributes identified in business analysis should also be specified as soon as they become known. Complete attribute specifications are not required until the end of logical design, but it makes sense to record information about attributes as soon as it becomes available. For this reason, we will discuss here all the issues surrounding the specification of attributes.

Attributes are data values associated with objects in an object class that have no independent existence or object identity. Each attribute identified should be atomic in the sense that it is either

---

[1] The only association for entity objects that is not usually added to the model until logical design is the communication association.

a single value or a group of values that always belong together, e.g., address. Objects can include arrays of a single attribute or arrays of a structure which itself consists of a number of attributes. Note that this means that objects need not be in first normal form.

Each attribute has an attribute type, e.g., name, which may be simple or more complex. Complex attribute types are modeled using aggregation, which shows the fact that the complex attribute type consists of more than one simple (or complex) attribute type. Inheritance can also be used in attribute type definitions, where one attribute type is based on another. It is useful to have a standard set of attribute type definitions including attribute types for name, address and other problem domain-specific attribute types.

The values an attribute may take (its allowed range of values or domain) and its initial value can be specified, where these are already known.

Some attributes are derived from the values of other attributes. Such attributes should be marked as *derived*. In some cases, it is not clear which of two or more related attributes should be derived. In this case, one can be marked as derived and the final decision left until later. It is not necessary to document all derived attributes. Indeed, it is often better to leave derived attributes out and to add them back in during logical design when it is clear that they are required. This helps avoid an overcomplicated model which gets in the way of understanding the analysis problem and also helps avoid including attributes which are never actually used. In some cases, a derived attribute is better modeled as a value which is returned by a given operation and no attribute is required.

Generally, it isn't necessary to identify all attributes at this stage. Attributes can be added as they are found. Only attributes relevant to the specification of requirements must be included. These are attributes that have a value that is not private to a single object, i.e., public attributes. Avoid attributes that are solely for implementation. Internal object identifiers and pointers to other objects should not be included. Each object implicitly has an internal object identifier and the potential requirement for an object pointer is shown by the existence of a relationship.

Specifying identifying attributes

Each object has an internal object identifier which can be used internally within the system to retrieve the object and which does not need to be included in the definition of each object class. However, this object identifier is never made public. Particularly for objects which users may wish to find and access (entity objects), it is useful to identify and document identifying attributes which can be used to find an object.

An object can be identified either using a single attribute belonging to the object, or a group of properties (attributes and/or relationships), which uniquely identifies the object and can therefore be used to retrieve it when its internal object identifier is unknown. The purpose of identifying and documenting identifying attributes is to make it possible to see how objects of a given object class can potentially be retrieved. Retrieval operations can then use these access paths. Identifying attributes are also relevant later for database design when a decision must be made as to what indexes should be maintained.

Specifying constraints

Constraints are used to specify rules which apply generally to the values objects in the object structure model may have. It is convenient to be able to state such rules once rather than having to repeat them in many different operation definitions with the consequent risk of omission or inconsistency. The central definition of constraints also results in an object structure model which communicates clearly what values the objects in the object structure may have.

Sometimes constraints can be implemented via application generators or database constraints or triggers. Where constraints are to be implemented in operations, the existence of a central definition of the constraint makes it easier to check that the constraints are consistently checked.

Constraints are specified declaratively, either formally[1] or informally. (Some constraints must be expressed informally because not all constraints are readily expressible formally.)

For attributes, the following types of constraint should be considered:

- attributes for which a value is mandatory for objects belonging to this object class,

- constraints that the values of other attributes place on the value of this attribute,

- constraints on whether a value may be updated if, for instance, the object participates in certain relationships, and

- constraints on the conditions in which the attribute value can be updated and accessed.

For relationships, the following types of constraint should be considered:

- whether deletion cascades, is restricted or nullifies a relationship, i.e., whether:

  - when an object is deleted, related objects are also deleted

  - an object may not be deleted if objects are related to it

  - when an object is deleted, the relationships to related objects are simply removed. Deletion generally only cascades within an aggregate. See the section on Aggregation.[2]

- under what circumstances the relationship can be created/accessed.

- whether other relationships place constraints on this one. For example, there could be a constraint that the relationship 'person chairs committee' should be a subset of the relationship 'person is member of committee'.

---

[1] A syntax may be used for expressing those constraints which are expressible formally, e.g., SQL.

[2] The corresponding update rules, which say what should happen if the primary key is updated, are not included here because relationships between objects are not implemented using a reference to the primary key of a related object, as in the relational model. Where an object's name, for instance, cannot be updated if other objects reference the object, this can be expressed as a constraint on an attribute value.

Note that it can also be useful to specify constraints for the relationship between an aggregate component and the aggregate in which it is contained.

Identifying and specifying operations

It is not necessary to identify operations during system requirements analysis as what is required for a complete specification of requirements is fully covered through the use of transaction sequences, object life cycle diagrams and constraints.

However, analysts who use the so-called shopping list approach to identifying operations may wish to document operations during system requirements analysis, at the point at which the need for the operation occurs to them.

See Chapters 14 and 22 for further information on the shopping list approach to identifying operations. Operations may also be identified during system requirements analysis as a by-product of considering object life cycles. See the section Defining Object Life Cycles.

Identifying inheritance

For each object class which has been identified, consider:

- what generalizations of this object class are possible, i.e., what possible superclasses, and

- what specializations of this object class are possible, i.e., what possible subclasses.

Consider also similarities between object classes. If two object classes share attributes and relationships, this could indicate that they could share a superclass.

If some attributes of an object class do not have a value for some objects of the object class, this could indicate that specializations of the object class are possible.

Consider whether the specializations and generalizations make sense in the problem domain. Is the distinction needed? Will there be attributes or operations which apply to all specializations? Will there be attributes or operations which apply to individual specializations only?

According to Rumbaugh[1], problems to avoid when setting up inheritance structures are:

1. Don't use inheritance for aggregation. For instance, an apple orchard is an orchard, but an apple orchard is not an apple tree even though some attributes of apple tree (e.g., harvest time) may also apply to orchard.

2. Don't confuse the medium with the message. For instance, consider a course which is attended by many people. Maybe this will eventually be implemented as a linked list, but there is no reason to represent linked lists, which are implementation constructs, in the object structure model, and still less to represent 'person' which is at a totally different level of abstraction, as inheriting from linked list.

---

[1] See "Disinherited! Examples of misuse of inheritance", James Rumbaugh, *Journal of Object-Oriented Programming,* Feb. 1993, Vol. 5, No. 9.

It is also advisable to keep inheritance hierarchies shallow and not too broad, in order to minimize their complexity. Also, static relationships may need to be reconsidered due to the addition of these structures.

Designing good inheritance hierarchies is not easy and it takes time to appreciate why this is so - to appreciate the ways in which inheritance differs from generalization/specialization as used in traditional data modeling techniques and also to appreciate how inheritance hierarchies should be designed to produce a maintainable and extendible system. Because good inheritance hierarchies are so important for a maintainable system and yet so full of traps for the unwary, we have included a chapter on inheritance in Part IV, Chapter 20.

Abstract classes

An abstract class is an object class that has no direct instances but whose descendent object classes have direct instances. These abstract classes specify semantics which are common to their descendent (concrete) object classes. Some of the superclasses you identify may be abstract classes, in which case they should be identified as such.

Aggregation

Aggregation can be used to model whole-part structures. The whole is called a composite object or aggregate and the parts are called component objects.

One way of deciding whether to use aggregation is to consider whether an object and its possible component objects are moved or copied as a whole. If they are, then it is usually appropriate to model the objects using aggregation. A useful by-product of identifying aggregation is that it draws attention to the need to consider whether operations other than Copy exist which should apply to the aggregate as a whole. Also, as a general guideline, messages from objects outside an aggregate should be sent only to the composite object, not to its components. This is discussed in detail in Chapter 21.

An example of a composite object is a bicycle. A bicycle consists of several parts - wheels, frame, bell etc. - all of which can be represented as component objects.

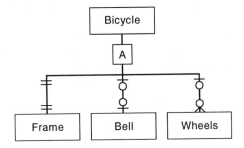

Figure 13-4: Composite object example

Cardinality can be used to show:

- whether the aggregate must include a component of the given type or not

- whether the aggregate may include more than one component of a given type

- whether a component object can exist independently of the composite object or not.

Figure 13-4 shows that in our view a bicycle must have a frame in order to be a bicycle and that a bicycle frame cannot exist independently of a bicycle. A bicycle does not have to have a bell and wheels, and the bell and wheels can exist independently of the bicycle. A bicycle cannot have more than one bell but can have more than one wheel.

It is useful to specify if components of an aggregate are ordered. It can also be useful to specify constraints on relationships between an aggregate component and the composite object.

Using aggregation is recommended where there is a close relationship between objects such that:

- the composite object is often viewed or handled as a whole,

- the composite object would (normally) be moved or "cloned" as a whole,

- there is an asymmetrical relationship between the composite object and its components such that the component objects can be regarded as being "part of" the composite,

- there is propagation of operations from the composite object to the components (this applies to the move and copy operations, but often also to other operations, e.g., save/restore, print, lock, display),

- there is propagation of attributes (for instance the position of the components of a window depends on the position of the window).

Aggregation should be used, rather than a relationship, where there is a whole-part relationship and not a relationship between two separate objects of equal status.

The decision to use aggregation rather than attributes to represent a complex object structure involves the same considerations as all decisions as to whether to model an item as an object or as an attribute. As stated previously, attributes are values that are closely associated with the containing object class such that they have no independent existence or object identity.

Often, identifying an aggregate means converting existing static relationships into relationships between a composite object and an aggregate component. When an aggregate is identified, it is also worth reviewing any other relationships, and also attributes, in the object classes in question in case they are in the wrong place. There may be attributes which should be in the composite object, or in the component object, or both.

See Chapter 21 for more information on aggregation.

Seminar registration system example

Figure 13-5 shows the final object structure model for system requirements analysis.

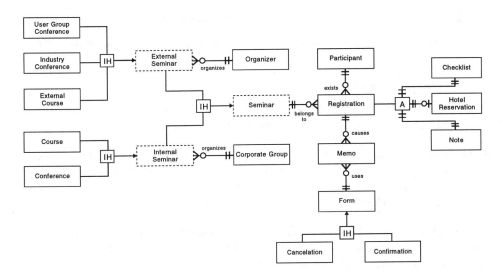

Figure 13-5: Seminar registration system - Entity object structure model

Defining Object Life Cycles

Whenever a new object is added to the object structure model it should be examined to see if an object life cycle diagram should be drawn for it. In this phase, therefore, all new entity objects should be examined.

In system requirements analysis, object life cycle modeling helps clarify system requirements by showing the significant states of the objects and the events that cause those states. The object has to cater for these states and that is typically done by adding operations to the object to handle the transition from state to state.

Life cycle models may also be used to help work out the details of transaction sequences in the same way as they are used to work out the high-level activities of the business processes. They will also be helpful later to developers and maintainers of the application who wish to understand the reasons behind the parts of the application's functionality which are based on the management of life cycles.

Using System Overview Diagrams[1]

System overview diagrams have two uses during system requirements analysis. Both of these uses are related to complexity management; they are:

- the partitioning of the problem space which is necessary if a large system is being built

- representation of system requirements at an overview level using system overview diagrams.

Partitioning the problem space

In this case, it is desirable to divide the system up into separately implementable subsystems, which can be handled in subsequent development stages by separate teams.

A system may be partitioned horizontally (into layers) or vertically. Vertical partitions are used for partitioning application functionality and may be useful during system requirements analysis. Horizontal partitions are more useful during physical design, where they are used particularly to isolate applications from knowledge of the operating system or database or hardware.

Usually a whole inheritance hierarchy or aggregation structure will be allocated to a single subsystem. The resulting subsystem should be such that it can be allocated a sensible name. It should be coherent and consist of tightly coupled objects.

Each subsystem should have a small, well-defined interface with the rest of the system. This interface is defined as one or more services, where each service groups functionality which the subsystem offers to other subsystems and defines the information which is passed across the subsystem boundary, without defining any subsystem-internal implementation details. Provided subsystem interfaces are well-defined, each system can then be designed independently, without affecting the other subsystems.

High-level overviews of system requirements

System overview diagrams are used to present an overview of a system, usually for the purpose of enabling business professionals and developers/maintainers to gain an understanding of the system and enabling business professionals to check whether the system requirements have been correctly understood. This usage of system overview diagrams is useful even for a very simple system, which can be adequately represented by a single overview diagram.

---

[1]   See Chapter 14 for the use of these diagrams in logical design.

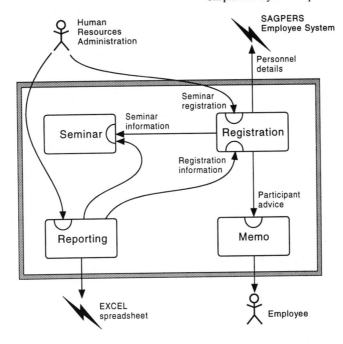

Figure 13-6: System overview diagram example

System overview diagram components

System overview diagrams can be used to summarize object structure diagrams and also to show the services which are offered by one object area to another. Subsystems group related object classes. Note that the grouping criterion is thus object (or data) based rather than being functionally based (e.g., based on functions carried out within a particular department).

System overview diagrams also show services offered by one subsystem to another or to actors. At this point, services offered by one subsystem to another cannot be derived bottom-up from a knowledge of what operations objects actually use, since the operations required have only partially been identified (if operations have been identified at all). Instead, if they are shown, they must be based on the understanding obtained from analyzing transaction sequences. Where system overview diagrams are used for communication purposes, it is best to regard these diagrams as draft documents which will be superseded when a later stage in design is reached.

Checking the System Requirements Model

Transaction sequence model

The following points should be checked:

1. Check that the actor hierarchy identifies all actors and that the division into types is clear and logical.

2. Check that all transaction sequences are identified and all system requirements covered.

3. Check that all transaction sequences which are not common sequences are associated with at least an initiating actor (unless they are initiated by a temporal event).

4. Check that all actors are associated with a transaction sequence.

5. Check that common sequences have been identified.

6. Check that transaction sequences are clearly named and are not overly complicated.

7. Check that the standard path description is meaningful on its own without reference to alternative paths.

8. Check that the standard path is not obscured by references to exception handling and variant paths which could better be explained under the alternative paths section.

9. Check that interface descriptions are clear.

Object structure model

The following points should be checked:

1. Check that the object classes are within the problem domain and required for the system.

2. Check that object classes are clearly named and that there are no duplications, and that there is a short description of the nature of each object class.

3. Check that inheritance hierarchies represent specialization hierarchies and not implementation inheritance.

4. Check that the semantics underlying each inheritance hierarchy are clearly defined.

5. Check that subtypes do not overlap and that, if the superclass is an abstract class, the set of subtypes completely covers all objects in the object class.

6. Check that inheritance hierarchies are not too deep (not to exceed a depth of 4 or 5.)

7. Check that the cardinality of aggregate components have been correctly defined and that dependent and independent components have been given the appropriate cardinality.

8. Check each attribute for cases where it is not applicable for some objects. This may indicate that there is a subclass within the identified object class and that the inheritance hierarchy needs reconsidering.

9. Check object classes with only one attribute. They may be legitimate, or the class may be redundant with the attribute belonging elsewhere.

10. Check each attribute for repeating values. These are allowed, but may sometimes point to a requirement for an additional object class.

11. Check that all the attributes of an object share the same life cycle. If they do not, there may be a requirement for an additional object class.

12. Check all relationships have been identified.

13. Check for relationships which are derivable from others. Can these relationships be removed from the model or should they be kept for the sake of the information they provide and marked as derived?

14. Check the cardinality of each relationship is correct.

15. Check that the meaning of each relationship is clear from its name and description.

16. Check many-to-many relationships and consider whether attributes should be associated with the many-to-many relationship and if so should they be modeled at one or the other end of the relationship or should a new object class be introduced?

17. Check multiple relationships between object classes. Sometimes multiple relationships are all subtypes of a single relationship type and can be mapped better by collapsing them all into an object which includes relationship type as an attribute.

18. Check for additional relationships by considering each pair of object classes.

19. Check that relationships and attributes are defined at the right place in an inheritance hierarchy, i.e., they apply to all objects of this type. If they do not, move them down to a subtype.

20. Check that identifying attributes uniquely identify the objects in question.

21. Check that any constraints which have been recorded are correct.

Object life cycles and system partitioning

The following points should be checked:

1. Check that life cycle diagrams are drawn for object classes with interesting life cycles.

2. Check that object life cycle diagrams are meaningful and correct. Eliminate redundant diagrams. Chapter 12 describes these checks in more detail.

3. Check that any division into subsystems is logical and clear.

Summary of Deliverables

1. Key deliverables
   - Transaction sequence descriptions
   - Object structure diagrams
   - Object class definitions including:

- attributes, relationships and constraints which are relevant for specification of requirements (and, optionally, identifying attributes and operations)
- first inheritance hierarchy definitions
- definition of aggregation structures
- Object life cycle diagrams for object classes with complex life cycles

2. Optional deliverables
   - Transaction sequence diagrams
   - System overview diagrams

Chapter 14
Logical Design

The purpose of logical design is to produce a complete design for the proposed system which is relatively free from detailed implementation constraints. It will be easier to port such a design to different user interface styles, languages, databases and computers. Hardly less important, where designers can avoid being distracted by detailed technical issues, they can produce a cleaner design.

The Relationship Between Logical and Physical Design

The aim of logical design is to produce a design which only requires relatively small, mechanical changes during physical design in order to be implementable. It takes experience however to understand which aspects can safely be left to physical design and which cannot. Experience with design, object-oriented techniques, and the specific target implementation environment is desirable.

It is a good idea to adopt an iterative approach, taking some portion of the design through to system construction so that lessons learned from this can be fed into the design. The development of a stable and adequate object structure model requires iteration and also experience. The object structure changes as design proceeds and also as lessons in object-oriented design are learned.

We recommend that you make strategic decisions relating to the choice of implementation environment and implementation tools before starting on logical design including:

- what target computer(s)
- what database
- what user interface
- what programming language
- what class libraries will be used
- planned use of batch and background jobs
- performance criteria
- possibly also, strategy with respect to error handling, garbage collection and other such detailed design issues which can often be handled in a standard way
- expected nature of distribution requirements, if any.

Such strategic decisions are discussed in more detail in Chapter 15.

Overview of Logical Design Activities

The following activities are undertaken as part of logical design:

1. Identifying interface and control objects.

2. Identifying operations.

3. Using object interaction diagrams to validate the design.

4. Refining the object structure model.

5. Refining the object life cycle model.

6. Defining subsystems.

Many logical design activities take transaction sequences as their starting point. Examination of transaction sequences is used to identify what control and interface objects should be added to the object structure model. Drawing of object interaction diagrams for individual transaction sequences is used to assist in identifying what operations object classes should support. Transaction sequences also provide the basis for deciding what the functionality provided by operations should be.

Identifying Interface and Control Objects

The three types of object, entity, interface and control, are used to assist in identifying object classes and assigning functionality to these object classes in such a way that a robust system is developed, with changes being localized as far as possible.

- Entity objects correspond to real-life objects or objects which are directly recognizable in the business domain.

- Interface objects are used to handle communication by the system with what is external to the system and to encapsulate environment-dependent behavior. They isolate behavior related to user and machine interfaces such that when details of interfaces are changed this affects only interface objects and not entity objects.

- Control objects are used for behavior which is not naturally placed either in interface objects or in entity objects. Such behavior typically relates to whole courses of events which may affect multiple objects and where it is not clear that the behavior should be owned by an existing entity object.

One benefit of the distinction between the three object types is that it makes explicit the fact that not all object classes identified in an object-oriented system design relate to real-world business objects. The distinction also assists when defining guidelines as to how to identify the additional interface and control objects which are required for a robust object structure and what behavior to assign to each. Such guidelines are given next.

Bear in mind, however, that the purpose of the three object types is to assist in the development of a maintainable system. There will be cases where it is really not important whether an object class is categorized as an entity object or a control object.

How to identify and define interface objects

Interface objects can be identified using the following guidelines:

1. Allocate one central interface object for each transaction sequence/actor/major device type combination. For instance, a warehouse supervisor may use a GUI interface to control stock movements and a printer to print stock movement details. For these activities, two interface objects can be identified.

2. For a GUI interface, allocate one interface object per window. The interface objects communicate with the central interface objects identified in Step 1. It is not useful to identify interface objects for individual window components as the definition of the window itself is handled via a GUI builder. Only define the contents of windows within interface object classes if the interface description capabilities of the GUI builder fall short of your requirements (for reuse of data definitions between windows or readable interface descriptions, for instance) and you consider that interface object descriptions can fill the gap.

3. For other device types, it may be useful to identify a central interface object which handles a particular type of output, e.g., long-distance communications, while additional interface objects are identified for the alternative types of long-distance communication, e.g., fax, e-mail or letter. This means that the choice of device can be independent of the output request. Similarly, a central interface object can handle all print requests, with associated interface objects being used to define individual printer types (color printer, for instance). The central interface object will then receive all print requests and will forward them to an interface object representing a printer of an appropriate type.

4. Interface objects can model layered communication protocols, e.g., the ISO seven-layer model. In this case, an interface object is defined for each layer, with each object only communicating with the objects in the layer above and below it. (Normal applications use a communications package and don't need to model all communication layers.)

5. Aggregation can be used for interface objects. For instance, some devices are best considered as composite. As an example, an ATM can be seen as consisting of a card slot, a display unit, a money dispenser and a receipt printer. This can be modeled by defining interface objects for the ATM and for its various components. The ATM interface object is defined as an aggregation of the interface objects for the various ATM components.

6. Inheritance can be defined for interface objects. This can be useful in the case where one type of actor has a set of capabilities which is a superset of the capabilities of another actor. E.g., a supervisor can carry out all functions allowed a workman, plus some additional ones. In this case, an inheritance hierarchy is defined where the supervisor

actor inherits from the workman actor. This can be mirrored in the interface objects, with the central interface object for the workman being inherited by the central interface object for the supervisor.

7. Once interface objects have been defined, central interface objects should be reviewed and any central interface objects which have similar functionality should be merged.

Once interface objects have been identified, it is necessary to consider what attributes and operations the objects require. Interface object classes for machine interfaces may have attributes such as communication speed, package size, etc. Requirements for operations are identified as described later in this chapter. The type of behavior allocated to interface objects is that which:

- requests information from outside the system,

- presents information to the world outside the system,

- changes if the user's behavior, in particular the required user interface, changes, and

- is dependent on a particular device type.

Changes to the functionality of the interface should be local to interface objects. Other types of change should not affect them.

There are often interface objects which have particularly complicated life cycles, in order to handle alternative input or navigation sequences. The life cycles of these objects can usefully be clarified by drawing an object life cycle diagram.

Details of how the user interface should appear is finalized during logical design, using a GUI builder and interface objects in combination. We suggest defining interface objects for GUI windows only. Finer details are better defined using a GUI builder, to avoid redundant definitions.

How to identify and define control objects

Control objects contain behavior which does not naturally belong to entity and interface objects. They are therefore usually identified after interface and entity objects.

Control objects are usually transient, lasting only for the duration of a transaction sequence. The logic in them could be spread over a number of entity objects. But the effect of distributing the behavior would be a lower resistance to change, because a change to the logic may then involve a change to several entity objects. If you identify such behavior, then you have identified a requirement for a control object. The logic contained in a control object may be system control logic, required because a computer system is being developed. It may also be application logic. It is often useful to use control objects for transaction logic, for instance.

Control objects can be identified by first assigning one control object for each transaction sequence. After behavior has been assigned to interface and entity objects, it can be seen whether all behavior has been satisfactorily assigned, leaving no requirement for the control object. Or if there is behavior that does not naturally belong to the interface and entity objects that can be placed in the control object. If there is very little functionality to assign to the control object, it is also undesirable to retain the control object. In other cases, it may be that complex behavior will be identified, which is better distributed between a number of control objects.

The type of behavior which should be allocated to a control object is:

- behavior which is unchanged if the object's surroundings change
- behavior which will not change much if entity objects change
- behavior affecting more than one entity object
- state-dependent logic
- control logic for a transaction sequence.

Control objects are linked with actors via interface objects. It is better for a control object to be associated with only one actor (to improve resistance to change). Control objects often act as a sort of buffer between interface and entity objects.

Control objects which are too complicated and lack functional cohesion should be split. Control objects which have strong functional cohesion (e.g., similar functionality required by different transaction sequences) should be merged.

Control objects may have associated attributes. They often do not possess public attributes, i.e., attributes the value of which should be visible outside the object.

The decision as to whether to regard some objects that contain calculations required in the problem domain, e.g., tax calculations or accruals, as control or entity objects may be relatively arbitrary. The rule is that an object that contains attributes and is persistent should be categorized as an entity object while one which does not contain attributes and is transient should be defined as a control object. Application calculations, while they may act on data in other objects, generally have data that clearly belongs to them and are therefore usually to be regarded as entity objects. Control objects should not be used to allow a lapse back into a non-object oriented separation of function and data. The role of the three object types is to assist in identifying the right object classes with the right scope. It is not significant whether borderline cases are classified as entity objects or as control objects.

The possible associations between interface, control and entity objects
Usually only associations of the following types exist between objects of the different types:

First Object	Second Object		
	Entity Object	Interface Object	Control Object
Entity Object	CO RE IH AG	*CO*	*CO*
Interface Object	CO *RE*	CO RE IH AG	CO
Control Object	CO *RE*	CO	CO IH *AG*

Italics indicate cases in which an association of the specified could exist but normally does not. The abbreviations used in the table are as follows:

Abbreviation	Description
CO	communicates with (dynamic link)
RE	relationship (static link)
IH	inheritance
AG	aggregation (consists-of)

Normally actors communicate with interface objects and not with entity and control objects. Relationships are usually modeled only between entity objects because these are the objects for which an analysis of static, intrinsic relationships is relevant. For interface and control objects, usually only communication associations are relevant. Modeling relationships is only really needed where it assists in clarifying relationships between objects which can be considered as relatively permanent.

Note that any given inheritance hierarchy or aggregation consists of objects of a single type - entity, interface or control.

One case where it can be useful to model relationships between interface objects is where it assists in understanding the relationships between interface objects which form a distinct structure, particularly where one interface object can be associated with a number of interface objects of another object class. Relationships between interface objects can, as one example of this type of usage, be used to model what windows can be reached from a given window.

Another case where modeling relationships for non-entity objects can be useful is where there are reasons for making interface or control objects persistent. This is often the case where a system should continue at the point at which it left off when it picks up after a system crash.

Particularly in this second case, it can be useful to use relationships between interface or control objects and entity objects to model cases in which interface or control objects need to retain information about the entity objects they are dealing with. The relationship should normally only be traversed from interface or control object to entity object.

Normally, entity objects should have no knowledge of interface and control objects. For this reason, the possible associations an entity object may have with interface and control objects are shown in italics in the table. Entity objects normally have no communication associations with interface or control objects. They respond to communications sent to them by interface and control objects and do not initiate communications. This protects them from changes or additions to the more volatile interface and control objects.

There is, however, an exception to this where interface or control objects need to be notified of changes that occur to an entity object. Consider, for instance, the case where a supervisor should be notified if an account limit is exceeded. When the entity object for the account sends such a notification, it should restrict itself to notification of the fact that the event has occurred. Knowledge of what the receiving interface or control object should do when the event occurs should not be built into the entity object's definition. The interface or control object should respond to the event notification by sending a message to the entity object requesting the information it needs.

The requirement for such event notification arises in a multi-user environment where it is important for updates by one user to be immediately reflected on another user's screen. It arises more frequently in a GUI environment where a user may have a number of windows open at once and wishes to see updates to one window reflected immediately in other windows. Where users have multiple update windows open, they are likely also to wish to see other users' updates as soon as these are committed.

A model-view-controller pattern was developed in the Smalltalk community that handles the updating of multiple windows and the handling of event notification such that entity objects do not incorporate unnecessary knowledge of the workings of interface and control objects. This pattern is described in detail in Chapter 23 and can be applied where event notification is needed.

Identifying and Defining Operations

An operation is processing which can be requested as a unit from an object. The same operation may be available from objects belonging to different object classes. For instance, the Create and Destroy operations are available for objects of all object classes.

An operation defines the service which is offered. This definition includes a description of the semantics of the operation, i.e., of what the operation does, and a description of the signature of the operation, i.e., how the service can be called. The core semantics of an operation should be the same regardless of which object class offers the operation and of whether the object classes in question are related via an inheritance hierarchy. The operation's signature consists of the information which must be supplied in order to invoke the operation, that is, its name and its input and output parameters and their types. For all object classes in an inheritance hierarchy which inherit a given operation, the operation's signature will be the same.[1]

A method is the implementation of an operation for a specific object class, and may vary for each object class.

Implicit operations

As explained in Chapter 4, some operations (e.g., Create, Destroy, Read and Update) can be assumed to exist and do not need to be specified for each object class.

Dot notation for referencing attributes

During logical design, explicit use of the Read operation is not necessary. You can assume that all public attributes are accessible. A dot notation can be used within the specification of an operation to identify which attribute is to be read. For instance, **Document.Author** references the Author attribute of the object Document. Relationships can be included in such attribute references, thus allowing navigation paths to be expressed. **Car.Driver.Name** refers to the name of the person who drives a given car, where **Driver** identifies a relationship between the object classes **Car** and **Person**.

The same dot notation can be used when updating attribute values.

How to identify operations

Three possible ways of identifying operations are as follows:

1. By considering the role and responsibilities of each object class, using either an approach based on the analysis of transaction sequences or a shopping list approach.

2. By identifying the object interactions required to support each transaction sequence, with the assistance of an object interaction diagram.

3. By looking at object life cycles and the requirements for operations which they imply.

All three methods of identifying operations are valuable and it is a good idea to use these methods in combination. If transaction sequences are used as the basis for identifying operations, consideration of roles and responsibilities combines very naturally with the use of object interaction diagrams.

---

[1] In C++, there can be multiple implementations of an operation within an object class that have different signatures. In our approach, all implementations of an operation within an inheritance hierarchy have the same signature. This conforms with Meyer's approach to inheritance.

Whichever method of identifying operations is used, the key issues which arise are:

- how should functionality be split between operations?
- which object class should be responsible for this operation?

Operation identification method 1 - Considering the role and responsibilities of each object class

According to Wirfs-Brock, each object class should have a single clearly defined and coherent role or function. In support of its role, the object undertakes certain responsibilities and behavior which it is logical for other objects to expect from the object, given its role. The operations an object has allow it to fulfill its responsibilities.

Responsibilities and hence operations are identified by analyzing the system requirements, as represented in transaction sequences. We have already identified the entity objects which participate in each transaction sequence and have also produced a first-cut allocation of interface and control objects to each transaction sequence. We can now consider each transaction sequence in turn in order to identify what operations should be assigned to each object class.

When doing this, use an object structure diagram which includes the object classes relevant to a given transaction sequence as the basis for considering the distribution of responsibilities between object classes.

Alternatively, responsibilities can be identified using the so-called shopping list approach. Using this approach, the analyst identifies operations by considering each object class in turn and considering in the abstract: "What is this object responsible for and what might I want to do with this data?"

Where an object class is clearly logically responsible for a particular item of behavior that is required for a transaction sequence, the operation should be assigned to that object class. Where it is not clear that a responsibility belongs to a single object class, you can:

- allocate the responsibility to the object class which is the most nearly appropriate,
- distribute the responsibility between more than one object class,
- introduce a control object and allocate the operation to the control object.

Which solution is the best depends on the context and is a matter of judgment. Because allocating operations correctly to the appropriate object class is the key to a well-designed, maintainable, object-oriented system, we have included a discussion of some of the issues involved in Chapter 22.

Operation identification method 2 - Object interactions required to support each transaction sequence

The object interactions required to support each transaction sequence can be modeled using object interaction diagrams. Generally speaking, one object interaction diagram is used to model each transaction sequence. First, concentrate on the standard path to ensure that basic requirements are covered. Later, alternative paths and exceptions can be considered. It is possible to use more than one object interaction diagram per transaction sequence and this is discussed in the section Advanced Modeling Techniques in Chapter 6.

The starting point for the development of an object interaction diagram is the extract from the object structure diagram. This should include all the entity objects which are relevant for this transaction sequence together with the interface and control objects which have been allocated to the transaction sequence.

The first step is to consider what object interactions are required to provide the functionality described in the transaction sequence. These object interactions are called events.

A transaction sequence is started by an event. An event may be external or temporal. External events are associated with an actor (either a person or a machine interface). Temporal events are triggered by a date being reached or other periodic processing.

If the event partitioning approach to the identification of transaction sequences is used,[1] the business event(s) to which each transaction sequence is a response will already have been identified. This business event initiates the transaction sequence if the originator of the business event also interacts directly with the system (e.g., a user of an Automated Teller Machine). This event, with its originator and the object class that receives it (which will be an interface object), can be entered on the object interaction diagram. If the originator of the business event does not interact directly with the system, then the event which starts the transaction sequence is the event in which an actor within the company reacts to the business event by initiating an interaction with the system.

Following the initial event, internal events are added to the object interaction diagram to represent the communications between object classes that are required to support the standard path of the transaction sequence. An internal event is effectively a message sent by one object class to another in order to invoke an operation.

Further events may be sent to, and received from, actors with whom the transaction sequence communicates. An example of object interactions is shown below, represented as a table (in no particular order). Italics are used to distinguish the actors in the table.

---

[1] See Chapter 13 for a discussion of event partitioning.

Sending Object	Event	Receiving Object
Order	CreateEntry	DepotAccount
Order	ConfirmExecution	*FinancialAdviser*
DepotAccount	CreateDepotEntry	DepotEntry
BuySellOrder	CheckBalance	Order
StockExchange	OrderExecuted	Order

The event names identify the nature of the event from the point of view of the initiator of the event. The messages which implement each event invoke an operation in the target object, passing a number of input parameters and expecting to receive certain return values. Each message is sent by an operation belonging to the sending object.

After identifing the object interactions, the next step is to identifythe operation associated with each event and the required parameters.

Sending Object	Invoking Operation	Event	Invoked Operation	Receiving Object
StockExchange		OrderExecuted	OrderExecuted	Order
Order	OrderExecuted	CreateEntry	CreateEntry	DepotAccount
DepotAccount	CreateEntry	CreateDepotEntry	CreateDepotEntry	DepotEntry
Order	OrderExecuted	CheckBalance	CheckBalance	BuySellOrder
Order	OrderExecuted	ConfirmExecution		FinancialAdviser

Note that the point at which a reply is returned in response to a message is only shown implicitly in the table. While in our example event names are the same as operation names, this is not necessarily the case. The same operation may be invoked for a variety of different purposes. There may be a sequence of invocations, where the use of different event names for the different invocations adds clarity to the description.

Figure 14-1 is an example of an object interaction diagram (in fence diagram form). An alternative net form can be used - see Chapter 6 for details.

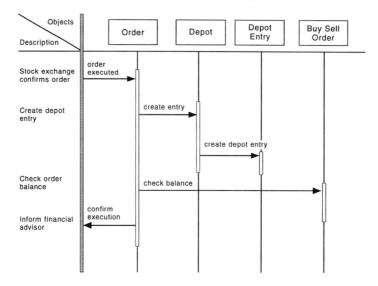

Figure 14-1: Object Interaction Diagram - Fence Style

Comments in the Description column can be used to assist cross-referencing with the text description of the transaction sequence and to make it clear which actors send and receive requests.

While an object interaction diagram shows events occurring in a linear sequence, the order in which events are received from outside the system may be random. For instance, a user might choose to enter customer name and address before entering details of the customer's order or vice versa. This needs to be considered when interpreting object interaction diagrams in which more than one event can be received from outside the system. (Our example does not illustrate this case.)

You can make it easier to identify blocks that can occur in random sequences, or conditionally, by marking such blocks on the object interaction diagram. You can also use an object interaction diagram in combination with an activity flow diagram to show the logic flow between the blocks. Generally speaking, this isn't necessary in order to achieve identification of operations.

In our use of object interaction diagrams, we used a white box approach. For each operation, we have considered what objects and operations that operation usees in order to provide its functionality. The white box approach is suitable where a new part of a system is being developed and details of each operation, and of the responsibilities of each object class, are not yet clear.

When an operation is used which has already been fully defined, e.g., because it belongs to an object class in a class library or existing system or because its design has been finalized for this system, then a black box approach can be used. In this case, there is no need to explode the operation to show its internal workings. The definition of the operation should clearly state whether it supplies the required functionality.

Operation identification method 3 - Object life cycles

Object life cycle diagrams can be reviewed to identify operations. Each event shown on an object life cycle diagram causes the invocation of an operation in the receiving object. Reviewing object life cycle diagrams does not reveal all operations, since life cycle diagrams normally model only events which cause a state change in the receiving object. It does, however, provide a useful cross-check that operations object life cycle diagrams require are indeed provided.

Naming operations

Use standard naming conventions for operations for the following reasons:

- It should be easy for other developers to identify operations which they could invoke. Note that operations in different object classes should have the same name if their function is the same, regardless of whether the object classes are related by inheritance.

- Similar operations should have similar names. If the same operation is identified during the analysis of different transaction sequences, it should easily be identified as being in fact the same operation.

Defining the operation's semantics and signature

Define the semantics for each operation. The name, signature and semantics of the operation should provide all the information potential users of the operation needto decide whether the operation is suitable for their purposes. It is undesirable for users to have to inspect the code of the operation in order to determine what the operation does. Users may then acquire information about the implementation of the operation which may affect how they use the operation. Any resulting reliance on the internal implementation of an operation damages encapsulation and the maintainability of the system. Changes to the internal implementation that are assumed to be safe, because they are encapsulated, can then have unexpected side-effects.The semantics of an operation should be carefully specified, so that users will not need to investigate the implementation.

The specification of the semantics may be expressed in text, decision tables, pseudocode, etc. Specification of any or all of precondition, post condition and invariant as part of the definition of an operation's semantics provides useful information which assists developers when considering whether they can invoke the operation for a given purpose.

The signature should also be specified, i.e., the input and output arguments which are required. The type of each argument and its possible range of values should be defined and also whether the argument is mandatory or optional.

Other attributes of an operation definition

An operation can be defined as a class operation. A *class operation* is an operation which is invoked on the object class itself rather than on its instances. Such operations may, for instance, return summary information (averages, totals etc.) about objects in an object class. A physical object class can be added later during physical design to handle class operations, if the chosen implementation language does not support them.

It's useful to specify an operation as public, private or protected. A *public* operation may be invoked by other objects. A *private* or *protected* operation may only be used by the object itself. Private and protected operations allow modular development of operations. Defining an operation as private or protected excludes it from the lists of operations available to clients of an object class. Implementation details and interfaces can be changed relatively freely. The difference between a private and a protected operation relates to inheritance. A protected operation may be used by subclasses of an object class. A private operation, on the other hand, may not be used by subclasses and can be used for purely internal modularization of operations. Public operations are always usable by subclasses.

Reviewing the identified operations

As operations are identified, a rationalization process is necessary to identify operations with different names that perform the same function, perhaps with a slightly different set of parameters. This process of rationalization is easier to carry out if consistent naming conventions are used.

Consider the operations in each object class and:

- Try to make each operation as widely applicable as possible.
- Try to make operations as orthogonal to each other as possible. They should have as little overlapping functionality as possible.

Note also that the reusability increases if the operations have relatively few parameters.[1]

Check whether other similar operations already exist, either within a single object class, within object classes belonging to the same object class hierarchy or within unrelated object classes. If similar operations exist, then consider:

- Are all the operations required or can the operations be generalized into a single operation?
- If the operations belong to object classes in an object class hierarchy, can the operation be defined in its most general form in a superclass and variants be defined in subclasses using operation redefinition?
- If the operations belong to unrelated object classes but effectively have the same semantics, then the operations should have the same name.
- Similarly, if the operations really have the same purpose, consider making their semantics as similar as possible and giving them a common signature.

---

[1] See Johnson and Foote, "Designing Reusable Classes", *Journal of Object-Oriented Programming*, June-July 1988, for this and other rules connected with obtaining reuse.

- For operations belonging to unrelated object classes, the existence of similar operations may indicate that the object classes should be related by inheritance.

It is also important to check the distribution of functionality between operations and object classes. The best distribution of functionality is the one which that localizes subsequent changes. This is a very important aspect of object-oriented design and is discussed in more detail in Chapter 22.

Inheritance of operations

Concrete, abstract and template operations

Abstract classes are classes for which no object exists which does not belong to a subclass. In any concrete class, operations must always have a method implementation since they will presumably be used and can't be used if they haven't been implemented. In an abstract class, a method implementation isn't needed, provided all concrete subclasses provide one. The following types of operation can be specified in an abstract class:

- abstract operation. An abstract operation has no method definition. Only the signature and semantics of the operation must be defined.

- template operation. A template operation is a concrete operation which is implemented in terms of one or more abstract operations.

- concrete operation. A concrete operation is fully implemented.

The developer of an abstract operation expects that subclasses will require an operation of a given type and specifies a standard name, semantics and signature for all operations of that type in the subclasses. The interface for the operation is inherited, and any concrete object classes that inherit the operation must supply their own implementation for the operation.

As part of logical design, it is useful to identify where concrete operations are required. Producing the method implementation itself (i.e., writing code) is not a logical design task but a physical design/construction activity.

Redefining inherited operations

Where an object class inherits a concrete operation from a superclass and uses it unchanged, no further specification of the operation is required in the object class. In practice, it is often unnecessary to change inherited operations.

In a well-constructed inheritance hierarchy, the only types of change required for an inherited operation are:

- addition of an implementation for an abstract operation.

- extension of the operation to add behavior or details specific to the way this object class handles the operation. For instance, a Create operation may be extended in a subclass to provide initial values for attributes that exist in the subclass but not in the superclass.

- redefinition of argument types and the range of values (domain) of each argument.

- code optimization.

A new implementation of an operation (a method specification) always overrides an inherited one. The new implementation may invoke the implementation in the parent (provided the operation is protected or public).

When behavior is added, the semantics should be extended not changed. Only state the additional behavior required. It is not necessary to restate the semantics of the inherited operation.

You cannot add or delete arguments for an inherited operation.[1] The type or range of values of individual input and output arguments can be changed. The range of values of an input argument should not be reduced. The range of values of an output argument should not be extended.

See the section Inheritance of Operations in Chapter 22 for a more detailed discussion of what lies behind the constraints on how an operation can be redefined.

Using Object Interaction Diagrams to Validate the Design

Earlier in this chapter we discussed how object interaction diagrams can be used to identify operations. They are also useful to validate the design.

Validating the design

A review of object interaction diagrams makes it possible to check:

- that operations exist which support the functionality described in transaction sequences.

- how centralized or decentralized the design is. It is usually better for intelligence to be evenly distributed between object classes.

- whether the distribution of functionality between operations allows changes to be localized.

Updating transaction sequence descriptions

During the course of examining transaction sequences to produce the logical design, it may be necessary to add details to transaction sequence descriptions that were not needed during system requirements analysis. If details were left out that are now found to be necessary to complete the transaction sequence, they should be added.

---

[1]   As mentioned previously, C++ does allow multiple implementations of an operation within an object class to have different signatures. We prefer Meyer's approach, in which all implementations of an operation within an inheritance hierarchy have the same signature.

Refining the Object Structure Model

Addition and removal of object classes

Usually the object classes from system requirements analysis are carried over one for one into logical design and additional interface and control objects are added.

As a better understanding of the system is obtained during logical design, you can make changes to the object structure model. Changes to the structure of the object structure model do not compromise the ability of the object structure model to represent system requirements.

In complex applications, you may need to change the level of abstraction at which object classes are viewed. For instance, from the requirements point of view it may be clear that a number of similar object types are required and that each should be described as a subclass of an appropriate superclass. From a logical design point of view, it might be clear that only the superclass is required in the final system design and that the subclasses are not required.

Here, the best approach is to ensure that the object structure model as a whole describes, without structural clashes, both the object classes required for an understanding in requirements analysis and any additional object classes added for logical design. Object classes required for requirements analysis and not for logical design and vice versa can be marked as such.

Identification of attributes

As logical design proceeds, the attributes required for each object class should be fully identified. Attributes required outside the object are defined as public. Attributes used internally to the object are defined as protected or private. *Protected* attributes are accessible by subclasses and *private* attributes are not accessible by subclasses. *Public* attributes are always accessible in subclasses.

Attributes that are identified should be described. It is useful to specify the attribute's type, range of values and initial value. If an attribute is derivable, it should be identified as derived and the derivation algorithm should be specified.

Specifying identifying attributes and constraints

Further identifying attributes and constraints may be identified. See Chapter 13 for details.

Defining Object Class and Attribute Persistence

Entity objects are generally *persistent* while interface and control objects are not. You need to identify entity objects which are not persistent, and interface and control objects which are.

It can generally be assumed that public attributes which are not derived are persistent and that private or protected attributes are not persistent. Any exceptions to this rule should be identified and marked as persistent or transient as appropriate. Specification of whether *derived* attributes are persistent is a technical issue which can be left until physical design.

Adjusting the Inheritance Hierarchy

As the definition of object classes is completed and operations are added to object classes, it is necessary to review the inheritance structure. Changes to the classification system may be desirable due to the design approach developed during logical design. Additionally, once operations have been added, the inheritance hierarchies should be reviewed to ensure that subclasses are substitutable for superclasses in each operation, i.e., that the *subtyping* type of inheritance is being used. See Chapter 20 for an explanation of substitutibility and subtyping.

It is also worth looking for object classes with similar attributes and operations and considering whether there would be any benefit in defining a common superclass. You should, of course, bear in mind the undesirability of using inheritance hierarchies to bind together object classes which have no real relationship to one another.

With existing inheritance hierarchies, consider whether attributes and operations are defined at the right level in the inheritance hierarchy. Maybe optional attributes should be moved down to a subclass where they are mandatory.

Seminar registration system example

Figure 14-2 shows the final object structure model for logical design.

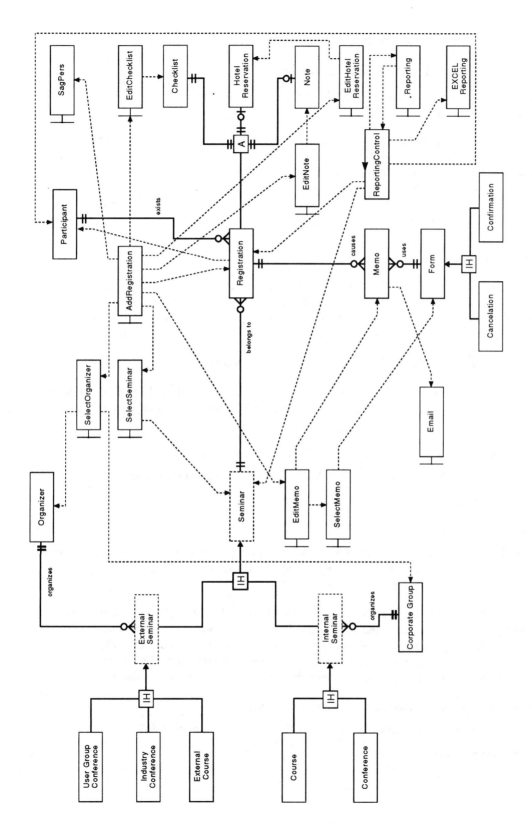

Figure 14-2: Seminar registration system ~ object structure model

Refining the Object Life Cycle Model

It can be useful to draw object life cycle diagrams for interface or control objects with complicated life cycles.

Object life cycle diagrams produced during analysis may be revisited to add detail identified during the identification of operations and to review for changes required as further information about object classes and their behavior has been obtained. This is an optional activity which is useful for objects with complex life cycles. As object life cycles are also used to identify operations, the process may be iterative, with the updated object life cycle diagrams potentially causing further operations to be identified.

Defining Subsystems

Subsystems may already have been defined or they may be defined at this stage in the development process. Even if they have already been defined, it is useful to check them at this stage, now that object classes and operations have been fully defined, to ensure that the subsystem does indeed represent a coherent unit.

During logical design, the main reasons for defining subsystems are:

- to define delivery units, i.e., units of functionality which can be delivered to customers on successive delivery dates, or optional or compulsory product components.
- to define units that are distributable.
- to define modules as a way of ensuring a robust system design.
- for validation purposes, to check the quality of the design of the system.
- for presentation purposes.

Defining the scope of a subsystem

Basically, object classes which have a high level of interdependency and serve a common purpose should be in the same subsystem. Note: objects that are always required and needed by multiple subsystems do not have to be in a subsystem.

It is desirable that the number of communications between subsystems should be small (low coupling between subsystems) and that the interface to the subsystem should be small (as little passing of data as possible). For this reason, it is also desirable that the number of objects which directly communicate across a subsystem boundary should also be small. Most objects in a subsystem should not send or receive communications across subsystem boundaries.

The following should be modeled as separate subsystems:

- existing products/subsystems with which the system communicates.
- optional components.

Some suggestions as to how to determine which objects are closely related and are therefore likely to belong to one subsystem are as follows:

1. Put objects which communicate with the same actor in the same subsystem.

2. Start from control objects and consider what interface objects and entity objects are closely related to the control objects.

3. Consider communications between objects. Objects which communicate frequently (via one or several message types) are closely related.

4. Consider whether changes to one object are likely to mean that another object should be changed. Where this is the case, the objects are closely related.

Having identified objects which are closely related, you can check if you have identified a subsystem by seeing if the grouping can be named, implying that it has a coherent function.

Identifying services

Once subsystems have been identified, services provided by one subsystem to another can be identified by looking at communications between subsystems and grouping these into services. The services can be documented with a name and a short description. They can be shown on system overview diagrams.

Some ways of using subsystem definitions

Defining delivery units

It is possible to see from system overview diagrams what subsystems depend on the services of other subsystems. This can assist in determining in what order to deliver subsystems and in identifying optional and compulsory product components.

Defining units that are distributable

Defining distribution is a physical design or configuration, issue. At the logical design level, however, subsystems can provide a useful definition of the units that are potentially distributable.

Typically a task will consist of one or more than one distributable unit. (See Chapter 15 for a discussion of tasks.)

Defining modules

Modules contain object classes directly and are defined as the next grouping level which is larger than an object class. They are defined in order to improve the maintainability of the system by defining cohesive units with small interfaces that are larger than a single object class. Typically, a module should contain between 5 and 15 object classes and not more than 20. It should also conform to the quality criteria for subsystems which are described in Chapter 8.

Using subsystems for validation purposes

The ability to define subsystems which conform to the quality criteria for subsystems can be used to check whether the system design will prove maintainable, with changes being localized.

Usage of system overview diagrams

System overview diagrams can be used to provide an overview of system functionality. The diagrams can be particularly useful if the subsystems are defined at a relatively fine level of granularity. The diagrams can give a relatively detailed view of what services are offered by the system.

Checking the Logical Design Model

Object structure model

1. Check that the object classes are within the problem domain and are required for the system.

2. Check that all interface objects have been identified, not including detailed window components.

3. Check that any control objects have a coherent function, are not too complicated, and do not contain functionality which would be better placed in entity objects.

4. Check that control objects are only linked with one actor (via interface objects).

5. Check relationships between entity objects and interface or control objects. Are these needed? Is the entity object insulated from knowledge of interface and control objects?

6. Check object classes for redundancy, i.e., object classes with similar relationships, attributes or operations.

7. Check relationships for cases where one relationship can in fact be derived from another.

8. Check all attributes and operations of an object class fulfill a role or responsibility of the object class.

9. Check that all roles and responsibilities of an object class have a strong functional connection with one another. If an object class can be broken up into groups of attributes and operations which have no strong functional connection with one another, the object class should probably be split up.

10. Check that inheritance hierarchies use subtyping and not implementation inheritance. (See Chapter 20 on inheritance.)

11. Check that inheritance hierarchies are not too deep. (As a guideline, try not to exceed a depth of 4 or 5.)

12. Check aggregates. Are cardinalities correct? Consider whether messages sent to component objects should be sent to the composite object. Make sure that the implications for the composite object of any operations invoked directly in a component object have been considered.

13. Check attributes and relationships as described Chapter 13.

14. Check identifying attributes and constraints.

15. Check for redundant, similar attribute types.

16. Check all objects either send or receive messages.

Support for transaction sequences

1. Are all actors associated with interface objects?

2. Are all transaction sequences supported using available operations?

3. Has the user interface been fully defined?

Definition of operations

1. Are similar operations which should be merged, made more consistent or related via inheritance?

2. Do all operations have a function and do not simply pass work on to another operation.

3. Are operations clearly defined so that their function is readily recognizable for reuse?

4. Is functionality well distributed between operations? Will the impact of likely changes tend to be localized?

5. Is all data passed as arguments to an operation directly relevant to the function of the object class?

6. For inherited operations, check that the range of values of each output argument is not extended and the range of values of each input argument is not restricted.

7. Are all operationsidentified as public, protected or private?

8. Are requirements for concrete operations identified?

9. Are all operations invoked?

Object life cycles

1. Check that operations take account of the different reactions required at different stages in the object life cycle. See also the section on object life cycles in Checking the Business Analysis Model in Chapter 12 for further checks on object life cycles.

System partitioning

1. Do subsystems represent functionally coherent units, with high cohesion and low coupling?

2. Do modules contain between 5 and 15 object classes but not more than 20?

3. Does most communication occur within a subsystem? Is the interface with the outside world small in terms of the number of objects communicating with the outside world and the amount of data passed?

Summary of Deliverables

1. Key deliverables

    •   Object structure diagrams

    •   Object class definitions including:

        •   all attributes, relationships and operations with the exception of ones introduced during physical design

        •   inheritance hierarchy definitions

        •   aggregation structure definitions

        •   definition of attributes and operations as public/private/protected

        •   definition of each attribute's attribute type, range of values and initial value

        •   definition of identifying attributes and constraints

        •   definition of object classes and attributes as persistent/transient

    •   Transaction sequence descriptions

2. Optional deliverables

    •   Transaction sequence diagrams

    •   Object interaction diagrams

    •   Activity flow diagrams

    •   Object life cycle diagrams

    •   System overview diagrams.

Chapter 15

Physical Design

The purpose of physical design is to add all the technical and platform-dependent detail required to build the system to the logical design. Construction involves putting together or generating the source objects required to implement object classes and then building the application with its user interface and data management components. Physical design and construction are often handled as a single phase.

As outlined in earlier chapters, we recommend adopting an iterative approach by taking some portion of the design through to construction before other portions. Experience gained from this can be fed back into the design before proceeding in the same way with the next portion.

Among the principal issues of physical design and construction are:

1. establishing a system architecture,

2. implementing the problem domain classes of the system,

3. building a user interface,

4. designing and implementing a data management component, and

5. designing for the integration of existing legacy systems.

This chapter describes each of these issues in detail. We incorporated many of the recommendations of Rumbaugh and Coad/Yourdon into our approach to physical design. Elegant solutions to some of these issues are also available in the form of well-known design patterns which contribute to a quality design. These are discussed in Chapter 23. To the extent that standard patterns can be defined, this opens up opportunities for automating the construction process.

System Architecture

System architecture is the overall organization of a system into components (or subsystems). Determining the system architecture usually represents the first step of the physical design phase.

Subsystems are usually defined during earlier phases of the development process to help control complexity, to assist in defining units which can be distributed to different processors, and for organizational reasons (separate development teams or subprojects, etc.). During physical design, these subsystems may be further refined in order to increase modularity and isolate implementation dependencies.

Note that a subsystem itself can also be viewed as an object which is an aggregation of the object classes in the subsystem. For a discussion of this alternative refer to the section 'Using an object class to encapsulate a subsystem' in Chapter 8.

System components

A system may be partitioned vertically or horizontally (into layers). Vertical partitions are used for subdividing application functionality, while horizontal partitions are used particularly to isolate operating system, database or hardware dependencies. Horizontal layering assists in safeguarding portability.

Vertical partitions should be weakly coupled and can be in a client-server or in a peer-to-peer relationship. Horizontal layers are in a client-server relationship, where the lower layer (server) supplies services to the upper layer (client). A layer is built in terms of the layer(s) below.

A layered architecture may either be open or closed. Open means that a layer can use the features of any lower level to any depth. Closed means that each layer only communicates with the next layer to it. (There is a trade-off between efficiency and modularity here.) Lower layers should not require knowledge of upper layers.

System architectures can be diagrammed using system overview diagrams which are also useful during all the other phases of the development process. These diagrams show subsystems and the services they provide each other with.

In their OOD model, Coad and Yourdon, aiming at a separation of concerns, proposed a basic system architecture. Our approach basically follows that model, extending it with two more components, one for interfacing with external systems and one for general utility services. Six major components of a system (modeled as subsystems) are considered:

- The *problem domain component* (PDC) represents the application or real-world part of the system and consists of all entity and control objects identified during previous development phases. The entire object structure model developed during the analysis and logical design phases becomes the "starting point" for the PDC; it is then modified and extended, as necessary, to deal with performance and implementation issues.

- The *human interaction component* (HIC) consists of all objects and object classes required for the user interface implementation. For a first cut, these are the interface objects used to define the interface with human actors defined during logical design.

- The *external interface component* (EIC) consists of all interface objects used to define the interface with non-human actors, like external systems, printers, etc. These will have been identified, as a first cut, during the logical design phase of the project; they may need to be refined or modified during the physical design stage.

- The *data management component* (DMC) provides the infrastructure for the storage and retrieval of objects in some data management system. This component is added during the physical design stage of the project, because typically only then does the development team finalize the choice of DBMS packages, etc.

- The *task management component* (TMC) handles concurrency, where necessary, within a system. In theory, this could be relevant in earlier phases of the development process, if the user's business requirements include explicit timing or concurrency constraints. However, it is quite rare to see this except in real-time systems. For business applications, the TMC is created during the physical design stage, when the developers are aware of the concurrency issues, and the capabilities provided by the operating system or run-time features of the programming environment.

- The *utility services component* (USC) provides general utility services that can be requested by all other components, such as for common handling of implementation data types, etc. This typically becomes relevant in the physical design stage of the project, when the development team has a complete inventory of available libraries, packages, and utility services provided by the hardware/software environment.

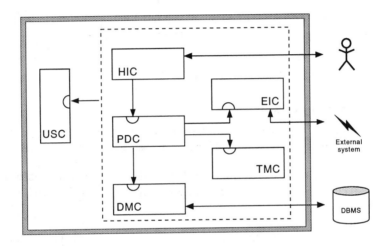

Figure 15-1: System architecture

Strategic decisions

The system architecture provides the context into which the more detailed design will later fit. It should contain strategic decisions on what type of data storage and user interface will be used, the way control will be implemented, what development environment will be used, and the use of reusable system frameworks.

Choosing a development environment

Some criteria for choosing the most suitable development environment for a project are:

- support for the easy development of user interfaces (GUI builder, GUI class library).

- support for the easy development of a database access layer (generator, database access class library) - the developer team may want to consider an ODBMS which unites DB management and OOPL technologies.

- tool support for easy location of available functionality to maximize reuse (browser).

- tool support for source code editing, compilation/interpretation, debugging, system integration, and testing have a big effect on productivity.

- adequacy of the environment for prototyping - interpreted languages are useful for rapid prototyping but are often inefficient compared to compiled languages.

- support for automatic garbage collection.

- support for multiperson projects - many products are typically conceived as one-developer environments.

- quality of tool and library documentation - the full functionality supported by a class library must be apparent from its documentation.

Chapter 16 describes alternatives for the mapping of an object-oriented design using NATURAL-OO, C++, Smalltalk, or a 'conventional' NATURAL environment.

Choosing a data management system

The type of data management system used for implementation depends on the type and amount of data to be stored. Obviously, there are tradeoffs between cost, access efficiency, capacity, etc.

Currently, the major data management approaches to consider are relational database management systems (RDBMS), object-oriented database management systems (ODBMS) and (flat) file systems.

Additionally, object-oriented extensions of RDBMS are now becoming available. Aiming at resolving some of the well known deficiencies of RDBMS, while preserving its benefits, relational functionality is augmented by object-oriented qualities in an evolutionary fashion. For an overview see Lockemann.[1]

While file systems are cheap, they do not offer the many infrastructure features provided by RDBMS, like transaction management, security, integrity, sharing between users and applications, and standard query language (SQL). On the other hand, ODBMS are just emerging and will become important in the future, but are considered less mature for supporting commercial applications today. For these reasons, we concentrate here on support for RDBMS.[2]

---

[1] Lockemann P.C., "Weiterentwicklung relationaler Datenbanken für objektorientierte Anwendungen", Informatik Spektrum (16), April 1993, pp 81-88

[2] ADABAS, Software AG's DBMS, is relational and as such implicitly mentioned whenever we write RDBMS. Only when addressing features generally not supported by other RDBMS will we make special mention of ADABAS.

Choosing a control style for the system

The object life cycle diagrams developed during logical design describe the most significant control aspects of the system. There are two major approaches for the implementation of control: procedure-driven and event-driven systems.

In a procedure-driven system, each operation is responsible for control within its context. When the system embodies complex object life cycles, this approach yields highly nested control structures in the program code with negative influence on maintainability.

For object-oriented development, an event-driven approach can be more direct and natural. State machines encapsulate event handling and manage the flow of control within the system. This approach is discussed in more detail later in this chapter.

While an event-driven approach yields more flexibility, the development of state machines also involves some extra cost. Many class libraries provide state machines (or event handlers) ready for reuse, in particular for user interface implementation. A combined approach, partly event-driven, partly procedure-driven, is also possible.

Deciding on reusable system frameworks

System architectures can often be based on previously developed systems. Rumbaugh discusses basic architectures which apply to system components or to whole systems. These include:

- *batch transformation* - inputs are sequentially processed in batch (e.g., a reporting subsystem),

- *continuous transformation* - changing inputs are processed continuously (e.g., a system processing changing stock exchange information),

- *interactive interface* - typically an event-driven interface for human interaction (e.g., the presentation layer of a GUI application),

- *transaction manager* - typically dealing with multiple users and concurrency (e.g., an airline reservation system).

Reusable system architectures can provide the infrastructure for a complete application, much as the application generation facilities of the NATURAL environment do for conventional NATURAL applications.

In general, decisions have to be taken as to how to achieve reuse of reusable components. This covers the selection of an existing reusable class library or framework (e.g., a GUI class library, a database interface), but also establishing the way reuse will be achieved and managed (e.g., to what degree the reusable components are to be changed by the reuser).

Reusable system frameworks

In this section we describe reusable system frameworks. It is important to note that improved reuse of software components will not result automatically just from using an object-oriented programming language. There are a variety of design techniques which must be taken into account in order to make object-oriented software more reusable (see Chapters 22 to 24).

Reusable software components can be classified in many ways, for example, according to their intended scope (which can be just the current project, or future systems too), or abstraction level (analysis and design results, or just code).

The development of components that are intended to be reused in future systems represents a capital investment, because they require a very high level of quality assurance. Usually, this investment pays off as components are reused in subsequent application development projects.

Abstract classes and frameworks

In conventional (procedurally-oriented) programming, reusable software components usually are provided by means of subroutine libraries (math functions, I/O, string manipulation, etc.), program code frames (or skeletons) or, on a larger scale, application templates like those provided within the application generators of the NATURAL environment. In object-oriented programming, class libraries (consisting of abstract and concrete classes) and frameworks perform a similar function to these techniques.

An abstract class defines a protocol or a template for a class interface. The abstract class can contain abstract (unimplemented) operations. An abstract class can also contain concrete or template operations. Subclasses inherit this protocol and fill in the template with implementations for any abstract operations. The collection object class is a common example of an abstract class which provides a common protocol for 'set', 'string', 'list' and 'array' classes (see the section 'Choosing types and data structures' later in this chapter).

A framework provides a template for a subsystem or even an entire application. It embodies the invariant part of some type of system. A framework consists of abstract and concrete classes and provides patterns for object interaction, constraints on behavior, invariants for object states and legal operation sequences. The best example of a framework is the implementation of the Model-View-Controller (MVC) design pattern in Smalltalk-80 (discussed in detail in Chapter 23).

Frameworks can be white box or black box. With a white box framework the user needs to understand how it is implemented. For a black box framework, the system developer only needs to know the external interface. Most frameworks are white box, although any framework can also contain black-box components (e.g., the MVC framework in Smalltalk-80 is white box but its 'pluggable views' can be seen as black boxes). Black boxes are easier to apply but are less flexible than white boxes. Also, it is possible that, during the course of its existence, the internals of a framework will become more and more encapsulated (or hidden) in such a way that the framework evolves from a white to a black box.

For easy application of reusable software components, a suitable reuse infrastructure is essential. This should consist of tools for retrieving object classes (browsers), cross-referencing, and change management.

Problem Domain Component (PDC)

The results of logical design are an integral part of the models developed during physical design. The problem domain component represents the 'real-world' part of the system. This component should not be affected by hardware, operating/windowing system, or DBMS dependencies.

The objects in the problem domain component ideally are traceable from system requirements analysis to logical design to physical design to construction. Traceability contributes to system stability, an argument for keeping the logical design model as unchanged as possible during the whole development process.

However, it may be the case that additions and changes to the logical design model become necessary for an efficient system implementation. Reasons for this can be performance, modularity, maintainability, or integration with legacy systems.

Implementation of object classes and operations

The problem domain component consists of all entity and control object classes defined during previous development phases. It can be extended with implementation classes during this phase of the development process.

The next physical design steps include implementation of object classes as well as formal specification and implementation of operations.

It is straightforward to implement an object class using an object-oriented programming language (OOPL) since most design constructs map one-to-one to language constructs. Most languages support *classes*, *attributes*, *operations*, *inheritance* and *polymorphism*; as well as object *creation* and *destruction*, *sending of messages between objects*, and procedural language constructs.

Many of the operations identified during logical design are not complex and are easy to implement. More complex operations require finding a suitable algorithm. See Chapter 24 for recommended design principles and programming guidelines which can help with this issue.

Operations can be formally specified using some pseudocode language, especially in combination with automatic code generation. But, generally, formal specification and implementation of operations are a single activity and can be done directly using an OOPL.

Not everything is easy when implementing object classes and operations. In the following sections we discuss issues which require special consideration, including:

- choosing types and data structures,
- implementing relationships,
- implementing object life cycle models,
- implementing constraints,
- implementing derived attributes and relationships, and
- exception handling

Choosing types and data structures

When formally specifying and implementing an operation, it becomes necessary to define the data structures it acts on. Most OOPLs, or their associated class libraries, provide an assortment of basic and more complex data structures, e.g., strings, arrays, collections, dictionaries, etc.

Most object-oriented languages support strong typing. The arguments and return values of operations and any variables used within an operation specification must be declared as belonging to a particular class or *type*. In contrast, a few languages (e.g., Smalltalk) have weak typing. A variable, an operation argument or an attribute value is only known to be an object. No particular class or type must be declared.

For our purposes, we assume strong typing during physical design. We also seek to use a set of logical data types which can be mapped to a number of different OOPLs. An example of such a standard is the ODMG object model.

The ODMG object model aims at setting a standard for the ODBMS and OOP industry. It supports strong typing. Built-in types provided by the model include:[1]

- simple types - Integer, Float, Character, Boolean, Date, Time and String

- collections - the parameterized type Collection[T] and subtypes Set[T], Bag[T], List[T] and Array[T]

- unnamed groups of elements - the parameterized type Structure[e1:T1, ... , en:Tn]

All elements of a collection must be of the same type T, where T can be any supported type. Examples of 'instantiated' collection types are Set[Integer], List[Array[String]], etc.

An example of an instantiated structure type is: Structure[street:String, zip-code:Integer, city:String] which defines an 'Address' type.

---

[1] Cattell R. ed., *The Object Database Standard: ODMG-93* (San Mateo, Calif.: Morgan Kaufmann, 1994)

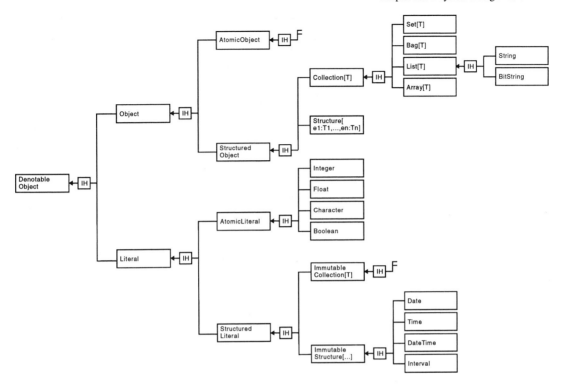

Figure 15-2: Example of ODMG built-in types (partially)

During the physical design stage of the project we add implementation details to the logical object structure model. In order to use object structure diagrams for representing the physical object structure model, the following additions to the notation are used.

Notation: The data type of each attribute is shown using the notation **attribute-name : type**. Each operation is shown with its signature (i.e., a data type for each argument and for the return value): **operation-name (arg1:type1, ... , argN:typeN) : return-value-type**. Class attributes and operations are shown in *italics*. Abstract operations are marked with the keyword {abstract} in braces.

An example of how to add implementation details to object classes is shown in Figure 15-3: data types are defined using the ODMG object model.

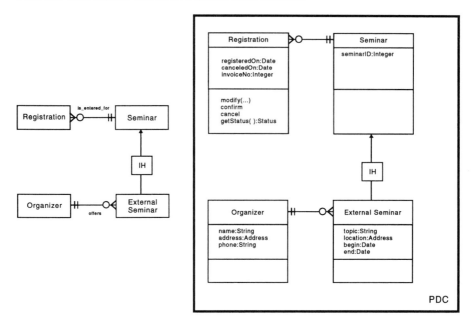

Figure 15-3: Example for implementing object classes

Implementation of relationships

Relationships between objects, defined during earlier phases of the development process, are bi-directional. They model properties of the objects rather than access paths between objects. For the implementation of object classes, however, it is necessary to determine how relationships are to be traversed. Relationships may be used in one or both directions, maybe with different frequencies.

Object interaction diagrams from logical design are a good starting point for the analysis of relationship traversal. These define what message sending between objects is needed in order to support the required system functionality. In order for an object to send a message to another object, the sender must have a way of identifying the message receiver and addressing it.

Relationships used in one direction are best implemented by including an attribute which holds a pointer to an object of the related object class. Depending on cardinalities and other constraints (such as ordering), sets, bags, or lists of pointers can be suitable.

Relationships traversed in both directions can be implemented by including pointers at both ends, with a consequent overhead on updates when the link changes. The relationship could be implemented at only one end if it is acceptable to search for the related object when coming from the other end. Finally, a bidirectional relationship can be implemented as a separate object class which manages a pair of pointers for each instance of the relationship. There is a trade-off between access and update efficiency when mapping relationships.

Notation: An attribute (or operation argument) that holds a pointer to an object of a related object class is denoted by **attribute-name : related-class-name**, i.e., the type of the attribute is the related object class. Depending on cardinalities and other constraints, the attribute can also be denoted by **attribute-name : Set[related-class-name], attribute-name : List[related-class-name]**, etc. An arrow from the pointer attribute shows the related object class.

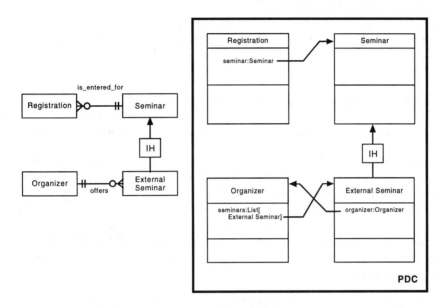

Figure 15-4: Example of the implementation of relationships

In Figure 15-4, the relationship 'is entered for' between **Registration** and **Seminar** is implemented by including a pointer at one end while 'offers' between **Organizer** and **ExternalSeminar** is implemented by including pointers at both ends.

How to implement relationships

The process for implementing relationships defined in an object structure model is as follows:

1. Analyze what messages are exchanged between the two related object classes.

2. Decide how a sender of a message should address the receiver:

    *   direct knowledge, the sender has a pointer to the receiver

    *   indirect knowledge, the receiver is passed as a message parameter

    *   searching for the receiver, by using identifying attributes, etc.

3. Whenever direct knowledge is required, add an attribute to hold the pointer. Depending on cardinalities and other constraints (e.g., ordering), use sets, bags or lists of pointers. Note that pointers in persistent objects to transient objects should not be persistent.

4.   Define any necessary integrity rules resulting from your decisions, for example:

- synchronization of pairs of pointer which implement the same relationship.

- referential integrity

Implementation of object life cycle models

The object behavior model, developed during logical design through the use of object life cycle and object interaction diagrams, captures the most significant control aspects of the system. While establishing the system architecture, a general decision should have been made on how to implement control (procedure-driven or event-driven).

Procedure-driven systems represent the traditional way for implementing control. The location of control within a program implicitly determines the program state. In a procedure-driven system, control is decentralized. Each operation, within its context, is responsible for (system) control.

When a system embodies highly interactive components, the procedure-driven approach has the weakness that deeply nested control structures within operations can considerably increase complexity. In object-oriented development, it can have advantages to centralize control within a state machine as is done in event-driven systems. State machines can be particularly useful for the implementation of user interfaces where the system has to process a huge variety of event-combinations triggered through the standard input devices (mouse and keyboard). The extra costs of implementing a state machine generally pay off as the event-driven approach highly contributes to changeability and extensibility (i.e., system maintainability).

Rumbaugh[1] discusses approaches for the implementation of a state machine and recommends implementing a state machine as an object life cycle diagram interpreter as the best and easiest way to proceed. Shlaer and Mellor describe a design pattern for the implementation of a state machine as an object life cycle diagram interpreter. We include a description of a State Machine design pattern in Chapter 23.

Implementation of constraints

All constraints specified as part of the object structure model (see the section 'Specifying constraints' in Chapter 13) must be implemented in one or more of the following:

- user interface logic

- database schema

- operations

Constraints specified as part of the object structure model can be implicit (such as those implied by an aggregation or by the specified cardinalities of relationships) or can be expressed explicitly in a declarative manner. Where constraints have to be implemented in operations (including user

---

[1] Rumbaugh J., "Controlling code. How to implement dynamic models", Journal of Object-Oriented Programming, May 1993, pp 25-30

interface logic), these have to be transformed into a procedural form so that they can be stated in a programming language.

Since OOPLs generally do not support relationships, a special case of an implicit constraint exists where a relationship has been implemented by including pointers at both ends (see the section 'Implementation of relationships' in this chapter). The accessor operations for this relationship, at both ends, are responsible for keeping both pointers consistent.

Implementation of derived attributes and relationships

A derived attribute or relationship specified during analysis or logical design will have a derivation algorithm expressed as a function of one or more other attributes and/or relationships. For example, within the object class **ExternalSeminar**, 'duration' is a derived attribute which is defined as **duration = endDate - beginDate + 1**.

A discussion of the implementation of derived attributes also applies to derived relationships since relationships are implemented in terms of attributes as described in the section 'Implementation of relationships' in this chapter. A derived attribute can be implemented as an operation which simply returns the derived value, or in user interface logic.

As a matter of efficiency, the value of a derived attribute can be saved in a separate attribute to avoid recomputation each time its value is needed. The attribute must be updated when 'base' attributes (i.e., attributes from which the value of the derived attribute is calculated) change. This can be done immediately whenever a base attribute changes or, as an alternative, all the derived attributes can be recomputed periodically.

Derived attributes can be implemented as either persistent or transient attributes.

Exception handling

An exception is an abnormal condition during program execution such as lack of available memory, usage of "dangling" references, arithmetic overflow, impossible I/O operation, etc. Exception handling relates to a mechanism for reacting to exceptions in a proper way. Usually, program execution will be terminated. In some cases an attempt can be made to change the conditions that led to the exception and reinvoke the failed operation again (e.g., with changed parameters) - a mechanism normally referred to as 'retry'.

Traditional exception handling involves a common protocol for passing error codes from one level to another. In object-oriented development such an approach can drastically increase the amount of code since the program code is generally spread over a large number of operations.

A few languages provide support for exception handling such as the ON ERROR statement in NATURAL or the *throw/catch* mechanism in C++ (not available with older versions).

Human Interaction Component (HIC)

Separating the object classes of the user interface in a separate component contributes to modularity and helps isolate operating/windowing system and hardware dependencies. This enables applications to be portable across platforms.

A general decision to use a particular graphical user interface (GUI) should have been taken while defining the system architecture. GUIs on different platforms look and feel different and in fact have core differences. Keeping an application independent of a specific windowing system is possible (and is supported by some GUI class libraries), but the costs of doing so can be to restrict the application to only a subset of the functionality supported by the GUI.

Usually, a GUI class library is available which encapsulates the low-level GUI functionality. Note that the presence of a specific GUI class library influences the design of the HIC.

A well known problem is that while GUIs are easy to use, they are hard to develop. Therefore, products that simplify the development of GUI-based applications are desirable. A GUI builder that makes it possible to paint screens based on GUI standards and to design dialogs belongs to this class of product.

The HIC consists, in a first cut, of all interface objects from logical design used to define interaction of the system with human actors. Normally, user interface layouts will have been specified during earlier phases of the development process.

During physical design, interface objects are refined by specifying detailed object interactions between windows, window elements (menus, buttons, etc.), and the related problem domain classes. Here, logical design techniques (like object interaction and life cycle diagramming) can be helpful. To what extent such a detailed design will be necessary depends on what kind of reusable components are available. Efforts can be reduced considerably by reusing standard dialog frameworks, for instance.

It is necessary to take existing GUI design guidelines into account (e.g., the Software AG Style-Guide, style guidelines for Microsoft Windows, OS/2 Presentation Manager (IBM's CUA), MacApp, etc.). Criteria considered include user interface consistency, number of user interaction steps, support for specific functions like 'undo', menu design, etc.

Adding detailed object interactions

Where complex user interaction is to be supported, detailed design of the necessary object interactions is required in order to meet the specific requirements. These interactions involve the interface object itself (window), the window components (text entry fields, list boxes, buttons, menus, etc.), and related problem domain objects.

The Model-View-Controller design pattern (MVC) supports the detailed design of interactions between objects of the problem domain and human interaction components. It is particularly useful where the same (problem domain) information is to be displayed by several different windows (or 'views') simultaneously.

Originally, MVC was implemented in Smalltalk-80 providing a complete framework for the implementation of interactive GUI applications. Today, most GUI libraries (e.g., also from C++ vendors) support some form of MVC.

MVC helps in increasing encapsulation and protecting the problem domain classes from changes to the user interface classes. The main idea is to separate object classes belonging to the problem domain (model classes), from object classes intended to display information (view classes), and from object classes in charge of user interaction (controller classes).[1]

The MVC terms relate to object types defined in our approach as follows.

	PDC		HIC
	entity	control	interface
model	✗		
view			✗
controller			✗

Model objects in MVC correspond to PDC entity objects which can be displayed via the user interface. PDC control objects are not supposed to be displayed via the user interface and have no correspondence in MVC. An HIC interface object unites both the display of information and user interaction. So, pairs of view/controller objects in MVC correspond to interface objects. Note: controller objects in MVC should not be confused with control objects in our approach.

Refer to Chapter 23 for a detailed description of the Model-View-Controller design pattern.

Simplifying GUI development

Using reusable GUI classes

For the construction of the user interface, each object class in the HIC can be implemented by reusing a suitable GUI class. The GUI class library may contain an exact match for a given HIC class in which case the GUI class can be reused just by creating instances of it. Such concrete GUI classes can be parameterized (also known as pluggable views) in which case the application developer supplies appropriate parameters when creating instances of the class. Pull-down menus are a typical example for pluggable views. If no exact match for an HIC class is available, a GUI class can be found that approximates the required functionality and which can be reused by building an appropriate subclass of it.

---

[1] A view object is in charge of displaying its associated model object's state. A controller object contains the interface between its associated model/view objects and the input devices (keyboard, mouse, timer, etc.). It also schedules the interaction with other view/controller pairs.

Note that existing GUI class libraries can differ considerably. Criteria for choosing the best suitable library for a project can be:

- full support for functionality of the underlying windowing system,

- support for portability across platforms,

- degree to which complexity of the windowing system is hidden or encapsulated,

- quality of the library documentation,

- tool support for easy reuse of object classes.

Using a GUI builder

GUI builders ease the development of GUI based applications by supporting visual programming. The developer can paint screens by combining standard GUI elements - in most environments called controls - and can add functionality by coding how the system has to respond to specific 'events' such as 'push-button clicked' or 'window resized'.

There are a number of commercial products available for C++, Smalltalk and also for non-OO development environments. Examples are Visual Basic and Visual C++ (Microsoft), PARTS (Digitalk), VisualWorks (ParcPlace), Galaxy (Visix), etc.

A GUI builder is included as part of the NATURAL workstation platform environment. Platform dependencies are hidden, making portable GUI based applications easy to develop.

Data Management Component (DMC)

The object classes of the DMC provide the infrastructure for the storage and retrieval of objects in a data management system, e.g., a database management system (DBMS) or a file system. Having these object classes in a separate component helps to isolate data management system dependencies and hence contributes to portable applications.

A strategic decision in favor of a specific data management approach should have been made while determining the system architecture. Usually, a relational DBMS (RDBMS) will be used. This is due to many infrastructure features provided, and because RDBMS technology is mature and currently dominates the marketplace.

During logical design, class and attribute persistence should already have been specified. Normally, all entity objects are persistent. For new object classes or attributes added during physical design and for derived attributes, persistence may have to be decided now.

Object-oriented programming languages and object-oriented DBMS (ODBMS) allow object attributes to be of complex types (e.g., class types) while most other data management systems usually only allow primitive data types. Therefore, when storing objects in an RDBMS, for instance, these must be 'flattened' by a transformation from the object structure model into a table oriented structure - the so-called *impedance* problem between objects and relations.

The main steps for the design and construction of the DMC are:

1. mapping persistent classes to data structures of the data management system (e.g., tables in an RDBMS).

2. designing object classes to handle the data structure transformations and for interfacing with the data management system.

3. designing the detailed object interactions needed to support storage and retrieval of persistent objects.

Techniques from logical design, like object interaction and life cycle diagramming, can be applied when designing the DMC classes. Ideally, parts of these object classes will be generated, or their construction will be simplified by means of reusable object classes.

Using an RDBMS

Most commercial applications are *data heavy* (i.e., have to cope with a large number of stored object instances) and have data shared among many users and applications. Furthermore, complex querying and advanced reporting on the stored information is usually required.

RDBMS provide many necessary infrastructure facilities such as transaction management, data sharing between applications and users, security, data integrity, and SQL. This is why, for object-oriented as well as conventional application development, RDBMS technology is currently being used in most cases.

Most programming languages currently support embedding of SQL statements for interfacing to an RDBMS. NATURAL provides a high-level application programming interface which enables the user to access a number of database systems and supports embedded SQL as well. For some OOPLs, e.g., C++ or Smalltalk, there are a number of commercial products available that provide object classes for interfacing with a variety of RDBMS.

Applications that use databases are usually organized into *transactions*, i.e., sequences of database operations that transform a consistent state of the database into another consistent state. During a transaction, inconsistent database states are possible. A transaction is *atomic* in the sense that it is either entirely executed or it is totally canceled. At the end of a transaction the DBMS performs one of two possible actions:[1]

- *commit* - the transaction was successful - all changes to the database made during the transaction are made permanent, or

- *abort* - unsuccessful end of transaction due to some abnormal situation - all changes must be undone, the database is restored to its state at the beginning of the transaction.

---

[1] A transaction can be terminated either implicitly (e.g., by an abnormal program termination) or explicitly (e.g., by SQL operations COMMIT and ROLLBACK).

Most DBMS are multi-user systems and support some kind of concurrency control mechanism (e.g., *locking*, *optimistic* and *timestamp-based* methods). A high level of consistency can only be achieved if concurrent transactions are *serializable*, i.e., the same result is obtained as if the concurrent transactions had been processed in some strict order.

Architecture of the DMC

It can be advantageous to split the DMC into two layers in order to isolate specific RDBMS dependencies. Such an architecture contributes to portability across many distinct RDBMS.

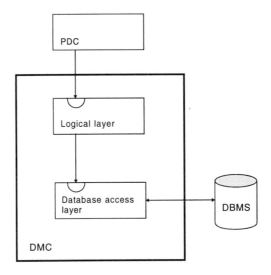

Figure 15-5: Architecture of the DMC

A *logical* layer can be used to contain object classes which handle the conversion of the object structure into a relational form. A *database access* layer is used to encapsulate the interface to a particular RDBMS, i.e., contains object classes which execute the actual SQL statements on database tables. Currently, most programming environments provide reusable object classes which ease the development of the database access layer.

The object classes shown in the following object structure diagram will be used as an example throughout this section. The relationships which are shown grayed are implemented by appropriate pointers (displayed by the arrows).

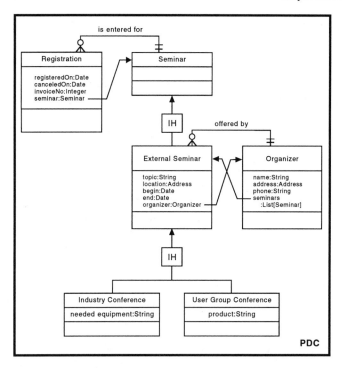

Figure 15-6: Logical design for part of the Seminar Registration System

Relational database design

If the application will not use an existing database, the first task is to design a suitable relational structure. This involves mapping object classes, attributes, relationships and inheritance hierarchies onto relations (tables).

It is recommended that a system-wide unique object ID be used for persistent objects. Object IDs ease the mapping of relationships to the relational model and contribute to stability. Note that the application itself is responsible for the generation and administration of the object IDs since most RDBMS do not provide support for this.

First, one object class can be mapped to one relation which contains one column for the unique object ID (the primary key of the relation) and a column for each *simple* attribute of the object class. Any *complex* attribute must be composed from primitive RDBMS data types and, depending on the situation, either maps to a group of columns within the relation, or to a separate relation. An attribute which holds a pointer to an object of a related object class can be mapped by including a foreign key (the object ID of the linked instance) in the relation. If identifying attributes have been defined during logical design, these can now be used for the definition of indexes.

If the DBMS in question is ADABAS, an attribute which is of a collection type (e.g., Set[T], List[T], etc.) can easily be mapped using *multiple fields* and/or *periodic groups* and does not necessarily need to be mapped to a separate relation.

The following diagram shows an example relational model (tables) for the two object classes **ExternalSeminar** and **Organizer**. Primary keys are shown shaded, the foreign key is shown using an arrow.

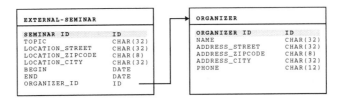

Figure 15-7: Example of mapping object classes to tables

Note that the attribute 'location' of **ExternalSeminar** (which is of a complex type 'Address') has been mapped to three columns in the table EXTERNAL-SEMINAR. The same holds for 'address' of **Organizer**. The relationship 'offered by' has been mapped using a foreign key.

In general, there are three alternatives for the mapping of relationships:

1. any relationship (whatever its cardinality) can always be mapped to a separate relation (relationship table) in which each row contains a pair of object IDs and corresponds to an instance of the relationship, or

2. one-to-many and one-to-one relationships can also be mapped by including a foreign key in one of the related tables (alternatively, with ADABAS, a multiple field to hold foreign keys can be included at the 'one' side of a one-to-many relationship), or

3. for one-to-one relationships, a third alternative is to merge both related tables into a single one in which each row corresponds to a pair of linked instances.

Decisions made as to the implementation of relationships in the object structure model (i.e., by including pointers at one or both ends) can influence the mapping of relationships to tables. A good match between the object and relational models reduces the need for structure transformations when reading and writing data. On the other hand, for an optimal relational structure - from the database point of view - it can be necessary to deviate from the object structure model by making independent decisions here.

The following diagram shows an alternative relational model (tables) for the mapping of the relationship 'offered by' between **ExternalSeminar** and **Organizer** which uses a relationship table. Primary keys are shown shaded, foreign keys are shown using arrows.

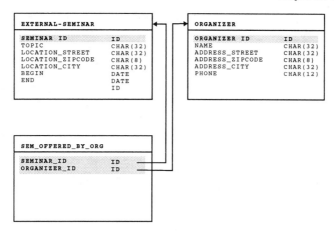

Figure 15-8: Alternative for the mapping of relationships to tables

For the mapping of aggregations, the same rules as for relationships apply since aggregation represents a special type of association between objects.

There are three alternatives for the mapping of inheritance hierarchies to the relational model:

1. each object class in the hierarchy is mapped to a separate relation, achieving object identity through a shared unique object ID, or

2. each non-abstract object class in the hierarchy is mapped to a separate relation which contains an additional column for each inherited attribute, i.e., superclass attributes are replicated for each subclass, or

3. all object classes in the hierarchy are mapped to a single relation containing columns for all attributes in the hierarchy.

The first alternative yields the cleanest design which also contributes to extensibility. Nevertheless, the second and third alternatives can be considered when a more efficient implementation (e.g., in terms of performance) is required.[1]

Figure 15-9 shows alternatives 1 and 2 for the mapping of the inheritance hierarchy in our example. Object class **ExternalSeminar** has been assumed to be abstract - otherwise alternative 2 would require a relation EXTERNAL-SEMINAR as well. Primary keys are shaded.

---

[1] Note: With alternative 1 the database state of a persistent object typically is represented by a number of records (namely one in each of the tables corresponding to the object class itself and to superclasses of this). With alternatives 2 and 3 the database state of a persistent object is represented by exactly one record.

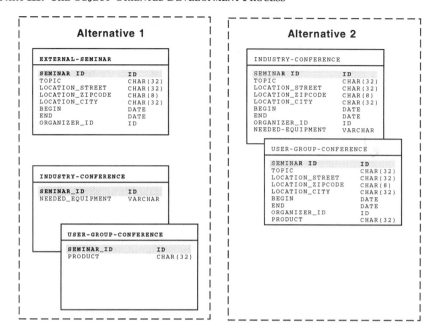

Figure 15-9: Example showing alternative mappings of an inheritance hierarchy

A good relational database design requires relational 'normalization' in order to eliminate data redundancies and to avoid certain so-called 'update anomalies'. Usually 3rd normal form (3NF) is considered sufficient.

Designing detailed object interactions for storing and retrieving objects

See Chapter 23 for a description of a basic *Persistent Object* design pattern for storing and retrieving objects in an RDBMS.

Simplifying the development of database access layers

There are a number of commercial products available from C++ or Smalltalk vendors which ease the building of an access layer to an RDBMS. Some are class libraries, others generate classes for interfacing to a particular RDBMS.

Application generation facilities within the NATURAL environment provide templates for the construction of object-based database access layers which can significantly ease the development of the DMC.

Using an ODBMS

Object-oriented DBMS (ODBMS) unite DB management and OOPL technologies. An ODBMS can reduce the development effort for the DMC. ODBMS are emerging and will gain importance in the future, but are less mature for supporting commercial applications today. The lack of a standard for ODBMS has been a major factor in discouraging their more widespread use. The ODMG standard may help address this problem.

Object-oriented extensions of RDBMS are available now and should be considered as well.

Using a flat-file system

Coad and Nicola[1] describe a design pattern for handling object persistence using a flat-file system which is based on a tag format.

This pattern assumes that all stored object instances of the application are loaded into memory at once (e.g., when the application is initiated) and all instances are saved together to the file, normally on a save command. This restricts the usefulness of the pattern to single-user applications where the total number of object instances in all object classes remains small.

External Interface Component (EIC)

The EIC consists of all interface classes from logical design used to define the interaction with non-human actors, like external systems, printers, etc., plus any additional interface classes introduced during physical design.

We distinguish between interaction with existing non-OO or OO systems (black box) and integration of existing object-oriented (sub)systems (white box).

Interacting with external non-OO or OO systems

Object wrapping is a technique for representing an external system using one interface object (called an *object wrapper*) which encapsulates the communication with that system. Usually, the external system acts as a server.

As an example, we assume that the Seminar Registration System will be implemented as a Windows application and that Microsoft's EXCEL will be used to produce monthly or yearly reports for all invoiced registrations.

The EIC of the system contains an interface class **ExcelReporting** which handles the communication with the spreadsheet program EXCEL. It contains no attributes and has operations for starting/ending the communication (connect/disconnect), for requesting data from a particular *topic* or spreadsheet (request), for putting data into a particular *item* or cell of a particular spreadsheet (poke), and for executing EXCEL macros (execute). All these operations use the *dynamic data exchange* (DDE) protocol to communicate with EXCEL.

The following object structure diagram shows some of the object classes involved. Arrows show communication associations.

---

[1] Coad P., Nicola J., *Object-Oriented Programming* (Englewood Cliffs, NJ: Yourdon Press, 1993)

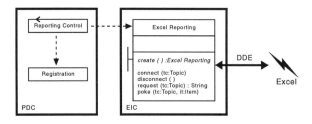

Figure 15-10: Interface object (wrapper) for interacting with EXCEL

Integration of existing object-oriented subsystems

In contrast to object wrapping, integration of an external OO subsystem involves direct interaction with its objects.[1] Therefore, knowledge of the relevant class interfaces is normally required. Depending on the circumstances, the external subsystem will be integrated as a layer (horizontal partitioning) or a vertical component of the system.

Normally, the subsystem to be integrated was developed using the same OOPL as chosen for the current development and *static linking* is used for the binding of the system. In some environments, e.g., Microsoft Windows, dynamic linking is possible by having the subsystem available in one or more *dynamic link libraries* (DLL). Furthermore, system integration can be implemented by using a client/server architecture, e.g., Microsoft's OLE or implementations of the CORBA standard.

Berlin[2] reports on problems resulting from integrating separately developed object-oriented subsystems. Even if a subsystem is well-designed, robust, and fulfills the specified functionality, there can be fundamental conflicts when integrating its classes with those of another system.

Many of the minor problems can be solved by providing glue code which translates protocols by combining arguments, transforming argument types, or translating operation names. But the real conflicts, as Berlin points out, result from fundamental differences in the global architectures of the systems - mainly the *pragmatic* decisions as to how information and control flow is implemented in the system. Examples of such conflicts are:

- error handling - conflicting styles of error handling, e.g,. passing error codes from one level to another versus error throw and catch mechanisms,

- argument validation - differing assumptions as to who is responsible,

- handling of aggregation - normally (and as described in our approach - see Chapter 21) aggregates handle control outside-in, i.e., communications related to components are

---

[1] An external subsystem can be an entire system in this context.

[2] Berlin L., "When Objects Collide: Experiences with Reusing Multiple Class Hierarchies", ACM OOPSLA/ECOOP '90 Proceedings, Ottawa, October 1990, pp181-193

always sent to the composite object; nevertheless, in an external system, the opposite pragmatic decision may have been taken, to handle control 'inside-out' within aggregates.

In object-oriented systems, the global architecture for information and control flow is usually not explicit, since class hierarchies disperse the code that embodies the pragmatic decisions.

Task Management Component (TMC)

The TMC contains all classes required to manage tasks. In a business data processing application, a TMC is required when the system has to cope with background or batch processes. We limit our discussion to those aspects related to the handling of concurrent tasks. The main ideas for this section are taken from Coad and Yourdon.

In this section we assume an environment with an operating system which supports multitasking (which can be implemented on separate processors or can be simulated on a single processor) such as UNIX, VMS, OS/2, Windows NT, etc. The purpose of the object classes of the TMC is to encapsulate the multitasking facilities of the underlying operating system.

There are a number of commercial class libraries available which aid in the design and implementation of the TMC by providing an appropriate framework. An example is Digitalk's Smalltalk/V for OS/2.

A task is a unit of activity which can be executed in a single thread of control. In our terminology, a task is represented by a group of interactions (messages/events) between objects, typically displayed in an object interaction diagram as a block. An object should not be accessible by two or more tasks concurrently because none of the tasks would have full control over the state of the object.

Most design patterns for the TMC use an object class **Task** to define tasks and an object class **TaskCoordinator** to communicate with the operating system. **Task** defines properties of tasks, such as whether a task is *event-driven* or *timer-driven*, how a task communicates (e.g., via a *mailbox*, a *semaphore*, a *buffer*, etc.), and what the priority of a task is (e.g., *low/medium/high*).

Figure 15-11 describes the life cycle model of a typical task.

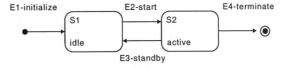

Figure 15-11: Life cycle model of a task

Utility Services Component (USC)

The USC contains all object classes that provide mechanisms used to implement the application classes and operations. Usually, all generic collection classes such as **Set[T]**, **Bag[T]**, **List[T]**, and **Array[T]**, as well as **String** and **Structure[e1:T1, ..., eN:TN]** can be placed in this component. If new data structure classes such as **HashTable[T]**, **Tree[T]**, or **Dictionary** are required, these should also be included in this component.

The object classes in this component should not be included in any of the other components. The object classes of the USC are on a different semantic level from entity, control and interface classes and normally do not emerge during analysis or logical design. Often an existing class library is available which contains most of the object classes of this component ready for reuse.

Checking the Physical Design Model

System architecture

1. Check that most object interactions are within subsystems and not across system boundaries.

2. Look for client-server decomposition because one-way interaction between components is easier to manage than two-way interaction.

Object structure model (physical)

1. Are all relationships, derived attributes/relationships, and constraints of the logical object structure model implemented?

2. Use delegation to avoid implementation inheritance.

3. Avoid deep inheritance hierarchies to reduce inheritance coupling.

4. Where possible, provide accessor operations (read and update) for attributes rather than making attributes public.

5. Check whether the object class provides full service coverage for better reusability.

6. To increase operation coherence, separate context-dependent decisions (control) from pure algorithmic and computational processing (procedure).

7. Consider the State Machine design pattern for object classes with a complex object life cycle model.

User interface implementation

1. Check conformance to existing GUI style guidelines.

2. Consider the Model-View-Controller design pattern for an efficient design of the interactions between interface and entity objects.

Data management component

1. Within the DMC, isolate the specific RDBMS dependencies in a separate *database access* layer.

Summary of Deliverables

1. Key deliverables

   - Object structure diagrams
   - Object class definitions including:
     - data types of attributes
     - signatures of operations
     - public/protected/private specifications for attributes and operations
     - attributes which implement relationships (pointers)
     - attributes/operations which implement derived attributes/relationships and constraints
   - User interface design
   - Database schema design

2. Optional deliverables

   - System overview diagrams (system architecture)
   - Object interaction and activity flow diagrams (e.g., for HIC or DMC classes)
   - Object life cycle diagrams (e.g., for HIC classes)

Chapter 16

Development of Object-Oriented Applications

With a physical design that describes the software architecture and the strategy for managing database accesses and user interface mechanisms, the application developer is ready to begin construction of the OO application. There are three paths the developer can follow:

- Traditional OO programming languages -- e.g., C++, Smalltalk, Eiffel, Ada9X, CHILL, Object Pascal, Object-oriented COBOL, etc.

- Higher-level OO languages and tools -- e.g., NATURAL-OO[1], PowerBuilder, Gupta's SQL Windows, and various "visual" forms of Smalltalk (e.g., IBM's VisualAge, Digitalk PARTS Workbench, ParcPlace System's VisualWorks, Easel's Enfin and Synchrony, etc.)

- OO CASE tools -- e.g., Software AG's NEW, Popkin's System Architect, Intellicorp's OMW, etc.

Traditional OOPLs are still the most common way of developing OO applications in the mid-90s, partly for historical reasons, and partly because of performance requirements for large, complex applications with high volumes of data and transactions. On the other hand, some of these languages (especially C++) are considered rather "low-level" for business applications, and the learning curve can be quite high.

The higher level OO languages and tools, which are sometimes referred to as OO-4GLs, are a practical choice for many small and medium client-server applications , especially where rapid implementation and user-interface prototyping are key issues. On the other hand, there is frequently a concern as to whether these languages and tools can "scale up" to be used on mission-critical, enterprise-wide applications (although NATURAL has a good track record so far as this is concerned).

Finally, there is the option of creating the OO analysis and design models discussed in this book directly using a high-level CASE tool which generates fully executable code; at the time this book was written, such CASE tools were not yet widely used. This is partly because OO developers have traditionally focused on programming issues, rather than analysis/design issues. It's also because the majority of widely available CASE tools still support only the older methodologies of structured analysis/design and information engineering.

This chapter describes the translation of a physical design into implementation. For the reasons discussed above, we concentrate on traditional OOPLs such as C++ and Smalltalk, as well as

---

[1] NATURAL-OO was not a released product as of the date of publication of this book.

Software AG's OO-4GL, NATURAL-OO. Also, we discuss how a physical design can be implemented in a conventional NATURAL environment. Though we certainly recommend the use of code-generating OO-CASE technology where available, we have chosen to avoid any vendor-specific details of CASE tools in this chapter.

The following diagram shows an extract from the object structure model for the Seminar Registration System which will serve as an example throughout this chapter.

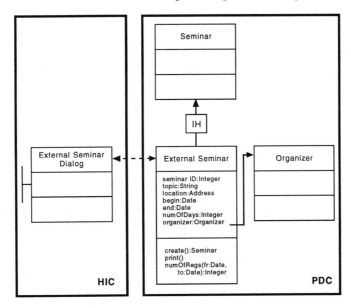

Figure 16-1: Extract from object structure model for the Seminar Registration System

Using NATURAL-OO

NATURAL-OO represents a seamless extension of the conventional NATURAL environment into a full object-oriented 4GL. It provides a class browser which supports the developer in finding available operations. A GUI builder is included as an integral part of NATURAL-OO on workstation platforms. With Microsoft Windows (or with Windows NT), OLE 2.0 is supported so that both the environment and NATURAL-OO applications can function as an OLE container or as an OLE server. The NATURAL-OO environment supports automatic garbage collection.

NATURAL-OO adds *classes*, a special type of NATURAL module, to the conventional environment. These can be used to implement the object classes of an object-oriented design. The NATURAL-OO *class editor* allows the developer to specify attributes, operations, and inheritance associations for each class.

For example, the entity class **ExternalSeminar** can be implemented by defining a NATURAL-OO class EXTERNAL-SEMINAR. The data types of the attributes and operation arguments specified during physical design are mapped onto NATURAL-OO data types. Operations are implemented using the NATURAL programming language. Attributes and operations specified in the design as being private, protected, or public can be mapped as such in NATURAL-OO.

NATURAL-OO adds to the conventional NATURAL programming language appropriate statements for the creation and destruction of class instances (*objects*) as well as for the sending of messages between instances. Each instance of a NATURAL-OO class is addressable by its unique identifier, the *object-id*. A special NATURAL data type is used for these object-ids. An attribute which implements a relationship with another class - such as the attribute 'organizer' in our example which implements a relationship 'offered by' between **ExternalSeminar** and **Organizer** - can be implemented using this data type.

NATURAL-OO supports single inheritance. The class editor allows the developer to specify a superclass for each class. All classes form part of a single inheritance hierarchy which has at its root a built-in *'base class'*. A class inherits all attributes and operations from its superclass. In order to overwrite an inherited operation, the developer needs only to enter new NATURAL code for the inherited operation at the subclass level. To enable the developer to extend an inherited operation, NATURAL-OO allows the explicit invocation of a superclass operation within an operation specification.

For the implementation of graphical user interfaces, *dialogs*, another type of NATURAL module, are available. A dialog is a special purpose class for GUI objects. In addition to attributes, operations, and an inheritance association, a dialog also includes graphical information in an associated GUI window that can contain a number of GUI elements (*controls*) such as menus, text fields, push buttons, etc. A dialog is equipped with a number of predefined *events* such as window resized, or push button clicked, to which developers can add their own user-defined events. What actions are to be performed when a given event occurs is defined within the operations associated with the dialog. A dialog inherits GUI information and all events from its superclass. Dialogs form part of a separate inheritance hierarchy which has at its root a built-in *'base dialog'*.

For example, the interface class **ExternalSeminarDialog** can be implemented by defining a dialog EXTERNAL-SEMINAR-DIALOG. The developer uses the NATURAL-OO *dialog editor* to specify the parent dialog, attributes and operations of the dialog, as well as to paint the associated GUI window by combining GUI elements (controls) as is usual in visual programming tools.

The creation and destruction of dialog instances is achieved by opening and closing the dialog. Message sending, of course, is supported between dialog instances as well as between a class and a dialog instance.

Using C++

C++ is a strongly-typed, hybrid language which is built on top of the C language. Unlike other OO languages, C++ does not contain a standard class library as part of its environment but many commercial class libraries are available, such as C++/Views (LIANT), OWL (Borland), Foundation (Microsoft), etc. Incompatibilities between these different libraries can be a problem. More recent versions of C++ support multiple inheritance. Automatic garbage collection is not supported. C++ is often regarded as a complex, rather "low-level" language which, on the other hand, is widely used. Next are alternatives for the mapping of design concepts of our approach to C++.

A standard practice in C++ is to place class interfaces in files named with a *.hpp* suffix; these are called header files. Class implementations are placed in body files which are named with a *.cpp* suffix. Linkages between these files are established using the *#include* directive.

So, the declarations for our object class **ExternalSeminar** would be placed in a header file *extsemnr.hpp* and would be of the form:

```
#include "seminar.hpp"
class ExternalSeminar : public Seminar
{
private:
        ... declaration of members ...
protected:
        ... declaration of members ...
public:
        ... declaration of members ...
}
```

A *member* has to be declared for each attribute (*data member*) and for each operation (*member function*) of the object class.

Attributes and operations specified in the design as being private, protected, or public can be mapped as such in C++.

For an attribute of a simple data type - such as Integer, Character, String, etc. - a data member can be declared using the C++ built-in types. Some examples are::

```
char * topic;       // String
int numOfDays;          // Integer
void * location;        // pointer to object of unknown type
```

In our example, there is a relationship 'offered by' with an object class **Organizer**. This is implemented by including an attribute 'organizer' in **ExternalSeminar** which holds a pointer to an organizer object. A declaration of this attribute takes the form:

```
Organizer * organizer;      // implements rel. 'offered by'
```

An attribute of a complex type - which includes other attributes which themselves can be simple or complex - can either be implemented by defining a new class to which the attribute points, or by using C++ *structures*. Using *user-defined* types - *typedef* declarations - helps in hiding the actual implementation. For example, declarations like:

```
struct Address {char* street, int zip, char* city};
typedef char* String;
typedef int ID;
```

included in *extsemnr.hpp*, allow member declarations such as:

```
Address location;              // attribute of complex data type
String topic;
ID seminarID;
```

To declare a member function (operation), the operation's name and signature are required.[1]

In C++, a member function can only be overridden in a subclass if it is declared with the keyword *virtual*. A virtual operation which is 'initialized' to '0' is called *pure virtual* and identifies an abstract operation. Examples are:

```
virtual int numOfRegs (Date from, Date to);
virtual void print () = 0; // pure virtual
```

Class attributes and class operations can be declared using the *static* keyword:

```
static int total;
static int getTotal (String aTopic);
```

In this case, all seminar objects share the same copy of the member 'total'. Within a function definition, such static members can be used as shown below:

```
int i1, i2;
i1 = ExternalSeminar::total;
i2 = ExternalSeminar::getTotal ('Principles of OO programming');
```

In C++ there are no standard class operations for the creation and destruction of instances of an object class. Instead, each class can have multiple *constructor* operations to initialize new objects and a *destructor* operation which performs any necessary cleanup before an object is destroyed. A constructor has the same name as the class and no return type. The same holds for a destructor but the name is prefixed with '~':

```
ExternalSeminar ();                             // constructor
ExternalSeminar (String aTopic);                // another
constructor
ExternalSeminar (Organizer anOrganizer);        // a third
constructor
~ExternalSeminar ();                            // destructor
```

The implementation of operations for our object class **ExternalSeminar** would be placed in an object file *extsemnr.cpp* and would be of the form:

---

[1] Note: C++ supports operation 'overloading' which allows distinct member functions to share the same name if their signatures differ (i.e., their arguments vary in number or type).

```
ExternalSeminar:: ExternalSeminar (String aTopic) {
        topic = aTopic;
        }

ExternalSeminar::~ ExternalSeminar () {
        ...
        }

int ExternalSeminar::numOfRegs (Date from, Date to) {
        ...
        }
```

C++ uses three kinds of memory allocation:

- fixed global (*static*) memory - allocated implicitly by declaring a variable outside of any function or by using the keyword *static*, deallocated when program execution ends

- stack (*automatic*) memory - allocated implicitly by declaring local variables within functions, freed when the function exits

- heap (*dynamic*) memory - allocated on an explicit request by using the *new* operator and deallocated when the *delete* operator is invoked; the *new* operator returns a *pointer* to the new object.

C++ distinguishes between the object *record* and a *reference* or *pointer* to the object. The notation for object creation, addressing and message sending depends on this distinction. In addition, the special pointer *this* makes it possible, within a member specification, to address the object for which the member was invoked. Examples:

```
ExternalSeminar aSeminar = ExternalSeminar ('OO Programming');
aSeminar.print ();   //invokes operation ExternalSeminar::print

Organizer * ptrOrganizer = new Organizer;
ptrOrganizer->print ();    //invokes operation Organizer::print

ExternalSeminar * ptrSeminar;
int i1;
i1 = ptrSeminar->numOfRegs (1-Jan-94, 31-Mar-94);
```

In the following table the mapping alternatives for C++ discussed above are summarized. The syntax column contains keywords shown in **bold**, tokens (operands, identifiers, etc.) shown in *italics*, and comments beginning with the //-sign.

Mainstream Objects	C++	C++ Syntax
object class	class	**class** *class-name* { ... }
abstract class	abstract class	// any class with at least one abstract operation
attribute - simple - complex	data member - basic - user-defined	*type member-name*; **typedef struct** { ... } *complex-type*; *complex-type member-name*;
operation	member function - no arguments - no return-value - virtual	*type member-name* (*argument*); type *member-name* ( ); **void** *member-name* (*arguments*); **virtual** *type member-name* (*argument*);
abstract operation	pure virtual member function	**virtual** *type member-name* (*argument*) = 0;
class attribute	static member	**static** *type member-name*;
class operation	static member	**static** *type member-name* (*argument*);
'Create' and 'Destroy' (standard operations)	- constructor - destructor	*class-name* (*arguments*); ~*class-name* ( );
- private - protected - public (attributes and operations)	- private - protected - public (members)	**class** *class-name* { **private**: ... ; **protected**: ... ; **public**: ... ; }
- subclass - superclass (only single inheritance)	- derived class - base class	**class** *derived-class* : **public** *base-class* { ... }
instance	object	**static** *class-name object-name*; *class-name object-name*; *class-name* * *object-pointer* = **new** *class-name*;
message sending	member function invocation	*object-name.member-name* (*arguments*); *object-pointer->member-name* (*arguments*);

Mainstream Objects	C++	C++ Syntax
	'this' pointer (addressing the current instance)	**this**->*member-name* (*arguments*);
	'scope resolution' operator **::** (explicit invocation of a superclass member)	*base-class::member-name* (*arguments*);

In the following table data types supported by C++ are summarized:

Mainstream Objects	C++
Integer	**int, short int, long int**
Float	**float, double, long double**
Character	**char**
Boolean	// supported by most C++ class libraries
Date	// supported by most C++ class libraries
Time, DateTime	// supported by most C++ class libraries
Collection types: Set, Bag, List, Array, String, BitString	// supported by most C++ class libraries

Using Smalltalk

Smalltalk is a pure object-oriented programming language. It is a dynamically compiled programming language combining the advantages of interpreted and compiled languages. Problems concerning the poor performance of the language have been nearly completely overcome. Smalltalk provides a highly interactive environment permitting rapid application development. A class library is part of the self-contained environment. An automatic garbage collection mechanism frees the programmer from the burden of memory management. The main implementations available are VisualWorks (ParcPlace), Smalltalk/V (Digitalk), and VisualAge (IBM), each of which is available for most common workstation and PC platforms.

In the following pages, alternatives for the mapping of design concepts of our approach to Smalltalk are outlined.

All code (declaration of classes, method specifications) is entered using the *Smalltalk Browser*. For our object class **ExternalSeminar** the following code would be added:

```
class name      ExternalSeminar
superclass      Seminar
class variables
instance variables
        seminarID topic location begin end numOfDays organizer
class methods
        new
        newWithTopic:
instance methods
        print
        numOfRegsFrDate:toDate:
        getTopic
        setTopic:
        getLocation
        setLocation:
        getOrganizer
        setOrganizer:
```

For each attribute an *instance variable* and for each operation an *instance method* must be added. Class attributes (class operations) are entered as *class variables* (*class methods*).

An instance variable is inaccessible to other objects except through accessor methods, for example 'getTopic' and 'setTopic:' are accessor methods for the instance variable 'topic'. However, an instance variable is inherited by subclasses. Smalltalk does not explicitly distinguish between private, protected and public methods. It is usual Smalltalk practice to designate protected/private methods using a comment in the method specification, but Smalltalk does not enforce privacy. So, in our terms, methods in Smalltalk are always public while instance or class variables are always protected.

Variables in Smalltalk are not typed. A variable is a container for an object of any class. In Smalltalk no distinction is made between simple and complex attributes since everything is an object: an integer, the Boolean values true and false, a string, etc.

Beside instance and class variables, there are *temporary variables* (method arguments and variables created during the activation of a method) and *global variables* (which are accessible from every object).

The basic unit of Smalltalk syntax is the *message passing* expression:

```
<object> <method-name> <arguments>
```

where <object> is the *receiver* and <method-name> <arguments> is the *message*. *Unary* methods, like 'print', have no arguments while *keyword* methods, like 'setTopic:' or 'numOfRegsFrDate:toDate:' can have one or more arguments. In the following examples for message passing 'sem1' and 'num' are variables, 'sem1' contains an object of class **ExternalSeminar** and '<-' is the *assign operator* (which is sometimes written ':='):

```
sem1 print.
sem1 setTopic: 'Database systems'.
num <- sem1 numOfRegsFrDate: '1-Jan-94' toDate: '31-Mar-94'.
```

All Smalltalk objects are allocated from heap memory and deallocated by an automatic garbage collection mechanism (objects cannot be explicitly deallocated). Smalltalk makes extensive *metadata* (data about the classes) available and modifiable at runtime. In particular each class is itself an object (namely of its corresponding *metaclass*). Therefore, Smalltalk does not require using any special object creation operators (such as *new* in C++) as the standard message passing mechanism. To create an object a message 'new' (class operation which could take arguments for object initialization) is sent to the class:

```
sem1 <- ExternalSeminar new.
```

or

```
sem1 <- ExternalSeminar newWithTopic: 'Database systems'.
```

Smalltalk provides a special variable *self* which makes it possible, within a method specification, to address the receiver of the message. Moreover, to enable the developer to extend an inherited method, the special variable *super* allows explicit invocation of a superclass method.

The following code segments show examples for method specifications. Temporary variables are defined between vertical bars 'I I'. The statement separator is a period '.' which is not used after a variable's definition or after the last statement of the method. The expression after the caret '^' is returned by the method. The default return value is the object itself.

```
setTopic: aString
        "Instance method which sets instance variable topic to
        string passed in aString"
        topic <- aString

newWithTopic: aString
        "Class method which creates a new seminar object and
        initializes its instance variable topic"
        | sem |
        sem <- self new.
        sem setTopic: aString.
        ^sem
```

In the following table the mapping alternatives for Smalltalk are summarized. The syntax column contains keywords shown in **bold**, tokens (operands, identifiers, etc.) shown in *italics*, and comments enclosed in quotes.

Mainstream Objects	Smalltalk	Smalltalk syntax
object class	class	"Class definitions are entered using the Smalltalk Browser"
abstract class		"Any class with at least one abstract operation"
attribute	instance variable	"Entered using the Smalltalk Browser" *variable-name*
operation	instance method - unary - binary - keyword	"Entered using the Smalltalk Browser" *method-name* "without arguments" *special-character* "e.g., +,*, etc.; has 1 argument" *keyw1:keyw2: ...keywN:* "has 1 to N arguments; method name is concatenation of all keywords"
abstract operation		"Programmers must ensure that undefined methods are invoked for an object"
class attribute	class variable	"Entered using the Smalltalk Browser" *variable-name*
class operation	class method	"Entered using the Smalltalk Browser"
'Create' and 'Destroy' (standard operations)	- instance creation method	*class-name creation-method arguments.* "Objects cannot be explicitly deallocated (automatic garbage collection)"
- private - protected - public (attributes and operations)		"Instance and class variables are always protected while instance and class methods are always public"
- subclass - superclass (only single inheritance)	- subclass - superclass	"Inheritance hierarchies are maintained using the Smalltalk Browser by supplying the name of the superclass"
instance	instance	
message sending	message sending	*object method-name arguments.* "*object* is the receiver; *method-name arguments* is the receiver"
	special variable 'self' allows addressing the receiver of the message	**self** *method-name arguments.*
	special variable 'super' for explicit invocation of superclass method	**super** *method-name arguments.*

Using a Conventional NATURAL Environment

Mapping object-oriented designs to a non-OO environment, such as conventional NATURAL, is not generally easy to achieve. The major impediment is the lack of support for inheritance.

However, NATURAL *subprograms* provide good support for encapsulation. Application generation facilities within the NATURAL environment have taken advantage of this fact by providing application templates which use subprograms for the construction of an object-based database access layer.

Furthermore, for the development of GUI-based applications, a GUI builder, included as an integral part of NATURAL on workstation platforms, supports a significant number of OO concepts such as instantiation (dynamic memory allocation) and event sending within the human interaction component of the application.

So, although the conventional NATURAL environment does not support object-oriented development, *object-based* development is certainly possible. Assuming an object structure design where inheritance hierarchies have been flattened, an interface class can be mapped to a NATURAL dialog and a persistent entity class to a NATURAL subprogram which encapsulates database access.

Figure 16-2 illustrates this approach. We use the same examples as in the previous sections.

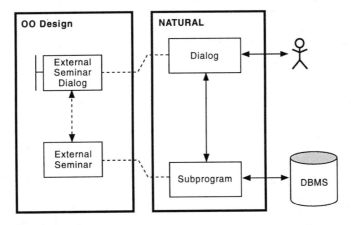

Figure 16-2: Mapping an OO design to a 'conventional' NATURAL environment

Chapter 17

Testing, Acceptance, Cutover and Operation

The software engineer who reviews the first generation of textbooks on object technology is likely to come to the following paradoxical conclusion. Either we know nothing about *testing* of object-oriented applications—so there is no ability to say anything about it—or we already know everything there is to know about OO testing, so there is no need to say anything about it. And yet this flies in the face of common sense: testing *must* be important in an OO system, and there *must* be something different about the way one performs it. Fortunately, several researchers, methodologists, and consultants are focusing on OO testing, and there is now a moderate amount of literature available on the topic[1]. By 1995 or 1996, we should begin seeing the first textbooks.

The Differences between OO Testing and Traditional Testing

The tacit assumption made by many methodologists is that testing will be easier if the earlier stages of analysis, design, and programming have been carried out in an OO fashion. Rumbaugh et al., for example, make the following comment:

> *Both testing and maintenance are simplified by an object-oriented approach, but the traditional methods used in these phases are not significantly altered. However, an object-oriented approach produces a clear, well-understood design that is easier to test, maintain, and extend than non-object-oriented designs because the object classes provide a natural unit of modularity.*

And Jacobson et al, begin their chapter with the comment that:

> *To test a product is relatively independent of the development method used. This chapter describes testing in a manner comparatively independent from the method, but we will nevertheless see that [Object Oriented Software Engineering] provides some new possibilities, but also some new problems.*

So if there are some differences, what are they? One obvious example is the fact that the basic OO test case is a message. Methodologist Donald Firesmith[2] draws a series of comparisons between traditional testing and OO testing, as shown in Figure 17-1:

---

[1] See, for example, the September 1994 issue of *Communications of the ACM*, which contains several excellent articles on the subject.

[2] Donald Firesmith, "Testing OO Software," presentation at Object Expo Conference, New York City, June 1994. Conference proceedings available from SIGS Publications, New York, NY. See also "Object Expo:

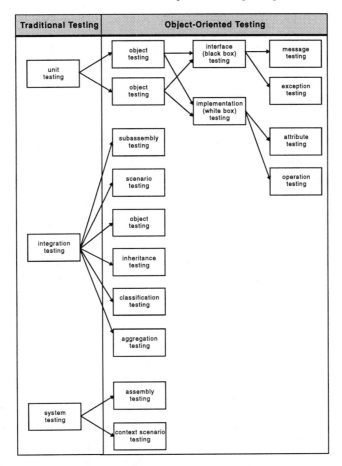

Figure 17-1: Comparisons between traditional testing and OO testing

Most software managers are familiar with unit testing, integration testing, and system testing in a traditional system, but it's not immediately obvious what stages of testing one should carry out in an OO system. As illustrated in Figure 17-1, Firesmith suggests more than a dozen levels or stages of testing that may be appropriate for OO testing. While many of the individual stages of OO testing are quite different than the comparable form of testing of procedural programs, system testing for OO-systems is still the same as before—because system testing is essentially a black-box form of testing that should be independent of the organization and architecture of the software inside the system.

The Marriage of Objects, Models, and BPR," *Application Development Strategies*, June 1994 (Arlington, MA: Cutter Information Corp.)

Here are some additional differences between traditional testing and OO testing:

1. OO testing puts more emphasis on state-based testing than procedural code does. Determining the correctness of an object involves determining whether it behaves properly when it is in different states. For example, if an object is in an initialized state, there may be certain messages that it can respond to, but other messages that should be rejected. The tester needs to verify that the object does behave in this fashion. This presumes that the application developer has created an object life cycle model for each object during the system requirements analysis and logical design phase of the project. Testers can use them to verify that the implementation of the object is correct.

2. In order to carry out state-based testing, we need testing and debugging tools that can force an object to be in the state that we want, in order to observe its behavior. This is one of several areas where it is likely that an application development project will need different kinds of testing tools than those used in traditional projects. One example of such automated OO testing tools is provided by Poston.[1]

3. One of the major sources of bugs in some OO programs (especially those written in languages like C++) is associated with garbage collection activities, since it typically is programmed manually. Thus, the testing process has to verify that objects are deleted when they should be, that "dangling pointers" are not created by the program, etc. Languages with automatic garbage collection—e.g., Smalltalk or Natural OO—typically won't require this kind of testing.

4. The classical approach to testing involves a series of test cases (based on transaction sequences in the OO environment) which are created by a separate test team, and used to exercise the system to see if it behaves properly. But an alternative approach recommended by Firesmith is the concept of built-in tests (BIT)—i.e., testing software that becomes a permanent part of the system, even when it is in operational use, that can provide an ongoing verification of the system's correct operation.[2]

5. In the area of inheritance testing, Firesmith makes the intriguing point that when the application developer creates a new subclass, he wants to be able to inherit all of the test cases and BIT logic from the superclass. This is something that many programmers overlook in the development of OO software.

---

[1] Robert M. Poston, "Automated Testing from Object Models," *Communications of the ACM*, Sep 1994, pp. 48-58.

[2] One approach to BIT is to design each object in the application so that it continually performs a self-check operation. This makes sense only in a concurrent-execution environment, where the various objects can take advantage of idle CPU resources to conduct their BIT. A second approach is to use assertions — combinations of preconditions, postconditions, and invariants—in the operations carried out by an object in order to discover failures and errors. Such an approach uses far less CPU resources and is usually the most cost-effective approach. However an object may not discover an exception within itself until long after it has occurred. A third approach is to provide each object with a BIT message that can be used when some client of the object wishes to determine whether the object is behaving properly—i.e., we can send the object a message that says, "test yourself". This approach requires an object to rely on its clients to ask them whether they are functioning properly before problems can be identified.

An OO Testing Strategy

The final stages of development of any large, complex system—whether or not it used object technology—involve many different forms of testing: system testing, acceptance testing, performance testing, failure/recovery testing, etc. The consensus in the OO community is that a combination of top-down and bottom-up testing is best—with the recognition that it may be different than in a conventional (non-object-oriented) project. Shlaer and Mellor, for example, offer the following recommendation:

> *Each module should be coded and tested separately, and then progressively integrated, each module with its callers or subordinates, to produce the program. This step should be interpreted literally to mean that coding is complete only when the program is also tested as a unit.*
>
> *...Integration consists of putting the various programs and data together to produce a system. The integration step starts with programs that have been tested, each by itself, and with data that has been verified, as previously discussed. Integration is the step that verifies that these separate units, each as correct as can be made on its own, will in fact fit together to make the required system. In other words, integration is the test of the system design.*

There is an additional problem with OO-based systems: *objects rarely stand alone*. Thus, while some testing can be done to ensure that an individual class and object does behave as specified, the relatively flat structure of an OO software architecture means that almost all of the interesting behavior will involve collaborations of several classes and objects.

Also, most object-oriented programs are message-driven, and most of the messages are initiated by an interaction between the user and the system. The sequence of execution (and object interactions) is difficult to predict; the straightforward testing approaches used in batch applications or even conventional on-line applications simply won't work for an OO application.

What does this mean, in terms of an OO testing strategy? Simply that, whether the project manager likes it or not, integration testing will begin much earlier than in a non-OO project. As McGregor and Korson observe:

> *...testing is continuously woven into the development process. This not only locates faults early, it makes subsequent phases less likely to create new faults based on existing ones.[1]*

As the project team develops more and more of the required objects in a relatively complete form, this integration testing involves hooking together real objects to exercise various parts of the system. However, in the earlier stages of development, when few such objects are ready for

---

[1] John D. McGregor and Timothy D. Korson, "Integrated Object-Oriented Testing and Development Process," *Communications of the ACM*, Sep. 1994, pp.

integration, there is often a greater need for scaffolding and testing environments; for examples, see Arnold and Fuson[1]. Also, note that many OO projects make extensive use of *existing* classes and objects from a reusable component library. This often provides a natural scaffolding and enables integration testing to begin even earlier.

So the primary thing that a project manager should expect from the testing phase of an OO project is more emphasis on integration testing, and earlier integration testing. It also means that regression testing and configuration management, are absolutely essential to maintain control of the testing process. As a result, the project manager may see some benefits that were associated with a top-down, incremental testing approach long before OO technology came along. On the other hand, the project manager should expect to develop an OO testing strategy that has its own unique characteristics; as Jorgensen and Erickson observe:

> *the implications of traditional testing for object-oriented integration testing require an appropriate construct for the integration level. This construct should be ... clearly distinct from the unit- and system-level constructs. We postulate five distinct levels of object-oriented testing:*

- *a method*
- *message quiescence*
- *event quiescence*
- *thread testing*
- *thread interaction testing*[2]

OO Unit Testing

As noted above, OO unit testing is complicated by the fact that objects frequently collaborate with other objects in the system. And there is another problem: the granularity of testing is different than in most traditional projects. Berard elaborates on this point:

> *...we are dealing with larger program units, e.g., a class. Further, the concept of a subprogram is not quite the same as it is in more traditional systems. Specifically, we tend to separate the specification (interface) for the subprogram from its implementation (body). We refer to the specification as a "method interface" (i.e., an advertised capability in the external interface the class presents to the outside world), and to the implementation as a "method" (i.e., the internal (hidden) algorithm by which the operation is carried out). We often further complicate matters by allowing one method interface to be supported by multiple methods.*

---

[1]   Thomas R. Arnold and William A. Fuson, "Testing 'In A Perfect World'", *Communications of the ACM*, Sep. 1994, pp. 78-86.

[2]   Paul C. Jorgensen and Carl Erickson, "Object-Oriented Integration Testing," *Communications of the ACM*, Sep. 1994, page 30-38

What does this mean for the project manager? First, it means that unit testing is likely to be more difficult in an OO project than in previous projects—*and that it may not be "finished" in the traditional sense, when the programmers tell you they are finished.* Because it is so difficult to thoroughly exercise an object in utter isolation, some of the bugs that you might expect to find in a unit test activity will *not* be found; they'll pop up later, during integration testing.

Second, because an object is bigger than a traditional module created with a structured design methodology, unit testing may take longer than the manager would otherwise expect. Remember, this is a question of granularity: an object contains a number of data attributes, encapsulated with a number of methods. Each of the methods might have been the subject of a separate unit-testing activity in older methodologies. To put it another way, an object brings together in one place several different functions which can be invoked in multiple, different contexts. By contrast, a program, in traditional development projects, has a single entry point.

OO Integration and System Testing

Integration testing obviously begins when objects are connected together. But as Jacobson et al observe:

> *...object-oriented systems are highly integrated and certain objects are dependent on other objects. Therefore it may be necessary to develop object simulators that simulate the behavior of adjacent objects. These supporting objects may be implemented with only operation stubs.*

Thus, the primary requirement for effective integration testing in an OO environment is a good suite of testing tools, which are likely to be domain-specific.

The very nature of the OO paradigm makes integration testing more difficult. The primary contributor to this difficulty is inheritance. A method that has been inherited may find that it is operating in a different context than in the superclass where it was first defined. For example, suppose that the subclass (which contains the inherited method) modifies an instance variable (perhaps also inherited) for which the superclass method assumed certain values. As a result, the method behaves differently in the subclass than it did in the superclass. Or, the superclass method may invoke other superclass methods which have been redefined in the subclasses.

The fact that an object, with its component attributes and methods, works properly does *not* necessarily mean that its descendants will operate properly when a class hierarchy is assembled during integration testing. Of course, the project team can establish various OO programming conventions to minimize these problems. Some guidelines can be derived from the discussions in Chapters 20 and 22, and can be added to the OOD guidelines discussed in Chapter 24. But the fact remains: the behavior of methods will have to be re-tested in the context of the subclasses that inherit them.

The distinction between integration testing and system testing may be one of degree. At a relatively early stage, many OO project teams attempt to exercise all of the major features of the system with skeleton objects whose attributes and operations will be fleshed out as the project continues, until the full system has been developed and can be tested *in toto*. Other OO project teams will concentrate on a limited aspect of the system's functionality, develop the necessary objects to implement that functionality, and perform appropriate integration testing to ensure proper behavior. Then they move on to the next set of system features, until they have finally developed all of the system requirements.

The interesting thing is that both groups typically use *transaction sequences* as the basis of their test cases for integration testing and system testing. Rather than invent artificial messages to be sent between groups of objects, the test team can create test transactions to exercise groups of collaborating objects. By making the set of test transactions broader and more comprehensive, the test team can exercise larger and larger portions of the object-oriented application, until the entire system has been effectively tested.

Acceptance Testing

As with system testing, *acceptance testing* of an object-oriented application should be carried out in the same way as a traditionally developed application.

Acceptance should be based on the requirements analysis model developed for the project. The users and specialists involved in creating the acceptance test cases should use the requirements analysis model as the basis for their work. To the extent that a new application incorporates reusable components that have been tested and accepted for previous projects, some portions of the acceptance testing can perhaps be minimized. However, even with reuse, acceptance testing usually cannot be eliminated, for several reasons:

- The acceptance test activity usually includes volume testing, recovery and fallback testing, and testing of various operational scenarios that may not have been thoroughly tested in previous applications, even though the same objects are being used.

- The new application may involve previously developed objects, but they may have been combined into different frameworks in the new application, which will require appropriate acceptance testing.

- The new application may use previously developed classes as a base class, and then create new subclasses. Even though the inherited properties of the superclass have already been tested, the behavior of the new inheritance hierarchy (with the new application-specific subclasses) will have to be tested.

Cutover

As with system testing and acceptance testing, the cut-over to install a new object-oriented application should be essentially the same as with traditional applications. Of course, all three of these activities are likely to be carried out within a larger framework of iterative development, which may involve extensive prototyping and delivering one feature set at a time to the user community. As such, it is reasonable to expect that the cut-over process will be smoother than with many traditional applications. On the other hand, the normal cut-over process involves a broad range of activities that are entirely outside the range of object-oriented methodologies: installation of new hardware, construction of new office facilities, training of users, delivery of documentation, integration of the new automated system with revised business procedures, etc.

This last point is crucial: cut-over to a new system involves much more than just installing a new application program on the user's PC and then walking away. Obviously, the various cutover activities should be planned in advance, and this can usually be done with the business process model discussed in Chapter 5.

Operation and Maintenance

Under normal circumstances, the user's operation of an object-oriented application should also resemble the operation of traditional systems. However, there are two areas where we may see some differences:

- Depending on the implementation technology used, an object-oriented system may behave differently when an unexpected error occurs. Obviously, it is particularly frustrating to users when an application program produces a message such as, "`SYSERR14: UNRECOVERABLE ERROR, TABLE OVERFLOW`" followed by the loss of all their work for the afternoon. Object-oriented applications have a tendency to degrade more politely, because the individual objects within the application are usually implemented to respond politely when they receive a message they don't understand. On the other hand, with languages like Smalltalk, errors can produce messages like "`Pen(Object) >>doesNotUnderstand: UndefinedObject>>Doit`", followed by several more lines of mysterious text.

- Depending on the physical design and the implementation technology, users may be more aware of the existence of pluggable objects which can be reconfigured to suit their day-to-day needs. This is a level of sophistication far beyond what most end-user applications provide today, but we are beginning to see the first signs of it from PC software producers like Microsoft, Borland, Apple, Lotus, etc. We believe that users will gradually come to expect this capability of *all* their applications, not just their word processors and spreadsheet packages.

Obviously, the major activity of concern to the application developers during the operational phase of the life cycle is the possibility of enhancements and modifications to the original application. To facilitate this kind of ongoing activity, we strongly recommend that the models discussed in this book be kept up-to-date, so that the enhancements and modifications can be planned, negotiated, and implemented in a more orderly fashion. The system requirements model should be the basis for discussions of any nontrivial changes with the user, and the impact of those changes should be explored within the logical design model and physical design model.

We recognize that many maintenance programmers prefer to make maintenance changes to the program-level source code. This increases the risk that the analysis and design models will become obsolete and will be discarded. We believe this will put more and more pressure on CASE toolmakers in the future to create facilities for bidirectional synchronization or for more complete integration—so that a change in either one will cause the other to be updated.

Finally, note that ongoing maintenance requires formal version control and configuration management. This is especially important in an object-oriented application, where changes to the attributes or operations in a superclass can ripple down to the subclasses below, through inheritance. Obviously, a careful impact analysis must be carried out for any proposed change to an object, including its descendants and collaborators.

Part IV

Thinking Object-Oriented - Analysis and Design Guidelines

Building on the basic modeling techniques described in Part II and the development life cycle described in Part III, Part IV discusses some of the less obvious conceptual issues of object-oriented analysis and design. The focus of Part IV is on object think, on acquiring the understanding needed in order to achieve a high quality object-oriented design.

Chapter Number and Title	Contents
Chapter 18 **Discovering Objects**	Describes various ways to identify objects.
Chapter 19 **Identifying Relationships**	Describes how to model relationships between objects.
Chapter 20 **Inheritance**	Discusses how to develop good inheritance hierarchies.
Chapter 21 **Aggregation**	Describes what aggregation is and when to use it.
Chapter 22 **Operations**	Discusses how to distribute functionality between the operations of different object classes.
Chapter 23 **Design Patterns**	Provides detailed descriptions of several fundamental design patterns using the seminar registration system for illustration purposes.
Chapter 24 **Guidelines for a Quality Design**	Provides guidelines which can be used for checking the quality of a proposed system design.

Chapter 18

Discovering Objects

There is a great deal of detail surrounding any OO model—messages and relationships, attributes and hierarchies, etc.—but the heart of any object-oriented application is its collection of object classes. Criteria for identifying objects are found in many sources—e.g., Rumbaugh et al, Shlaer and Mellor, Wirfs-Brock et al., Coad, Yourdon, and Jacobson and it is well worth consulting these sources.

Aside from the requirements of the methodology itself, our motivation for discovering objects is the belief that an object-oriented *technical* representation of the system is closer to, and more compatible with, the user's conceptual view than with any other kind of model. This is tantamount to saying, "Users think in terms of *objects*, not in terms of functions or third-normal-form entities. Objects correspond to real things that the users see in their world, things with descriptive attributes *and* behavior." However, remember that some users (and some novice application developers) may resist any abstract model, favoring a working prototype instead.

Aside from the user's conceptual mindset, expressing requirements in terms of objects is typically based on the nature of the application itself. Objects provide a natural metaphor for describing some kinds of applications—and this is becoming more and more common for systems that involve GUI front-ends, event-based processing, client-server architectures, and distributed data and processing. Indeed, it may also be a better metaphor for the organizational environment in which our systems are built, as the enterprises of the 1990s move from a hierarchical control-oriented structure to a flat, decentralized group of communicating clusters.

The discovery of essential objects in a system depends a great deal on our perspective. Are we looking at the system from a data perspective, from a functional perspective, or from a behavioral perspective? The system often exhibits a dominant characteristic: a business application, for example, tends to be intrinsically data-oriented, while a real-time process-control system is intrinsically behavioral. This does not mean that we should ignore the other perspectives altogether, but merely that the dominant perspective will usually suggest the starting point in our search for object classes.

Also, the user's mindset often has a dramatic influence on our search for objects. Despite the suggestion that users find the object-oriented model intuitively appealing, it may still be true that when we first begin interviewing them, their mental model, or frame of reference, may be intrinsically functional, or behavioral, or data-oriented in nature. Unless the systems analyst is as expert in the underlying application as the users, it is folly to fight the users' way of thinking when carrying out these interviews. The information thus gleaned may be packaged and rearranged in other forms, but the object discovery process can be made easier and more pleasant if it follows the users' natural way of thinking. This is one reason why the use of transaction sequences provides such a good means of communication with users.

This chapter discusses the task of object discovery from all three perspectives. Then we will discuss some criteria for evaluating the reasonableness of candidate objects that have been discovered through the analysis process. As always, standard naming conventions should be observed. A standard vocabulary should be defined for the problem domain. It is recommended that object class names should be singular nouns or an adjective and noun.

Finding Objects: The Data Perspective

In many business applications, data is the dominant characteristic of the system, even from the first moment of requirements analysis. As a result, the most common technique for identifying objects is basically the same as the standard technique for identifying entities in entity-relationship modeling. This is almost a disappointment to many systems analysts who have been reared in ERD-based methodologies. The beginning steps of an object-oriented project look so familiar, they are apt to complain, "What's so different about OO? Isn't this the same old stuff we've been doing all along?"[1]

Shlaer and Mellor were among the first to popularize guidelines for data-oriented object discovery. In this technique, all nouns in requirements specifications (which, in our approach, are described using transaction sequences) are regarded as representing candidate object classes and the actual object classes required for a system are selected from these candidate object classes. Aside from transaction sequences, there is usually a wealth of existing information that the systems analyst can use to search for potential objects:

- written policy statements
- company procedures
- product descriptions
- service descriptions
- business plans
- statements of business goals and objectives
- existing files
- existing applications
- forms, screens, and reports
- models from related business area applications

---

[1] What *is* different is the inheritance features of class hierarchies, which are typically more powerful and extensive than the subtype-supertype concept in data modeling methodologies. Even more important is the encapsulation of data and function within objects, and the message communication between objects, which the data modeling methodologies lack entirely. Also, ER-oriented approaches typically only find the obvious domain objects; some of the most useful objects to find, which fully use object-oriented features such as polymorphism and inheritance, are not so obviously apparent in the problem domain.

- diagrams, pictures, and drawings which the users have pasted on their wall
- information requirements documents

If the documents exist in a computer-readable textual form, they can be subjected to a formal linguistic analysis to extract a list of candidate objects; see Argila's description for more details.[1] This has the advantage of minimizing what is otherwise a tedious, error-prone task.

In addition to formal, written documents, the analyst will normally be able to use discussions, interviews, JAD sessions, and direct observation of the user's environment to find candidate objects. In these discussions, *collective* (plural) nouns are often good clues to the existence of useful objects. For example, the user will often talk about:

- *persons*—as groups of individuals (Joe, Mary, and Susan), or as members of a group (clerks, salespeople, engineers, accountants), as well as roles played by people in the organization, and organizational units that may be relevant to the system.

- *places*—as individual locations (New York, London, Berlin), or as instances of important organizational locations (field offices, regional sales headquarters, customer repair centers).

- *things*—as individual, unrelated tangible items (trucks, pencils, ice cream cones), or as instances of a class (products, parts, machines, desks) which are relevant to the organization's activities.

- *events*—especially recurring events (monthly sales conference, annual shareholder meeting, weekly planning session) and "external stimuli" to which the system must have a preplanned response (customer orders, inquiries, cancellations).

- *concepts*—as abstractions for which there are no physical, tangible counterparts, but which are nevertheless important to the organization (plans, strategies, mission-statements, objectives, specifications).

- *other systems*, which communicate or interact with the system being modeled, as well as *physical devices*, which will exist in the environment and interact with the system, regardless of the technology used to implement the system itself.

In our own modeling work, we have found that basic entity objects follow a "30-30-30" rule: 30 percent are generic, 30 percent are industry-specific, 30 percent are environment-specific, and the remaining 10 percent cannot be readily categorized at all. For each of the primary categories, we offer the following observations:

- *generic objects*—these are fairly obvious, and typical of almost any kind of business environment. They are typically physical objects that can be observed in the environment—e.g., customer, product, employee, etc.

---

[1] Carl Argila, "Finding and Keeping Good Objects," *American Programmer*, October 1994.

- *industry-specific*—these are more abstract and not always observable. The analyst must delve deeper into the problem domain to detect them, but they are important components of the model. A commercial airline business, for example, might have objects such as schedule, passenger, fare, etc. An insurance company would have an entirely different set of industry-specific objects, such as policy, claim, etc.

- *environment-specific*—these are the objects that are unique to a specific business or organizational environment; they may involve products, policies, organizational groups or other aspects of the business. They are the Loch Ness monsters of object discovery: very abstract and very obscure. Rigorous analysis, and/or deep knowledge of the user's business application, are required to detect and identify these objects.

It is best not to start by considering possible inheritance hierarchies. Similarly, we recommend that the analyst avoid any attempt to produce abstract classes. Instead, start by collecting the specific object classes which are required; at a later stage, the object classes can be examined and inheritance structures can be created. This helps avoid ill-advised decisions concerning inheritance based on insufficient data, which can prove to be awkward to rectify later in the development of the system.

There is no guarantee, of course, that this checklist will discover all of the objects in a system. All it can do is provide analysts with a starting point for their investigations. Even with an OO perspective, the classic problems of systems analysis remain: users may not know exactly what they want their system to do, and may be unwilling or unable to articulate their needs. If the analysts are unfamiliar with the underlying application, they may not know what questions to ask—even with the assistance of this checklist. Thus, a prototyping life cycle may continue to be an extremely important safety factor to ensure that no essential objects have been left undiscovered when the final version of the system goes into production.

On the other hand, a common problem with object-oriented analysis is the discovery of too many objects. Enthusiasm and a naive belief that more is better when it comes to adding objects to the OO model may lead the analyst to the creation of objects that really don't deserve to exist. We discuss this problem further in the next section.

Finding Objects: The Functional Perspective

During an OO presentation at Apple Computer a few years ago, one of the authors presented a standard data-oriented perspective on discovering objects. Besides talking to users and examining any textual documentation they may have, he suggested that analysts look for nouns as a good indicator of the existence of an object in the model.

"Wrong!" bellowed a software engineer in the back of the room. "Look for *verbs*!"

Later we realized that the engineer was looking at the object world from a different perspective: to him, what characterized an object is what it does, not what it is. Identification and documentation of attributes comes later; the first question is, "What does this object have to *do* in order to exist?"

For example, most of us would immediately accept the notion that a person is an object. For some, the essential nature of "person-ness" is the combination of such attributes as height, weight, name, age, etc. But for others—perhaps those thinking of a person object within a corporate environment—the essential nature of "person-ness" is what he or she does. When you're introduced to someone at a social gathering, for example, are you more likely to ask, "Where do you live?" or "What do you do for a living?" Both questions are usually appropriate and socially acceptable; but they reflect two very different perspectives.

Apple Computer is not alone in this perspective; many OO enthusiasts use a method of documenting their objects known as "CRC" cards, originally developed by Ward Cunningham of Wyatt Software Services, Inc., in Lake Oswego, Oregon. "CRC" is an acronym for "Class-Responsibility-Collaboration" and it addresses three fundamental questions about an object: What class does it belong to? What responsibility does it have? And how does it communicate with other objects?

Identifying the responsibility of an object is another way of asking what function(s) it performs; discovering objects by asking about responsibilities thus leads one to focusing on verbs in a problem statement, rather than nouns.[1]

What does this have to do with systems analysis and object-orientation? As mentioned above, many systems cry out to be examined from a special perspective. More importantly, as we observed earlier in this chapter, the perspective depends a great deal on the mindset, personality, and orientation of the user. If the user is most comfortable talking about the requirements of the system, that may be the most appropriate one to use when discovering objects. This is particularly common in business reengineering projects, when the user's essential question is, "What business are we really in? What do we really *do* around here?"

The primary danger of a function-oriented OO perspective is that it can corrupt the analyst or the user into building a completely functional model of user requirements[2]. As a starting point for object discovery, it's fine—but if it leads to a final analysis model that looks like a HIPO diagram, or a functional decomposition diagram, or a structure chart, then the OO analysis process has gone badly awry. (It may also indicate that the application was ill-suited to an object-oriented approach, and that a function-oriented approach would be better.)

---

[1] The most eloquent description of the "responsibility-driven" approach to OO analysis and design is provided by Rebecca Wirfs-Brock et al.

[2] Don Firesmith points out that a business-oriented function can often involve multiple objects.

Finding Objects: The Behavioral Perspective

There is one last perspective that can be helpful in discovering objects: *behavior*. Our primary questions here are: how do objects communicate? With whom? How fast? How do they respond to messages, signals, interrupts, or other forms of communication?

The applicability of this perspective to real-time or distributed systems is obvious. But it can be helpful if the analyst entices a group of users to adopt a role-playing attitude in acting out the behavior of the overall system. Thus, if the analyst suspects that there is a customer class in the system, he might ask one of the users to pretend that he *is* a customer. It is easy to imagine how questions like "Who do you interact with?" and "How do you respond when the accounting department sends you an overdue invoice message?" could evoke a healthy analyst-user dialogue to help determine whether customer really is an appropriate class for the system.

As we will see in subsequent chapters, a closer examination of the behavior of objects typically introduces an object interaction diagram. In addition, we may find it helpful to draw object life cycle diagrams to illustrate the behavior of the objects.

For the initial task of discovering relevant object classes, these diagrams are unnecessary. Instead, we often find it more useful to describe transaction sequences or, in the initial stages of analysis, we might focus on a simple textual list of the events to which the system is required to respond. When interviewing the user in an accounts receivable application for example, the analyst might hear the casual comment, "Sometimes we get a request from the customer to find out whether an invoice that we've sent him has, in fact, already been paid." The relevant event, then, might be described succinctly as **QueryInvoicePaymentStatus**, and it suggests questions such as: Which object initiates such an event? Which object within the system must respond to that event? Does that external event trigger a chain of events within the system—and if so, which objects are involved in that chain of events?

Structured analysis veterans may recognize this line of thinking: it is very similar to the event-partitioning strategy proposed by McMenamin and Palmer[1] as part of their methodology of essential systems analysis. Their strategy for clustering bubbles together turns out to be object-oriented in nature. Look for a group of DFD bubbles clustered around a common data store, and aggregate them upward into a higher-level bubble. There is some commonality between the older and newer methodologies. This is a comforting thought for systems analysts who spent their first ten years practicing structured analysis and who now wonder whether everything they learned is fundamentally incorrect.

---

[1]   Stephen McMenamin and John Palmer, *Essential Systems Analysis*. (Englewood Cliffs, NJ: Yourdon Press/Prentice Hall, 1984).

Criteria for Evaluating Candidate Objects

Having discovered numerous object classes using various strategies, it is important for the systems analyst to pause and subject each candidate object to careful scrutiny. The identification of object classes involves a mental abstraction process. It involves our categorizing objects, and objects can be categorized in many different ways. The system developer has the task of deciding which categorizations are relevant and selecting object classes from the candidate object classes which have been identified.

As mentioned earlier, there is a tendency for enthusiasm to run rampant. Everything becomes an object. More dangerously, there is a "macho" attitude: "my OO model is better than your model because it has more objects." The head of one large Silicon Valley computer company boasted recently in a public forum that his company's latest creation had *ten thousand* classes; while most in his audience gasped with delight, a few grizzled veterans shook their heads in despair.[1] Whether it's bubbles, boxes, objects, or functions that we use as our measure of atomic units in a system, smaller is better. Software is hard enough to develop without turning its architecture into a bureaucracy the size of the Federal Government.

What do we look for when critically reviewing proposed objects in an object-oriented model? Coad and Yourdon propose a number of criteria that are familiar to many systems analysts who have used data-modeling methodologies based on ERDs:

- *Necessary remembrance*—make certain that the proposed object has *some* data that it must remember. It's not necessary at this point to identify all of the attributes, but it is useful to verify that some do exist.

- *More than one attribute*—if the proposed object consists of only one attribute, then perhaps that's what it is: an attribute in some other object. This is not intended as a rule, but merely the basis for a challenge to the existence of a proposed object. There are indeed legitimate examples of objects containing only one attribute, and there are (especially in real-time and control systems) objects with *no* attributes. But the vast majority of objects will have multiple attributes.

- *Needed functionality*—it should be possible to identify one or more operations, for the proposed objects: the object has to *do* something to justify its existence. As noted above, it is possible (though uncommon) for an object to have no attributes; but it is highly implausible for an object to have no operations.[2]

---

[1] What does this mean in practice? If each of the 10,000 classes has an average of 10 operations, and if each operation requires an average of 10 lines of code, then the entire system involves approximately 1 million lines of code (one million for the operations themselves, plus another 10-100,000 for class declarations and attribute definitions). If each operation requires an average of 100 lines of code, such a system then represents more than 10 million lines of code.

[2] Consider the dilemma of an object that contains attributes but no operations. How can other objects modify or interrogate the value of those attributes? More bizarre is the concept of an object that has no attributes *and* no operations.

- *Essential functionality*—the functionality, or behavior identified for the proposed object should be relevant regardless of the hardware/software technology used to implement the system. Otherwise, the proposed object is a *design* object, or *implementation* object, and it should be deferred until a later stage of the project.

- *Common attributes*—all of the attributes of the proposed class should apply to each of the instances of the class. If the analyst hears comments from the user such as, "Well, this attribute of **Person** doesn't apply to left-handed people," it's a strong clue that the model should contain an inheritance hierarchy. In such a case, we probably have one or more subclasses which have been muddled together into a common superclass.

- *Common functionality*—all of the operations associated with the proposed class should apply to each of the instances of the class. The rationale is the same as for common attributes.

Rumbaugh et al., contribute the following guidelines:

- Eliminate any duplicate object classes, retaining the most expressive name.

- Eliminate any object classes that are not relevant to the system being developed.

- Make sure object classes are specific.

- Don't model attributes as objects. Attributes are items that are primarily used to describe other objects. They do not have an independent existence. If, on the other hand, the item's independent existence is important then it should be modeled as an object. (Attributes are discussed in more detail in Chapters 13 and 21.)

- Check that object classes really identify objects. Sequences of actions which can be applied to objects are not objects unless there is also information which has to be retained about the sequence. For example, a telephone call would be modeled as an object for a telephone billing system, but not for a telephony system where it is solely to be seen as a possible transaction sequence for the system.

- Check object class names. The name of an object class should reflect its intrinsic nature and not a role it plays in an association. **Person** is a better object class than **CarOwner**. The issue of representing roles is covered in Chapter 20.

- Eliminate implementation constructs such as linked list. Similarly, beware of objects whose names are window, scroll bar, menu, etc. These may be objects that are necessary for the user interface, but have little or nothing to do with the fundamental nature of the application.

Abstracting Objects into Object Classes

It is easy to recognize objects that are visible, real concrete things. However, the identification of object classes often also involves a mental abstraction process. It involves our categorizing objects, and objects can of course be categorized in many different ways. The system developer has the task of deciding which categorizations are relevant to the system being built and thus of selecting object classes from the candidate object classes which have been identified.

There are no right or wrong categorizations, merely more and less useful. In most cases, the categorizations involve inheritance structures; in some cases, they may also involve abstract classes, for which there are no instances in the real world. The abstract classes serve as templates, and allow us to factor out common attributes and operations; this is modeled with inheritance structures, which are discussed in more detail in Chapter 20.

Chapter 19

Identifying Relationships

An object relationship is a *static* representation of user policy—e.g., a user policy that says, "For every invoice that we deal with in our company, there must always be exactly one customer; but for every customer, there may be zero to many invoices." Relationships between objects can be modeled, so that user and the analyst can be certain that they have understood and documented this very important aspect of the system requirements.

Relationships can be viewed as a type of attribute. Both relationships and attributes model information about an object—i.e., the things that an object knows about itself. They are properties the object has, and the values of these properties define an object's state. Both attributes and relationships are used to model information which is relevant in the context of the problem domain and of the planned system's responsibilities. For entity objects, both attributes and relationships are generally persistent. While an attribute links an object class with a literal value, a relationship links two object classes.

Object relationships are not the same as the concept of collaboration discussed in various OO methodologies. A collaboration between objects, as the term is normally used in OO methodologies, is an *active, dynamic* relationship that typically involves a message being sent from one object to another, as opposed to the *static* relationship we model using object relationships. The existence of an object relationship almost always implies the existence of an active, message-based collaboration—but they are nevertheless separate concepts.[1]

A careful consideration of the logical, structural connections between objects results in a stable, logical object structure. The relationships often identify good paths for communications between objects (i.e., which object classes send messages to which other object classes) and thus assist in the production of a maintainable, stable system. The relationships are also important during the physical design phase discussed in Chapter 15, when the object model is mapped to a database.

How to Discover and Specify Relationships

Relationships often correspond to verbs in transaction sequence descriptions. They describe lasting relationships, where it is important to document which object is associated with which other object, rather than transient connections. Thus, for instance, the relationship "**AutomatedTellerMachine** accepts **CashCard**" would normally be considered a transient connection, not a structural one. (If you consider the circumstances where it is relevant to model it as a relationship, you see that what should be modeled as a relationship depends on the planned

---

[1] To put it another way, an object relationship will typically be implemented as a pointer, whereas a message is typically implemented with something more akin to an operation invocation.

scope of a system.) Relationships can be named in a sentence of the form "object relationship object" where the relationship is named with a verb phrase. Thus, for example, "A car is driven by a person".

The cardinality of a relationship should be specified and if the objects on the many side of a relationship are ordered then this should be specified. As an example, a flight (from New York City to Missoula, Montana) may involve several segments (e.g., New York to Salt Lake City, and Salt Lake City to Missoula), and the order of the flight-segments is rather important if we want the airplane to arrive in the desired location. While the cardinality notation of our method documents both the participation constraints (optional versus mandatory relationships) and the multiplicity constraints (e.g., 1:1, 1:N, N:N, etc.), it is usually a good idea to explore these constraints separately with the user. First determine whether *any* relationship exists between a pair of classes, whether the relationship is optional or mandatory (as seen by either side of the bidirectional relationship) and whether that relationship is structural rather than transient. Then determine the multiplicity of the relationship.

It's important to recognize that relationships model properties of objects rather than access paths, or the ability of one object to send a message to another object. Access paths, i.e., routes where specific objects are accessed given one or more start objects, are inherently unidirectional and are mapped later in the development process, usually as pointers. Using object pointers to represent relationships during the requirements analysis phase is undesirable as it preempts an implementation decision. Also consider the case where two pointers are used—one at either end of the relationship. The fact that both describe the same relationship is obscured.

In our methodology, all relationships in the model are bidirectional. The fact that the cardinality of the relationships is documented from both directions emphasizes that the relationship *is* bi-directional. Regardless of how we intend to implement this model in a programming language or database package, it is important to document the user's policy regarding relationships between one object class and another. Rumbaugh et al., observe:

> *Although associations are modeled as bidirectional they do not have to be implemented in both directions. Associations can easily be implemented as pointers if they are only traversed in a single direction.*

The bidirectional nature of the relationships suggests an obvious strategy for discovering and documenting them. The analyst can interview users in an exhaustive fashion to determine the policy (or lack of policy) regarding each possible pair of objects. This can be quite illuminating, for it may point out areas where users realize that they *should* have a policy, but have never bothered establishing one because the particular relationship pair has never occurred in the existing business.

However, the problem with this kind of exhaustive analysis is that it becomes unwieldy in large applications. The number of object pairs in a model with N object classes is the familiar formula of $(N*(N-1))/2$, which means that if there are more than about 19 object classes in the model, it's unlikely that the user will tolerate the monotony of examining each of the several hundred possible combinations of pairs. In most cases, the initial discovery of objects will have occurred in logical "clusters".

Of course, there are potentially many variations on the basic approach, and the graphical notation for relationships that we have presented in this book. The differences in graphical notation are largely cosmetic; however, there is one issue which may influence the process of *discovering* the relationships. We noted in Chapter 4 that the relationships in the object structure diagram are allowed to show any one of the following:

- the name for each direction of the relationship,
- the name for one direction of the relationship,
- a single name that represents both directions,
- no name at all.

In many OO analysis projects, the last option is the one implicitly chosen by the user and the analyst. They'll draw a line between two objects to indicate that there is some relationship between the two, but they won't bother providing a textual description. In many cases, this is perfectly understandable. The textual description of the relationship is trivial—indeed, so trivial that it insults the reader's (and the user's!) intelligence. Furthermore, while the analyst can usually find a (trivial) meaningful term to describe the relationship from one direction, the "inverse" relationship is artificial and redundant. Thus, if one decides to describe a relationship between a customer and a product as "**Customer** orders **Product**," it probably doesn't add any value to the model by annotating the object structure diagram with the inverse relationship of "**Product** is ordered by **Customer**."

However, there are a few times when the textual description provides an explanation of a relationship that might not otherwise be obvious. Also, if there are multiple relationships between two objects (e.g., "**Customer** orders **Product**" and also "**Customer** recommends **Product**"), then a name is necessary in order to distinguish them. There are analysts who feel very strongly that the only way to be really confident that one understands the nature of a relationship is to enforce the discipline of providing a name.

Additional Forms of Relationships

There are several special cases of the basic concept introduced in this chapter. For completeness, we discuss several more in this section:

- Many-to-many relationships
- Recursive relationships
- Multiple relationships between object classes
- Mandatory relationships when adding/deleting objects
- Derived relationships
- N-ary relationships

Many-to-many relationships

Our basic notation for documenting relationships in the object structure diagram allows the analyst to describe N:N relationships as well as 1:N and 1:1 relationships. While some analysts (particularly those with a data modeling background) may feel nervous about allowing N:N relationships in an OO model, they are perfectly legal. To the extent that they need to be converted into a series of 1:N relationships, it can be accomplished in the physical design phase discussed in Chapter 15. (The conversion of N:N relationships is only necessary if you don't have an object-oriented database.)

However, it is in this kind of situation that we are likely to find the phenomenon of relationships which have attributes of their own. To illustrate this, consider the situation where a **Customer** purchases a **Product** (ignoring the possibility of a **Salesperson** being involved in the process), where we might have begun with a simple N:N relationship as shown in Figure 19-1.

Figure 19-1: A typical N:N Relationship

As soon as we see the N:N nature of the relationship, we should consider it a clue that an attribute may have been improperly assigned to one of the connecting object classes. Thus, we discover that the date/time of the relationship is important, and that it's inappropriate to place the attribute in either **Customer** or **Product**. We decide that it is more appropriate to introduce a new object class, **Purchase**, with a new set of relationships as shown in Figure 19-2:

Figure 19-2: Introducing a new object class in an N:N relationship

Keep in mind that the existence of a many-to-many relationship in the OO model is a strong clue that it should be examined more closely by the analyst. Some of the many-to-many relationships have associated data. If so, the analyst needs to consider whether the data belongs in an object at one end of the relationship or whether the relationship itself should really be considered as an object. A **Purchase** is used to order quantities of one or more **Products**. In a typical structured data analysis method, this many-to-many relationship is resolved by introducing a separate **PurchaseLineItem** entity which is associated via a one-to-many relationship with **Purchase** and via a further one-to-many relationship with **Product**. In an object structure model, it is more obvious to consider a **Purchase** as an integral object which includes its line items, the data which is therefore modeled within the **Purchase** object. In the context of object orientation, avoid making object granularity too fine, which often happens with analysts who are accustomed to normalizing data. Objects can and do contain repeating groups of data.

Recursive relationships

What about relationships between instances of the same class? The situation is often described as a "recursive" relationship. It is part of the standard notation of our method, though it may be useful to include a role name for each direction, in order to avoid confusion.

Consider, for example, a **Person** object class for an organization where we wish to model the fact that some people are managed by others. Figure 19-3 shows one possible model of this situation; the textual annotation on the relationship is useful, as can be seen, so that we can distinguish the cardinality of the "managed by" relationship from the "manages" relationship.

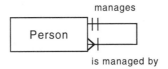

Figure 19-3: A recursive relationship

Multiple relationships between classes

So far the examples in this chapter have involved only one relationship between pairs of classes. This is the norm, and a systems analyst could experience dozens of projects without ever feeling the need for anything else.

To illustrate something more elaborate, let's imagine that we want to keep track of customers who have *ordered* products as well as customers who have *recommended* products to their friends and associates. For the moment, let's assume that we don't need to store any attributes about the ordering and recommendation activities. All we need to know is which customers have recommended which products, and which customers have purchased which products. In this case, our model might look like the one shown in Figure 19-4.

Figure 19-4: Multiple relationships between classes

Note that this is another case where it is convenient to annotate the relationship so that we can tell one from the other. The reason we *must* distinguish one relationship from another, in this example, is that they have different cardinality constraints. Our user has told us that the "purchase" relationship is an N:N situation; but the user policy for recommendations is somewhat more involved. The user has decided that every customer must recommend one, and only one, product; and every product must be recommended by one, and only one, customer.

Consequences of mandatory connections when adding/deleting instances

The presence of a relationship between two object classes may imply certain actions when an object in either one class or the other is added or deleted. Suppose that a member of royalty, as modeled in Figure 19-5, dies and his or her object is deleted from the class. What happens to the citizens he or she knew? Should they all be executed and deleted? Presumably not. The relationships should be deleted, but the instances of **Citizen** to which they were attached should not (to the great relief of the citizens thus affected!).[1]

Figure 19-5: Adding and deleting objects with relationships

On the other hand, we might have an OO model which includes an object class called **Manufacturer** and another object class called **Product**. Assume for the moment that a **Product** is manufactured by only one **Manufacturer**, which suddenly goes bankrupt and is deleted from the system. Should the related **Product**s also be deleted? What about the case where the **Product** is manufactured by multiple **Manufacturers**, *each* of whom goes bankrupt, one after the other—should the related instances of **Product** be deleted when the last **Manufacturer** has disappeared? Depending on the nature of the business, the user's response might well be, "Yes!"

In such a situation, one of the classes could be considered a *controlling* class. If an instance is deleted, then the instances it is connected to via a relationship should also be deleted; the relationship itself is known as a *controlling relationship*. This is illustrated in Figure 19-6.

Figure 19-6: Controlling relationships

---

[1]   This example is based on the rhetorical question posed by Ivar Jacobson et al., "What if you know about the king of Sweden? Does that mean that he knows about you? Normally not." But Jacobson's question actually refers to two separate bidirectional relationships; one of them (for example, the one shown in Figure 19-5) might be described as "Royalty knows Citizen, Citizen is known by Royalty." The other relationship mentioned by Jacobson, which is not shown in Figure 19-5, might be described as "Citizen knows Royalty, Royalty is known by Citizen."

A similar question arises when a new object is created within a class, when the object structure model tells us that the class is related to another class. For example, if a new instance of **Manufacturer** is created in Figure 19-6, what can we say about the products it manufactures? If we look closely at the cardinality constraints in Figure 19-6, there is a chicken-and-egg problem: each instance of a manufacturer is required to be associated with at least one product; and each product must be associated with exactly one manufacturer. The obvious interpretation is that an instance of **Manufacturer** and one or more instances of **Product** must be created (and associated with one another) at the same instant.

To some users this will seem like an irrelevant detail; for others, it will be regarded as a programming question. They might respond to the question posed above by saying, "Do whatever you want when you program it; just make sure it works." But for some, there may be legal, political, or contractual implications—and they will care deeply about such details. If they care, then we must have a way of representing it in the model.

To pursue the example above a little further, let's assume that our user allows us to have **Product**s that are not associated with any **Manufacturer**—e.g., we will continue to carry an inventory of the **Product** even if the **Manufacturer** has gone bankrupt. This means that we will represent the product-to-manufacturer relationship as a 0:1 relationship, and we can delete the "C" notation for the controlling relationship.

Having done this, our model would allow us to *first* add instances of a new **Product** without necessarily associating the **Product** with a **Manufacturer**. As a separate step, we could then add instances of **Manufacturer**, and as part of *that* instance-creation activity, we could establish the relationship with the appropriate product(s). In this case, the relationship would be called a *dependent relationship*, and would be diagrammed as shown in Figure 19-7.

Figure 19-7: A dependent relationship between two classes

It is evident that the details of controlling and dependent relationships involve substantial knowledge about the *state* and *behavior* of classes and objects. Indeed, some systems analysts prefer to bury this detailed information in the object life cycle diagrams that we discussed in Chapter 7 rather than highlighting it on the object structure diagrams. Alternatively, it may be appropriate to specify the details in the description of operations associated with adding and deleting objects within a class. This is a matter of choice. Our only advice is that consistency is crucial: if dependent and controlling relationships are documented in the model, they should *all* be modeled on the relationship diagram or in the details of the object's internal life cycle diagrams and operations. This is likely to be domain-specific knowledge and should be documented by the model. Otherwise it may fall through the cracks and never be implemented by programmers unfamiliar with the application domain.

Derived relationships

Some relationships are redundant—because they can be derived from other relationships. For example, the relationship, grandparent, can be derived from the parent relationship. In most cases, it is preferable *not* to include such derived associations in the object structure model, as it just adds complexity without adding useful information. However, if the derived association is particularly meaningful for the application domain, it can be included in the object structure model, marked as derived with the notation shown in Figure 19-8. Inclusion of a derived relationship in the object structure model may also be useful where the decision as to which relationship should be considered as derived is, for requirements analysis purposes, arbitrary.

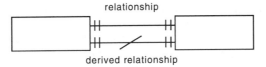

Figure 19-8: Derived relationships

N-ary Relationships

Finally, we note that all of the relationships in our methodology are binary. They represent relationships between members of exactly two object classes. In the vast majority of cases, simple binary relationships are sufficient to document the user's policy in an OO model.

However, there are a few limited cases where the analyst may feel the need to express relationships involving three, four, or more classes and objects. Such a situation can occur, for example, if the analyst begins with a simple binary relationship and then begins to realize that there is important information that needs to be stored about that relationship.

In a simple order-entry system, for example, the user and analyst might begin by discussing the relationship between a **Customer** and a **Product**; the relationship might be described as orders or purchases. But it soon becomes evident that we need to keep track of *when* the purchase was made. This is not a proper attribute for either **Customer** or **Product**, but rather an attribute of the relationship itself. Thus, we would be prompted to create a new class and object (assuming that it didn't already exist) called ORDER, and document a three-way relationship between **Customer**, **Product**, **Order**. Indeed, it might occur to the user that an essential component of a purchase is the **Salesperson** who convinced the **Customer** to buy the **Product**. We might end up with a four-way relationship shown in Figure 19-9.

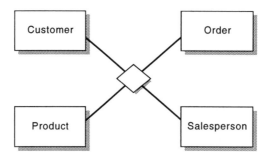

Figure 19-9: Example of a four-way relationship between classes and objects

Note that the relationship (shown by the diamond) is not named, and that the diagram does not show the cardinality of the participating members. It is far more difficult to describe, and great care would have to be given to ensure that the notation on the diagram was understandable. Each instance of an **Order**, for example, is probably associated with exactly one **Customer**, exactly one **Salesperson**, and one-to-many instances of **Product**. But what is each instance of a product related to? How do we describe the relationship from the perspective of a **Customer**? As Rumbaugh et al. observe:

> *Higher order associations are more complicated to draw, implement and think about than binary associations and should be avoided if possible.*

Thus, we recognize that there are circumstances where n-ary relationships may be useful to accurately model a complex problem. In the overwhelming majority of cases, it will be unnecessary. The situation shown in Figure 19-9, for example, could be modeled instead as a combination of six separate binary relationships. Consequently, our methodology, and all of the examples in this book, use only binary relationships.

Chapter 20

Inheritance

This chapter discusses inheritance, what is tricky about inheritance, and what mindset is needed for using inheritance as opposed to that needed for generalization/specialization. Following this, various pragmatic modeling issues are discussed, involving cases where generalization/specialization should not necessarily be modeled using inheritance.

For the standard procedure for identifying inheritance, see Chapter 13.

The Importance of Good Inheritance Hierarchies

The development of good inheritance hierarchies is a particularly critical part of the development process because the inheritance hierarchies have such an important influence on the subsequent reusability of the design and its robustness in the face of change.

One reason for this relates to the question of the impact of a change to an object class in the inheritance hierarchy. If an operation is changed or added to an object class, what is the impact of this on object classes which inherit the operation? If the classification structure is a good one, the change should have few or no undesired side-effects. If it is a bad one, the impact of the change could be complicated to deal with.

Another reason is the difficulty of adjusting an inheritance hierarchy once it is in use. If the class hierarchy requires extension to accommodate a new category of objects, then the ability to add the new subclass into a logical place in the hierarchy depends on how well the inheritance hierarchy is constructed. Ideally, the classification structure should not need to be changed. If changes are however required, the effect of this on the affected subclasses and all lower levels of the inheritance hierarchy must be considered. This can involve substantial work and can be extremely difficult for an implemented system which is already in use.

It has often been remarked that the use of inheritance violates the principle of information hiding. Objects support information hiding since they know no more than they need to know about the workings of other objects and are (or should be) designed such that the interfaces between objects are as small as possible. Objects also, by linking data and function, seek to bind together, into a cohesive unit, details which are so closely related that a change to one item is likely to results in a need to change another item. These factors mean that requirements for change should tend to be localized in their impact.

However, object classes that inherit from a superclass inherit all the details of the superclass and are, therefore, also affected when changes are made to the superclass. Inheritance can thus be seen as violating the principle of information hiding. This means that particular attention needs to be given to the question of how inheritance should be used in order to create a reusable, maintainable design. It also means that overuse of inheritance should be avoided.

Basically, the fundamental principle in developing inheritance hierarchies is that the semantics of the hierarchy should be clear. It is likely to be much easier to extend and maintain an inheritance structure and classification of objects into object classes which has a clear organizing principle, rather than one which has a confused or unclear classification principle behind it.

For the design to be maintainable, it is also important that the criteria used as the basis of a classification structure are clearly communicated. They should therefore be documented. For instance, in our seminar registration system, we have an inheritance hierarchy for seminar. We classified seminars first on the basis of whether they are internal or external and second according to the type of seminar organization. The type of seminar organization is important because it affects how seminar costs are handled. This is the sort of information which needs to be documented. These criteria have to be clearly understood if object classes in the inheritance hierarchy are to be changed in a way which is compatible with the hierarchy's original meaning, or if the hierarchy is to be extendible.

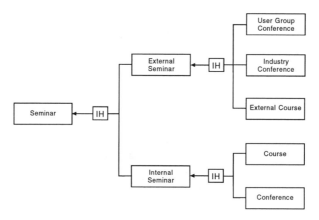

Figure 20-1: Inheritance hierarchy for Seminar

Inheritance and Generalization/Specialization

For those from a structured methods background, a first reaction to inheritance is likely to be "Oh yes, we recognize that - inheritance is generalization/specialization under another name". It is true that there is an overlap and that the use of generalization/specialization is one basic way of building an inheritance hierarchy. However, inheritance in the object-oriented world has been arrived at by a different route, and it is important to understand the differences, as well as the similarities. Understanding the differences between inheritance and generalization/specialization is an important milestone in learning to think object-oriented.

The most important difference is that inheritance and generalization/specialization arise from different needs, needs which emphasize different parts of the development life cycle.

Generalization/specialization is a conceptual modeling tool. It is an analysis and design technique, that is used to describe relationships between classes of object. When the design is implemented, it is mapped to an implementation which will take another form. It is understood that there will be a transition between design and implementation and that the design does not predetermine what the implementation should be.

Inheritance, on the other hand, is fundamentally an implementation concept. Because object-oriented development ends with an object-oriented implementation, and because *transitions* between models are not regarded as desirable, any inheritance structure which is designed must work at the code level. Inheritance is not simply a conceptual modeling tool. Even if you are an analyst or designer, you need to understand the implications of this, because it affects what the best logical design will look like.

We discuss the consequences of this in the next section.

Inheritance and Subtyping

What special implications does it have that inheritance is used for implementation purposes?

The key issue, in our view, is that, in the context of a programming language, object classes have to be able to function in a similar way to data types, e.g., like an integer or a string in a conventional programming language.[1] Integer and string are fixed data types which come predefined with the programming language. Object classes can also be regarded as data types - they are effectively user-defined types, which are available in addition to the programming language's predefined, fixed types.

To appreciate why object classes should be regarded as being like data types, consider how they are used in an object-oriented programming language. In most programming languages, you can use an integer as a parameter in a function call. In an object-oriented programming language, this is also true of an object class - you can use an object class as a parameter in an operation invocation just as you can an integer.

In the case of operations such as   `IntegerA = IntegerB + DecimalC`
it is obviously desirable to be able to predict how the data types involved will behave when an addition is carried out. Does the result get truncated if the result field has no decimal places or does it get rounded up? Whatever the answer is, we would like it to be consistent.

---

[1] Object classes also have to function like modules, e.g., like subroutines. This, however, is not relevant to our current discussion.

What are the implications if Decimal and Integer are object classes? Suppose you design a system so that Integer truncates results which are too large for it. Later, two subclasses, IntegerTruncates and IntegerRounds are introduced. This is fine, except for all the places in the system where you've used the superclass Integers assuming that they will truncate.

The situation is even worse if you are extending a system which is frozen, maybe because it is a framework from a third-party vendor. In this case it is undesirable, and may not even be possible, to change the predefined classes.

It is possible to add subclasses in the way we have outlined. But it does raise problems for maintenance that we wouldn't have to deal with if we took the view that object classes are like data types and that objects belonging to a given object class should be substitutable for each other just as variables of a given data type are. With data types, we can assume that all integers will behave in the same way. If we have an object class Integer, we want to be able to make the same assumption.

When you invoke an operation in an object of a given object class, it is a good rule that you should not need to know whether the object belongs directly to the object class or to one of its subclasses. If you have to know about the quirks of how the subclasses behave, then you have a lot of additional checking to do every time you invoke an operation. What is more, it would no longer be possible simply to add a new subclass to an inheritance hierarchy in an existing application without changing all the object classes which communicate with the superclass so that they can handle the new variant.

The more the behavior of existing object classes can be relied upon, as one can rely upon the behavior of data types - at least, usually, these days! - the better the maintainability of the application. And we are more likely to achieve the goal of a component-based approach to building software.

This means that it is a good design rule that an object belonging to an object class should always be substitutable for an object belonging to the superclass - it should always have the behavior of its superclass object as a subset of its own behavior.

This is what lies behind the concept of substitutability, which the OMG defines as follows:

> *Substitutability means being able to substitute an object of some type S when an object of type T is expected, where T is a supertype of S, while guaranteeing that the substituted object will support the same operation as specified by the supertype T.*[1]

---

[1] *Object Management Architecture Guide.* (Framingham MA: Object Management Group, 1992).

We regard substitutability as an important concept, and while its use is not mandatory for an object-oriented system, we recommend that you always try to make your subclasses substitutable for their superclass.

In the object-oriented literature, the use of inheritance such that object classes are substitutable is usually called *subtyping*.

Implementation Inheritance

The most basic definition of inheritance is as a relationship between object classes that allows an object class to include the attributes and operations defined for another more general object class. It is simply a mechanism to allow reuse of another definition.

This means that inheritance can be used for what some people call *implementation inheritance*. For this type of inheritance, the rationale is that there is useful code in the superclass which can be reused by creating an object class as a subclass. The questions of shared semantics or of substitutability are not considered. An example of implementation inheritance would be the definition of **Binary File** as a subclass of **ASCII File** simply because it is convenient to reuse some of the object definition implemented for **ASCII File**.

This type of inheritance leads to designs which are difficult to understand and to maintain, and there is now an almost universal consensus that it should be avoided.

The use of inheritance is often advocated as a way of extending an existing application without disrupting code which is already in operational use. If different functionality is required, inheritance allows this to be added without disturbing the current implementation by simply defining a new subclass. This is a valid usage of inheritance where the change really is an extension. However, it is not a good use of inheritance where the subclass is really being introduced as a quick fix - a way of fixing an error in one part of an application while avoiding the overhead of correcting the error throughout the application. Such quick fixes are sometimes needed where an error has widespread ramifications, but is critical only in a given context in which it is urgent that it should be fixed. Effectively, inheritance is being used for versioning, to enable a new and old version of a module to exist side by side. This is a misuse of inheritance which, in our view, developers are likely to regret later when any further maintenance is required or when the inheritance hierarchy needs extending for semantically valid reasons.

Using Different Types of Inheritance in Different Phases

The three types of inheritance we introduced in the previous sections also have alternative names which are sometimes used in the literature. We show below the names we use together with their alternative names:

Name used in this Book	Alternative Name
generalization/specialization	is-a
subtyping	specification inheritance
implementation inheritance	subclassing

These three types of inheritance can be associated with the analysis, design and construction phases.

- Generalization/specialization is readily identifiable during analysis.

- Subtyping has its roots in design considerations. In order to determine whether an inheritance hierarchy uses subtyping, it is often necessary to be able to consider the operations associated with object classes. This can readily be checked during design.

- Implementation inheritance is mentioned here only for completeness. Its use is strongly discouraged. It leads to maintainability problems.

Start analysis by identifying inheritance hierarchies based on generalization/specialization and check and modify these during design to ensure subtyping is used.

Generalization/specialization is well known from semantic modeling techniques and is fairly easy to understand. It describes one kind of object as a special case of another. For instance, a car is a special kind of a vehicle.

Subtyping often overlaps with specialization. Many specializations are also valid subtypes. Our example of specialization (a car is a specialization of a vehicle) is also (almost certainly) a valid subtype. We say almost certainly because it is easier to prove that a subclass is not substitutable - by producing an example of a case in which it is not - than to prove that it is.

As an example of the different inheritance hierarchies which can be produced using generalization/specialization and inheritance, we consider sets, integer sets and bags. This is a technical example but it is also a widespread example which is easy to grasp.[1]

Figure 20-2 shows a possible inheritance hierarchy for sets, integer sets and bags, based on generalization/specialization.

The subclasses produced using generalization/specialization are not also valid subtypes.

---

[1] We have taken this example, together with much of our discussion, from Lalonde and Pugh. See W.R.LaLonde, J.R. Pugh " Subclassing =/ Subtyping =/ IsA", *Journal of Object-Oriented Programming,* January 1991, pp 57-62

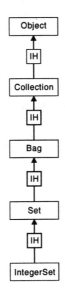

Figure 20-2: An inheritance hierarchy based on generalization/specialization

Consider any operation, in some other object class, which takes a set as an argument. Can an integer set be substituted for the set argument? No, since the operation should only need to know that it is dealing with a set, not what type of set it is, and on this basis could try to add a non-integer to the set. Can a bag be substituted for a set? No, since the operation might be relying on the fact that duplicates cannot exist in a set, whereas the bag can contain duplicates. An integer set is thus not a subtype of a set (using the definition of subtyping from the previous section on subtyping) even though it is clearly a specialization of a set. Nor is a bag, although a bag has similarities with a set.

Sets, integers and bags could however be defined, using subtyping, as subclasses of the object class **Collection**. In Figure 20-3, we show an inheritance hierarchy for sets, integer sets and bags which uses subtyping.

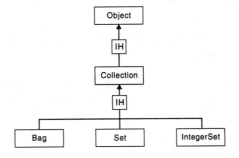

Figure 20-3: An inheritance hierarchy based on subtyping

Subtyping involves the consideration of a logical relationship between types of object, namely whether an object of one type can be substituted for another. In order to determine this, only specification issues need to be considered, in particular the interface to the object class and its semantics. (These specification issues are clearly defined during logical design, which is why logical design is the best point at which to check that subtyping is used.)

Figure 20-4 shows an example of implementation inheritance. As previously explained, we discourage implementation inheritance since it results in a less maintainable system.

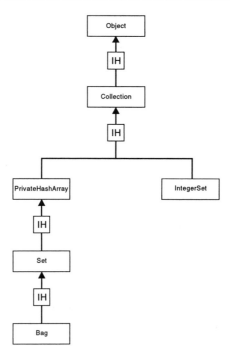

Figure 20-4: An inheritance hierarchy based on implementation inheritance

Aspects of Generalization/Specialization not Supported by Inheritance

The specializations which are best modeled using inheritance are those which do not overlap and are not time-dependent. For example, **One-Off Order** and **Standing Order** might be modeled as subclasses of **Order**. See Figure 20-5.

Overlapping and time-dependent specializations on the other hand are best not modeled using inheritance. We discuss alternative ways of modeling them using object-oriented concepts in the sections which follow.

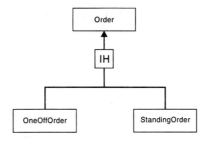

Figure 20-5: Mutually exclusive subtypes

Overlapping Specializations (Inclusive Hierarchies)

Generalization/specialization allows modeling of the following types of hierarchy:

- An exclusive hierarchy (is one of), where an instance is not only a member of the supertype, but must be a member of one and only one of the subtypes.

- An inclusive hierarchy (is any of), where an instance is a member of the supertype and at least one of the subtypes, but possibly more than one of the subtypes, i.e., specializations may overlap.

- A conditional hierarchy (maybe), where an instance is a member of the supertype, but does not have to be a member of any of the subtypes.

Of these types of inheritance hierarchy, inheritance supports the first and third variants. Taking these in turn:

- Inheritance hierarchies are always exclusive hierarchies. If a superclass has a number of subclasses, then an object can only be a member of one of the subclasses.

- Inheritance hierarchies can also be conditional and non-conditional hierarchies. If the superclass is concrete, then objects may be a member of the superclass without being members of any of the subclasses. If the superclass is abstract, then any object must always belong to a subclass and the hierarchy is not conditional.

- The second variant, the inclusive hierarchy, where an object may belong to more than one subclass, is not normally catered to in object-oriented languages. The general rule is that an object can belong directly to only one subclass.

It is possible to model inclusive hierarchies using multiple inheritance, but each possible combination of subtypes has to be modeled explicitly. See Figure 20-6.

Generalization/Specialization

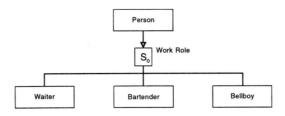

Inheritance

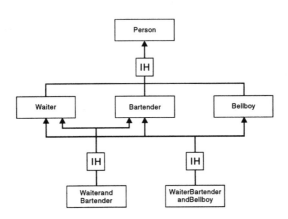

Figure 20-6: Using multiple inheritance for inclusive hierarchies

With multiple inheritance, the subclass always inherits from *all* its superclasses. This makes it a clumsy way of modeling inclusive hierarchies since each possible combination has to be modeled as a separate subclass. In any case, it is a good idea to avoid the use of multiple inheritance. It is difficult enough to produce a good inheritance hierarchy using single inheritance. Using multiple inheritance increases the scope for producing a design which is difficult to maintain. The fact that inheritance violates the principle of information hiding, as we said at the beginning of this chapter, makes it advisable to use it with caution.

Next we give some suggestions as to how to model types of inclusive hierarchy which do not have a direct counterpart when inheritance is used.

Modeling multiple roles}

Overlapping specializations often occur where an object can play more than one role. For example a **Person** object class could be specialized into doctor and nurse subclasses. However let us assume that in our environment a **Person** can be both a doctor and a nurse. (We assume, for the

purposes of this example, that this is a valid use of subtyping - that the doctor and nurse
subclasses are substitutable for **Person**.)

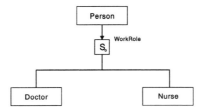

Figure 20-7: Generalization/specialization of Person

This case is best modeled using a separate **WorkRole** object class. A **Person** may have one or
more **WorkRoles**, e.g., may be both doctor and nurse. **Doctor** and **Nurse** are modeled as
subclasses of **WorkRole**. We had originally viewed **WorkRole** as an integral part of the **Person**
object, which indicates that they are closely connected. So it is logical to use aggregation to link
WorkRole and **Person**.

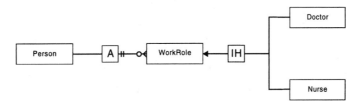

Figure 20-8: Modeling roles using aggregation and inheritance

Multiple partitions

Objects can often be classified according to more than one criterion. As we mentioned at the
beginning of this chapter, each inheritance hierarchy should have a single clear classification
principle behind it. This is true for generalization/specialization also and means that, theoretically,
multiple generalization/specialization partitions are possible. Within each partition, subtypes are
mutually exclusive. But often an instance can belong to one subtype in each of the partitions.

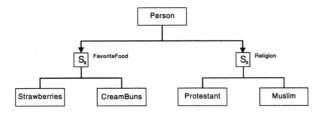

Figure 20-9: Multiple partitions using generalization/specialization

A good way of handling this using inheritance is to use aggregation, such that one aggregate
component is used to represent each partition. We show how this would work in Figure 20-10.

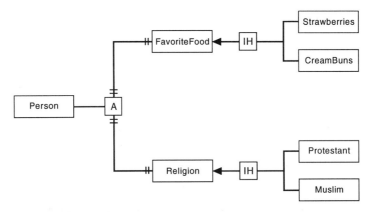

Figure 20-10: Handling multiple partitions using aggregation and inheritance

Time-Dependent Specializations

Another aspect which generalization/specialization supports but inheritance doesn't is the modeling of objects which change their type during the course of time. With generalization/specialization each type is modeled as a subtype. Instances can, from a conceptual point of view, switch between these subtypes. Most commonly used object-oriented languages, however, do not allow an object to switch between subclasses. The only way to change a class in most object-oriented languages is to destroy the object and create a new one. For this reason, it is best to avoid modeling such that objects need to change their class.

Below we give suggestions as to how to model two cases where specializations are time-dependent. These two cases call for different solutions.

First, consider the case where **Approved Order** and **Shipped Order** could be modeled as specializations of **Order**. Over time, an **Approved Order** changes into a **Shipped Order**. In effect, what is being modeled is a change of state. In an object-oriented design, this should be modeled simply as an attribute of the object class **Order**, without inheritance being required.

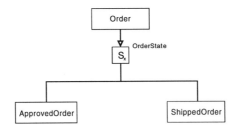

Figure 20-11: Modeling changes in state with generalization/specialization

A more complicated case exists where the attributes and operations associated with each "state" are significantly different. Consider the case where an employed person becomes an unemployed one. Clearly there is significantly different data associated with an employed person and an unemployed one. Such cases are best modeled using aggregation, in the same way as we suggested for multiple partitions.

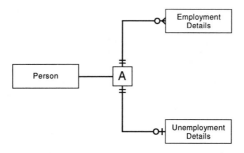

Figure 20-12: Modeling objects which change their type

Chapter 21

Aggregation

Chapter 21 provides an overview of what aggregation is and when to use it. It concludes with a discussion of the following more detailed aspects of aggregation:

- fixed, variable and recursive aggregates,

- dependent and independent aggregate components, and

- whether outside objects should send messages to aggregate components (i.e., issues relating to the encapsulation of aggregate components).

We recapitulate, for reference, the description of the basic notation for aggregation which was introduced in Chapter 13. This chapter incorporates many of Rumbaugh's recommendations.

Notation

Aggregation is used to model whole-part structures. The whole is called a **composite object** or **aggregate** and the parts are called **component objects**. One example of a composite object is a bicycle. A bicycle consists of several parts - wheels, frame, bell etc. - all of which can be represented as component objects.

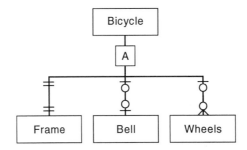

Figure 21-1: Bicycle as a composite object

Cardinality can be used to show:

- whether the aggregate must include a component of the given type or not.

- whether the aggregate may include more than one component of a given type.

- whether a component object can exist independently of the composite object or not.

Figure 21-1 shows that in our view a bicycle must have a frame in order to be a bicycle and that a bicycle frame cannot exist independently of a bicycle. A bicycle does not have to have a bell and wheels and the bell and wheels can exist independently of the bicycle. A bicycle cannot have more than one bell but can have more than one wheel.

It is possible to specify that the components of an aggregate are ordered. An example might be **PackageTours** in a **TravelBrochure**. The **TravelBrochure** contains **PackageTours** in an ordered sequence.

It is also possible to specify that a relationship with an aggregate component is *ordered* and to specify constraints on relationships between an aggregate component and the composite object. Ordered relationships are described in Chapter 4 and constraints in Chapter 13.

What is Aggregation?

Aggregation is a concept used to describe relationships between objects. Aggregation allows a composite object to be described in terms of the objects of which it consists. Aggregation can be seen as a type of relationship which is less close than the relationship between an attribute and the object it describes and closer than the type of relationship between two objects which is described by a static relationship.

Attributes have no independent existence apart from the object they describe. Objects, on the other hand, have an independent existence, but can be brought together via aggregation into assemblies or composite objects, which then appear externally to be like a single object.

We find it useful to associate a fixed semantics with aggregation. This is so that a composite object and its components are moved or copied as a whole. The copy operation is propagated from the composite object to its components, so that, for instance, when a document is copied, all its paragraphs are copied. (The operation is not propagated in the reverse direction - copying a paragraph does not imply copying the whole document.) This provides a good rule to consider when deciding whether to use aggregation.

Identifying aggregation also draws attention to the need to consider propagation of other operations and of attributes for the aggregates which are identified. It also has implications with respect to encapsulation which need to be considered, which we discuss later in this chapter.

Aggregation differs from inheritance in that aggregation represents the relationship "a-part-of" while inheritance represents the relationship "a-kind-of". The components of an aggregate are all potentially present in an aggregate, while subclasses in an inheritance hierarchy are in an "OR" relationship with each other. Sometimes, an inheritance hierarchy is mistakenly used where an aggregation is in fact appropriate. Considering whether the lower level object is "a kind of" the higher level object or "a part of" it should enable any confusion on this head to be resolved.

Aggregation and inheritance can be combined. If a composite object has subclasses, then each subclass inherits its aggregation structure.

When to use Aggregation

Basically, use of aggregation is recommended where there is a close relationship between objects such that:

- the composite object is often viewed or handled as a whole.

- the composite object would (normally) be moved or cloned as a whole.

- there is an asymmetrical relationship between the composite object and its components such that the component objects can be regarded as being "part of" the composite.

- there is propagation of operations from the composite object to the components (this applies to the move and copy operations, but often also to other operations, e.g., save/restore, print, lock, display).

- there is propagation of attributes (for instance the position of the components of a window depends on the position of the window).

Aggregation should be used, rather than a relationship, where there is a whole-part relationship and not a relationship between two separate objects of equal status.

The decision to use aggregation rather than attributes to represent a complex object structure involves the same considerations as all decisions as to whether to model an item as an object or as an attribute. As stated previously, attributes are values that are closely associated with the containing object class such that they have no independent existence or object identity.

In the following sections, various concepts which are relevant to aggregation are described.

Fixed, Variable and Recursive Aggregates

Aggregates may have a fixed, variable or recursive structure. In an aggregate with a fixed structure, the number of components of each type is fixed. For instance, a bicycle has a fixed structure (it has two wheels).

In a variable aggregate, the number of components of one type may vary. For instance, the number of chapters in a book depends on the book in question.

Aggregate components may themselves be aggregates. Aggregation is transitive in that an aggregate consists of both its direct components and also of all components of those components. The whole composite object consists of all objects at all levels in the aggregation structure.

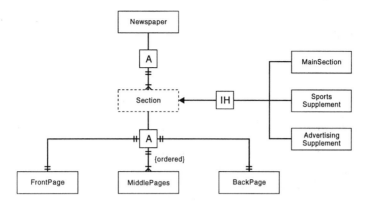

Figure 21-2: Aggregate which includes aggregates: Newspaper

A recursive aggregate is an aggregate which contains, directly or indirectly, a component which is of the same object class as itself. Recursive aggregation is often associated with the use of subclasses. An example is that of statements in a computer program. A program includes statements which may be compound or simple. Compound statements in turn may include compound statements or simple statements. Compound statements thus include compound statements recursively. We show this in Figure 21-3.

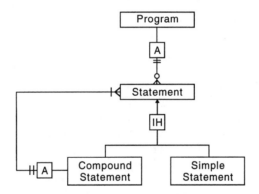

Figure 21-3: Recursive aggregate: Computer Program

Aggregate Components Exclusive to a Single Composite Object

Any individual component object is used exclusively within a single composite object. It cannot belong to more than one composite object.

It is important to note that this applies at the object or instance level. At the object class level, the same object class may be used to describe aggregate components for more than one aggregate. For instance, a bolt or a screw could be included in objects of different types. The same bolt or screw cannot however be included in more than one manufactured object (either of the same type or of a different type).[1]

Aggregate Components - Dependent and Independent

An aggregate component can have an optional relationship with the composite object of which it is a part. If the relationship is optional (which can be seen from its cardinality), then the aggregate component can exist independently of the composite object. It can be created before the composite object comes into existence and can survive the deletion of the composite object.

An aggregate component with a mandatory relationship with the aggregates in which it may occur can only exist within an aggregate. It cannot be created until the composite object of which it is a component is created and must be deleted either before or at the same time the composite object is deleted. Dependent components that have no separate life cycle can often be modeled as part of an object's complex data structure, i.e., as attributes, rather than as objects.

Aggregate Components - Encapsulation

We use aggregation to model cases in which objects are so closely related that one object can be considered to be a part of the other. Object orientation emphasizes the encapsulation of objects and that access to the attributes of an object should only be possible via the object. If we regard an aggregate as a composite object then aggregates should also be encapsulated as a whole and aggregate components should only be accessed via the composite object. This seems like a desirable goal. However, we need to consider the implications of this. These differ depending on whether the aggregate components are dependent or independent and on what kinds of association an independent aggregate component has with other objects before it becomes part of an aggregate. We discuss these different cases next.

Dependent components can be fully encapsulated, and they should be. That is to say, any communications which either query or modify the dependent component should always be

---

[1] There are alternative definitions of aggregation that do allow an individual component to be included in more than one aggregate. However, this tends to make the exact definition of an aggregate more difficult. Should a component included in more than one aggregate be copied when the aggregate is copied? If an operation is propagated to the component, can this lead to clashes with what the other aggregate requires? We would suggest that where a potential component is not exclusive to a potential aggregate, aggregation should not be used. A static relationship should be used instead. There may also be exceptional cases in which the same object is part of two component objects within a single composite object. For instance, if a shape is divided into areas and lines separating those areas, then a line may border on (and be a part of) more than one area. Again, it is better to use relationships within the aggregate to model these links.

directed to the composite object and not to the component. This allows the composite object to deal with the implications of the event for the object as a whole and allows better information hiding.

Independent components on the other hand are not so unconditionally encapsulatable. While an independent component is leading an independent existence, its identity may be known to other objects, which communicate with it. While it is independent it is not encapsulated. Once the independent component becomes part of an aggregate, communications relating to it should usually be sent to the composite object, in order to allow the composite object to handle the implications of events for the composite object as a whole. More specifically, it is good practice to ensure that all communications which can only occur while the component is in the composite object are sent to the composite object. Thus that part of an independent component's behavior which only applies while it is part of an aggregate should be fully encapsulated, just as the behavior of a dependent component is encapsulated.

The situation is more complicated for operations which the object made available while it was independent. How these should be handled depends on the specific semantics involved.

As one example, after an engine has been assembled into a car, it is unlikely that any other object will still have knowledge of the engine independently of the car in which it is assembled. All subsequent operations can be directed to the composite object which represents the car. This can be regarded as the most desirable case. While the component is part of the car, it is fully encapsulated and receives no messages from objects outside the aggregate.

There are, however, more complicated examples of independent components. Consider the case where different departments or individuals submit order requests. The department responsible for handling purchases gathers the order requests into a purchase order that is sent to the relevant vendor. Once an **Order Request** has been included in the composite object **Purchase Order**, communications relating to it should as a matter of principle be sent to the **Purchase Order**.

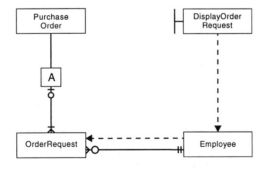

Figure 21-4: Order Requests and Purchase Orders

But we may also have a display to allow the people who submitted order requests to see how their orders are progressing. This display will still be available after the purchase order has been submitted and should show both order requests which have not yet been included in a purchase order and those which have. It is logical for this display to be produced by communicating directly with the relevant order requests. Queries answered by communicating with the object directly before it became part of a composite object will normally still be answered like this.

Similarly, update requests may be sent to the component object, either before or after it becomes part of a composite object. In this case, once a component object is part of a composite object, update requests received by the component object from outside the composite object should normally be forwarded to the composite object to allow it to deal with any implications of the event for the object as a whole. The composite object may or may not allow the update. It may also not allow a component object to be deleted while it is part of the composite object.

Thus the correct functioning particularly of update operations in objects which may be independent for part of their life cycle and then become part of a composite object should be carefully considered. The use of object life cycle diagrams to clarify the life cycles of such objects is to be recommended. If messages can be sent directly to an aggregate component by objects outside the aggregate, the composite object should normally be informed so that it can deal with any ramifications of changes for the composite object as a whole.

Chapter 22

Operations

How well functionality is distributed between the operations of different object classes is one of the most crucial issues for a good object-oriented design.

Why is the distribution of functionality between operations so important? It goes back to the basic arguments in favor of object orientation. Object-oriented systems are more likely to be correct and robust in abnormal conditions, are easier to change, and are more likely to support reuse.[1]

Object-oriented software can achieve these benefits because it encapsulates data and function in objects. But if you fail to package data and function together in the right object classes, then you fail to achieve the localization of change and the ability to substitute one object for another which are required in order to achieve robustness, maintainability and reusability.

Because a good distribution of functionality between operations is so important for a good object-oriented design, we include guidelines on this topic which we hope will give some tools for thinking about the issues involved. Hard and fast guidelines are not easy to give, because there is currently little objective evidence about what constitutes a good object-oriented design.

Difficulties in Allocating Operations

Why is it difficult to allocate operations appropriately? The answer is quite simply that associating operations and data together in objects is an artificial thing to do. Objects are not naturally associated with operations in the real world, or, to the extent that they are, the rationale which allocates an operation to an object is not the same as the rationale we need for allocating an operation to an object in a computer system.

It is easy to get carried away by analogies between objects in the real world and objects in a computer system. However, software isn't the real world. This becomes immediately apparent if we try to model the real world in terms of objects and then try to allocate operations to these objects. For instance, suppose we take the sun as one object and try to model birds who start singing when the sun rises. How should we model this? Which object sends the sun a message telling the sun to rise? Does the sun send a message to each bird individually telling them it has risen? The sun rising on its own is only one factor in determining when a bird starts singing. What additional factor causes them to sing? We can model this situation using messages and we can think of ways of allocating responsibilities for sending the relevant messages, such that we produce a good object-oriented design, but it is obvious that what we are doing is something artificial. The sun doesn't actively send messages, and it certainly doesn't have to worry about

---

[1] Bertrand Meyer, *Object-Oriented Software Construction*. (Englewood Cliffs, NJ: Prentice Hall 1988)

whether messages have to be sent individually to each recipient or can be broadcast. Software, unlike the real world, operates under the constraints of instruction sequencing on a von Neumann architecture. Software has to be maintainable and this influences how we design it. And objects which we regard as passive in the real world (e.g., **Order**) can have active responsibilities in a software system.[1]

This is why we need some conceptual framework when thinking about how to allocate operations to objects. We seek to discuss some of the issues involved in this chapter.

Localizing Change

When searching for criteria to assist in distributing functionality between operations, various goals can be suggested - we want to achieve reusability, extendibility, robustness, maintainability. Which of these goals provides the best guidance? When considering how object-oriented software achieves its key benefits (ignoring inheritance for the moment), we would argue that it achieves these benefits principally through encapsulation. We would also argue that if we want to achieve encapsulation, then, pragmatically speaking, maintainability provides the best target to pursue. If you think about maintainability, imagine changes which might be made, and design such that if these changes were to occur, they would be localized as far as possible. This kind of thinking will help improve the level of encapsulation. Once this has been achieved, then we expect other benefits such as reusability, extendibility and a level of robustness to follow.

Roles and Responsibilities

The idea of associating responsibilities with object classes is described in Wirfs-Brock. This forms part of a responsibility-driven design approach, which is based on the use of class, responsibility and collaboration (CRC) cards.[2] This approach is valuable in terms of teaching object think.

The first principle of this approach is that each object class should have a single clearly defined and coherent role or function. In support of its role, the object undertakes certain responsibilities. It assumes responsibility for items of behavior which it is logical for other objects to expect from the object, given its role.

---

[1]   We have taken the example of the sun and the argument with respect to the real world from Steve Cook and John Daniels, "Designing Object Systems: Software isn't the real world", *Journal of Object-oriented Programming*, May 1994.

[2]   CRC cards are attributed originally to Beck and Cunningham. See K. Beck and W. Cunningham, "A laboratory for teaching object-oriented thinking", *OOPSLA '89 ACM Conference on Object-Oriented Programming Systems, Languages and Applications* (ed. N. Meyrowitz). (Reading, MA: Addison-Wesley, 1989).

You can use role-playing as a lighthearted way of assigning responsibilities to object classes. Each member of a team plays the role of an object and considers what he or she is responsible for. As you work through a scenario, which can be based on a transaction sequence, the people playing individual object classes accept responsibility for items of work that fall in with their view of their role and reject items of work they feel they aren't responsible for. Playing this sort of role game assists in grasping the basic principles of object-oriented design - that each object class has a role, accepts tasks which fit in with its role, and wants as little knowledge of any other extraneous information as possible. Each object class seeks to mind its own business.

The most important way of identifying responsibilities is by analyzing system requirements, which we have represented in transaction sequences. Drawing object interaction diagrams is a good tool for doing this, which we have described in Chapters 6 and 14.

It is useful to use the Bertrand Meyer shopping list approach in addition to this, as a checking mechanism. It provides a way of considering what else the object class might be responsible for and also how easily likely changes can be accommodated.

In the shopping list approach, the analyst identifies operations by considering each object class in turn and considering in general terms: "What is this object responsible for? What might I want to do with this data?" This is a bottom-up approach whereas the analysis of what specific functionality is required in a system (as is done, for instance, in the analysis of transaction sequences) can be seen as a top-down approach.

The benefit of the shopping list approach is that it assists in generalizing operations and object classes such that the system will be more flexible in the face of change. It takes into account the possibility of further uses for object classes which are not currently planned.

Obviously some common sense is needed. Energy should be spent on ensuring that the system's requirements can be fulfilled rather than on writing operations to provide functionality that is never likely to be required. Nevertheless, it is useful to use the shopping list approach as well as an analysis of current requirements, as a way of checking how widely applicable the object class is and how easily it could be changed to accommodate other functionality that could be required of it.

Allocating Responsibilities to Object Classes

So how do you decide which object class should be responsible for a particular item of behavior? Here are some guidelines:

- It is better to distribute intelligence evenly between the object classes so that each object class knows about relatively few things, making it relatively easy to modify.

- The behavior should fit in with the definition of the object classes role.

- Behavior should be kept in the same place as information it uses.

- Keep information about one thing in one place, rather than spreading it across object classes.

- Object classes should avoid requiring knowledge of the ways other objects behave. It is enough to know that objects of a given type can be printed or displayed. It is undesirable to know anything about how they do this.

- Allocate behavior such that the effect of changes will be localized.

In many cases it is clear that one object class is logically responsible for a particular item of behavior which is required for a transaction sequence, and in this case there is no problem assigning the operation to that object class. Where it is not clear that a responsibility belongs to a single object class, this can be dealt with in a number of different ways:

- Maybe an object class is missing that would be the logical home for the operation.

- It may be that trying out the alternatives - considering the consequences if one object class is responsible for the operation and then considering the consequences if the other is - will make it clearer which alternative is better.

- It may be that the responsibility should be distributed between more than one object class. Consider, though, what the effect of this would be. If the result would be that little pieces of what is really a single coherent function are spread between object classes, this may have a bad impact on maintainability, as any change to the function will tend to affect all the separate object classes. If this is the case then you have probably identified a requirement for a control object. (See our next point.)

- It may be that the responsibility should be allocated to a control object. (We mention this separately, because introducing a control object can feel more like inventing an object than identifying one that is missing from the design.)

As a concrete example of the problems involved in deciding which object class to allocate a responsibility to, consider an elevator system with multiple elevators. When a would-be passenger calls for an elevator, should the individual elevators decide whether to respond to the call or would it be better to have a controller decide which elevator to send? As with all design decisions, there is not necessarily a single correct answer. Both alternative strategies may well have been used in the architecture of different elevator systems. Sometimes, only time and experience bring the best solution to light.

Control Objects

Like Jacobson, we divide object classes into three types, *entity*, *interface* and *control*, because we feel that the explicit identification of these three types of object helps with an understanding of object-oriented design.

One of the initial problems when learning object think is that there is a tendency to think or design as if there will only be entity objects in a system - only objects relating to real-world things. This is understandable because these are the easiest objects to identify. However, it tends to lead to object-oriented designs which are difficult to maintain.

Recognizing the existence of control objects as a type can assist with the recognition that there are other types of objects in an object-oriented system. They are there not because they are identifiable in the real world as what we normally think of as objects but because they function in the encapsulated way we wish objects to function in an object-oriented system.[1]

Often, control objects are used to contain transaction logic, e.g., logic relating to a group of updates which should either occur as a whole or not at all. Thus an end of transaction statement is often (but not necessarily) to be found in a control object.

As stated above, the key to identifying control objects is that a requirement for one arises when it is not clear which object class should be responsible for a function and the results of spreading the behavior between a number of object classes would be that, when changes are made, they are likely to affect more than one of the object classes in question.

Use of control objects should, however, be the exception rather than the rule. They should of course never be used to separate data into entity objects and processing into control objects. Associated data and behavior should always be together in a single object class.

Control Strategies

Using object interaction diagrams to draft a design makes it possible to identify how control is passed between objects for a transaction sequence and to consider whether the control strategy used is appropriate. The best control strategy for a given case is the one which will localize subsequent change better.

Control strategies which are possible include:

- centralized control where one object controls the flow and operates on other objects.
- decentralized control where decisions are delegated to those objects which are expected to have the necessary context to make these decisions.

Decentralized control, distributing control evenly, is more in the spirit of an object-oriented development approach, in which objects are conceived of as independent agents, capable of taking responsibility and playing an active role, rather than acting only as passive performers of requests which are sent them.

Centralized control can, however, be better if the sequence of operations may change or new operations may be inserted. In this case, there will often be no very strong semantic connection between the operations in the sequence of operations. Often, such sequences relate to the control logic for a transaction, and can be allocated to a control object.

---

[1] Wayne Haythorn has an interesting discussion of the difficulty of recognizing the less obvious objects, particularly events, in the article "What is object-oriented design?", *Journal of Object-Oriented Programming,* March-April 1994.

Decentralized control may be appropriate in order to isolate the original caller from details of a decision. Consider Jacobson's example where pallets are moved around a warehouse. The move is controlled by a transporter object, which must determine whether a pallet can be moved or not. There may be various conditions determining whether a pallet may be moved or not, e.g., the stability of the load on the pallet or what the contents of the pallet are. It is better to make the pallet responsible for determining whether it can be moved than to include in the transporter the responsibility for knowing all the rules governing whether the pallet can be moved or not.

You can see from an object interaction diagram how centralized or decentralized your design is. If all operations are invoked by a single operation, and do not tend to pass control on, then you have a very centralized design and it is worth considering whether it could be improved.

Minimizing Dependencies between Object Classes

Another way of looking at the same issue of control strategy is described in the Law of Demeter, formulated by Lieberherr[1] which suggests rules as to which object classes an object class should communicate with.

It is a general objective that dependencies between object classes should be minimized as far as possible. The fewer dependencies an object class has on other object classes, the less likely it is to be affected by changes and the more likely it is to be reusable.

In Sakkinen's[2] formulation, the Law of Demeter states that, to ensure encapsulation and thus reusability of operations (or methods) "the methods of a class should not depend in any way on the structure of any class, except the immediate (top-level) structure of their own class. Further, each method should send messages to objects belonging to a very limited set of classes only."

In particular, a message sent to an object class should avoid incorporating knowledge of the structure of any further object classes with which the receiving object class may communicate in order to accomplish its task.

As an example, when searching an archive, you should avoid sending messages to the **Archive** object which explicitly specify a given archiving method (e.g., microfiche or CD-ROM). If an object class incorporates knowledge of the structure of object classes with which it does not communicate directly, then, if the structure of one of these object classes is changed, the change will affect not only object classes which communicate directly with the object class but also those object classes which communicate indirectly, multiplying the effects of the change.

---

[1] K.J. Lieberherr, I.M. Holland "Assuring Good Style in Object-Oriented Programs", *IEEE Software*, September 1989, pp. 38-48

[2] M. Sakkinen, "Comments on the Law of Demeter and C++", *SIGPLAN Notices*, **23**(12), 38, 1988.

We give the specific details of the Law of Demeter in Chapter 24. Note that the law is to be regarded as a suggestion, rather than a hard and fast rule. Note also that operations should not normally be used simply to pass control on to another object. An operation should have some functional content. This requirement has to be balanced with the requirements of the Law of Demeter which can tend to produce operations which simply act as mediators between two object classes which should not communicate with one another.

Generalizing Operations

We have already mentioned the use of the shopping list approach as a way of generalizing operations. We generalize operations in order to make them more reusable and maintainable and in order to avoid introducing unnecessary redundancy into our design.

When you identify operations, or after drafting a first possible design, opportunities for generalizing or rationalizing operations should be considered. As far as possible:

- Operations should be as widely applicable as possible.

- Operations in different object classes which perform the same function should have the same name, should operate as similarly as possible and should have as similar a signature as possible.

- Operations which have different functions should be orthogonal to each other, i.e., their functionality should not overlap.

- In an inheritance hierarchy, an operation used by all subclasses should be defined in the superclass, to ensure that subclasses use a common definition of the operation.

- As a general rule, operations with few parameters are more likely to be reusable.

Inheritance of Operations

Operations can be defined in abstract superclasses as abstract, template or concrete. In subclasses, operations can be redefined, subject to various restrictions, and method implementations can be added. These basic aspects of operation inheritance and redefinition are described in Chapter 14 and are not repeated here. In this chapter, we discuss in more detail the thinking behind the restrictions on how operations can be redefined.

As mentioned in the chapter on inheritance, if we wish to design a maintainable system, wherever an object class is used, either as the receiver of a message or as a parameter in an operation, its subclasses should be substitutable.

This is important because a user of a given object class should be able to invoke an operation on objects of that object class without needing to know that some of the objects belong to one subclass and some to another. To achieve this, any changes to an inherited operation in a subclass should be restricted to changes which will not result in a requirement for a user of the operation to distinguish between subclasses.

This means that, when an operation is redefined, the meaning and purpose of the operation must stay the same. Furthermore, the types and domains of the input and output arguments of a redefined inherited operation must be compatible with those of the original operation definition.

When considering how the arguments of an inherited operation may differ from those in its original definition, it is useful to think of the original operation as constituting a contract in which the supplier of the operation agrees to provide the user with a given service. If the supplier of the operation completely subcontracts the work to a subclass, then the subclass must provide the service promised by the original supplier.

This is similar to the situation where a builder contracts to supply a house. If the builder completely subcontracts the work, then the customer will not be satisfied with the result unless the subcontractor supplies at least what the original builder promised. (If the subcontractor supplies more than was originally promised, the customer may not mind - apart from being somewhat surprised!)

Applying this analogy to an operation, the original operation offers to provide a given service such that, provided the user supplies input arguments within a given range, the operation will produce output values which lie within a given range. The inherited operation must at least meet this original requirement. That is, it must be capable of handling at least all the possible input values for which the original operation offered a service, and must guarantee not to produce output values lying outside the range produced by the original operation, as users of the service may be relying on this. Thus the domain of input arguments must be at least as great as that of the original operation while the domain of output arguments may not be greater than that of the original operation, but can be more restricted.

Theoretically, the domain of input arguments could be extended - the subcontractor could offer to do more than the prime contractor. So far as system development is concerned, however, such an extension has little practical use and it is enough for all practical purposes to say that the domain of input arguments must remain the same in an inherited operation.

An understanding of substitutability is particularly important in cases where an operation is defined in general terms in a superclass, perhaps as an abstract operation, and is then redefined in subclasses. It is then important to be careful that the redefinitions of the operation are such that the subclass will still be substitutable for the superclass.

Chapter 23

Design Patterns

In this chapter we provide a detailed description of the design patterns referred to in Chapter 15. These patterns are:

- the *Model-View-Controller* pattern,
- the *Persistent Object* pattern for an RDBMS, and
- the *State Machine* pattern.

Recently, design patterns have received increased attention in the software reuse area. For more detailed accounts of the topic see the books by Coad et al[1], Gamma et al[2] and Pree[3].

Design patterns are more useful than simple design guidelines because they provide an example of a solution to a given problem. Our intention is to convey some of the key ideas rather than to give instructions which should be followed literally.

Each pattern is explained with the help of an example from the Seminar Registration System, together with an object structure diagram (showing the required abstract and concrete classes) and an object interaction diagram. We also include a "how-to-apply" checklist at the end of each pattern description.

We repeat for convenience the notation we introduced in the section "Choosing types and data structures" in Chapter 15, which facilitates the usage of object structure diagrams for the representation of the *physical* object structure model.

Notation: The data type of each attribute is shown using the notation **attribute-name : type**. Each operation is represented with its signature (i.e., showing data types for each argument and for the return value of the operation): **operation-name (arg1:type1, ... , argN:typeN) : return-value-type**.
Class attributes and operations are shown in *italics*. Abstract operations are marked with the keyword {abstract} in braces.
An attribute (or operation argument) which holds a pointer to an object of a related object class is denoted by **attribute-name : related-class-name**, i.e., the type of the attribute is the related object class. Depending on cardinalities and other constraints, such as ordering, the attribute can

---

[1] Coad P., North D., Mayfield M., *Object Models: Strategies, Patterns, and Applications* (Englewood Cliffs, NJ: Prentice-Hall, 1995).

[2] Gamma E., Helm R., Johnson R., Vlissides J., *Design Patterns: Elements of Reusable Object-Oriented Software* (Addison-Wesley, 1995).

[3] Pree W., *Design Patterns for Object-Oriented Software Development* (Addison Wesley, 1995).

also be denoted by **attribute-name : Set[related-class-name], attribute-name : List[related-class-name]**, etc. An arrow from the pointer attribute shows the related object class.

The Model-View-Controller Pattern (MVC)

The Model-View-Controller pattern is used for details the design of interactions between objects belonging to the problem domain and human interaction components. Chapter 15 describes the advantages of using MVC in the section Human Interaction Component - Adding detailed object interactions.

A detailed description of the pattern in terms of interface and entity objects follows.

Description of the pattern

The main idea of MVC is to separate object classes belonging to the problem domain from object classes intended to display information and/or to manage the interaction with the user (interface classes). An interface object requires direct knowledge of the entity object(s) it represents. On the other hand, an entity object can be represented by many interface objects of which it does not need direct knowledge and, indeed, should not have such knowledge.

Object interactions of the pattern

A change of state in an entity object results from its receiving a message from the same or another object (e.g., a currently active interface object, another entity object, a control object, etc.). To reflect this change in all related interface objects, MVC uses a broadcasting change mechanism.

This mechanism is based on each entity object having a list of dependents in which all related interface objects are registered. Normally, when an interface object is created (e.g., when the window is opened) it immediately registers itself as a dependent of each associated entity object. On a change of state in an entity object, a message (which can have parameters) is sent to all dependents to notify them of the change. This allows the related interface objects to react in an appropriate manner, such as accessing the entity object to retrieve its new state and updating their display accordingly.

The following object interaction diagram illustrates the broadcasting change mechanism. Note that the diagram shows instances (objects) rather than object classes. As an example, we use an entity object of the class **ExternalSeminar** and a related dependent interface object of the class **ExternalSeminarDialog**. Two more dependent interface objects are involved. Suppose that the user has triggered a "topic-changed" event (where topic is an attribute of **ExternalSeminar**).

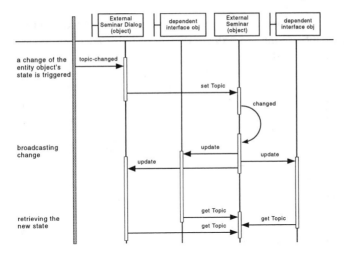

Figure 23-1: Example of Model-View-Controller pattern (object interactions)

The object classes of the pattern

The pattern is implementeded by providing the following classes: class attributes and operations are shown in *italics*, abstract operations are marked by the keyword {abstract} in braces.

- **Model**: Abstract class from which all entity objects inherit the "broadcasting change" mechanism and the ability to have "dependents".

  - Attributes:
      dependents : List[View]

  - Operations:
      changed ()
      register (v:View)
      de-register (v:View)

- **View**: Abstract class from which all interface objects inherit the generic behavior of view/controller pairs.[1]

  - Attributes:
      model : Model

  - Operations:
      update ()   {abstract}

---

[1] Views are often composed of more than one part with one application view containing multiple subviews (composite view). Moreover, various concrete subclasses of **View** implement more specific types of view/controller behavior providing the pieces where user interfaces can be plugged together. Many concrete **View** subclasses can be parameterized. Rather than building new subclasses for each new view, the application developer creates an instance of an existing object class (pluggable view) with appropriate parameters. Most view behavior is provided within a GUI class library or can be generated by a GUI builder.

The following object structure diagram shows the object classes of the pattern. Our example object classes **ExternalSeminar** and **ExternalSeminarDialog** are also shown (grayed). Class attributes and operations are shown in *italics*.

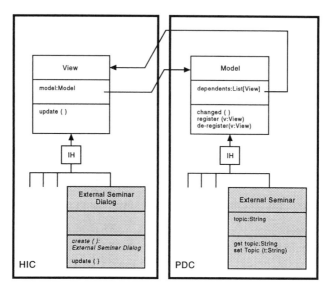

Figure 23-2: Model-View-Controller pattern (abstract classes)

Model defines a protocol such that subclasses can contain a list of dependents. The class defines the operations "register" and "de-register" which are in charge of adding and removing dependent interface objects from the list, and "changed" for broadcasting change (it sends an "update" message to each member of the dependents list).

View can be made a subclass of some existing class in the available GUI class library. It should include a protocol for the operation "update" which is in charge of retrieving the new entity object's state and displaying it (to be implemented in each concrete subclass of **View**).

How to apply the pattern

If the development environment does not directly support MVC, follow steps 1 to 3. Otherwise, only steps 2 and 3 are required:

1. Make the framework available for use. Implement the abstract classes **Model** and **View**.

2. Make each PDC entity class a subclass of **Model**. Be sure to initiate broadcasting change within each operation that changes the entity object's state by sending the "changed" message to the current object (i.e., to self - the object for which the operation was invoked).

3. Make each HIC interface class a subclass of **View**. Remember that the operation in charge of initializing the interface object after creation (e.g., "openDialog") must register the object in dependent lists by sending "register" messages to all related entity objects (a reference to the current object is passed as an argument). Similarly, "de-register" messages must be sent to related entity objects before an interface object is deleted (e.g., "closeDialog"). You may of course need to register/deregister during the life of the interface object, at the point at which a given entity object becomes relevant or irrelevant. Finally, an update operation must be implemented individually for each interface class.

The Persistent Object Pattern for an RDBMS

The main activities for the design and construction of the DMC of a system (using an RDBMS) are outlined in Chapter 15.

In the following, we describe a basic pattern for storing and retrieving objects in an RDBMS. The main ideas are taken from Jacobson. We assume that the design will be implemented using an OOPL which provides RDBMS interfacing facilities, e.g., support for embedded SQL.

There are a number of approaches of different levels of complexity for such a pattern. It is not within the scope of this book to discuss the most complex of them nor to go into all the details. The intention is to convey an understanding of the main ideas for such a pattern. For our purposes we establish the following premises:

- We use a system wide unique *object ID* for persistent objects.

- We deal with two states of a persistent object: one in "volatile" memory, the *volatile state*, and one stored in the database, the *database state*. The volatile state of a persistent object is defined in its PDC class (e.g., the object class **ExternalSeminar**), while its database state is described by the corresponding tables of the relational model (e.g., the table EXTERNAL-SEMINAR). The correspondence between both states is established through the unique object ID. In general, only a few of the persistent objects stored in the database will exist in volatile memory at any point in time. A maximum of one copy of a volatile state for a persistent object is allowed for each user/session of the application.

- Volatile states can survive database transaction limits. However, at the end of a transaction (commit or abort) we do not allow a persistent object to exist in volatile memory without having a stored state in the database. When a transaction commits, volatile and database states are consistent and a new transaction begins.

- We deal only with queries which return objects, e.g., all seminars on a specific topic (in contrast to queries returning values, e.g., all the distinct values occurring in the "topic" column of the EXTERNAL-SEMINAR database table, or database views which join data from more than one object). Retrieved objects are *instantiated.*[1]

---

[1] If the resulting set of retrieved objects is large, instantiation of all objects in the set will not be possible. So-called *database lists*, which are not explained in greater detail here, can be useful in such cases.

- Database queries only take into account stored database states, not uncommitted changes to the volatile state.

- We do not assume any particular concurrency control model.

Description of the pattern

For each concrete persistent PDC class the pattern requires an associated so-called *database class* which knows the conversion rules for converting persistent objects to the relational model and which contains the actual database access operations, e.g., embedded SQL. For example, the persistent class **ExternalSeminar** has an associated class **DatabaseExternalSeminar**:

- which knows how to transform a seminar object's volatile state into the corresponding database state (and vice-versa), and

- which contains operations for accessing the EXTERNAL-SEMINAR database table.

All the database classes together form the database access layer of the application. At runtime, only one instance of each database class, the *database object*, will exist in volatile memory.

A special object, the so-called *object manager*, is in charge of managing persistent objects currently existing in volatile memory (it is the unique instance of the object class **ObjectManager** described below). The *object manager* is responsible for:

- translating object IDs into pointers,

- initiating the retrieval of persistent objects from the database that are needed in volatile memory (e.g., to receive a message from some other object), and

- handling backup/recovery in situations where a transaction sequence involves the updating of multiple objects, all of which have to be successful at updating the database before a final "commit" can be considered successful.

The *database objects* and the *object manager* could be created and initialized, for instance, when the application is initiated. Figure 23-3 is an example of objects involved in the pattern.

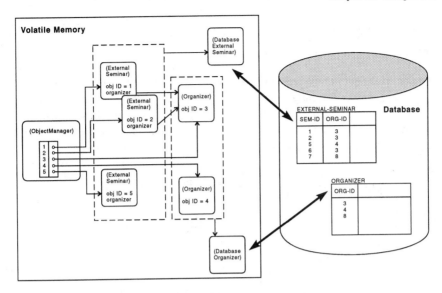

Figure 23-3: Example of persistent objects, database objects and object manager

Object relationships and weak pointers

In some cases related objects, such as an aggregate and its components, are always stored or retrieved as a unit, i.e., within one database transaction. More generally, however, there is a problem with respect to object relationships. When a persistent object which references other persistent objects is retrieved from the database, do all referenced objects need to be retrieved as well in order to avoid dangling pointers? This, of course, presents a problem when the number of objects to be retrieved becomes too large.

One possible solution to this problem is to use *weak pointers* instead of direct pointers in the object model (only, of course, for relationships between persistent classes). A weak pointer does not point directly to another object but instead contains the other object's unique object ID. To traverse the relationship, the corresponding accessor operations request the actual reference to the object from the object manager which either knows the actual pointer, or in fact initiates the retrieval of the required object.

For example, consider the relationship "offered by" between **ExternalSeminar** and **Organizer**. Using weak pointers, the attribute "organizer" of a seminar object contains the unique object ID of the related organizer object instead of a direct pointer to it. The accessor operations "getOrganizer" and "setOrganizer" use the *object manager* to convert weak into direct pointers. If the required organizer object is not yet in volatile memory, the object manager will initiate its retrieval from the database.

The object classes of the pattern

The pattern is based on the following object classes.

- **ObjectManager**: The unique instance of this class, the *object manager*, manages all persistent objects currently existing in volatile memory. It translates weak into direct pointers, initiates the retrieval of persistent objects from the database which are needed in volatile memory, and handles backup/recovery in situations where a transaction sequence involves the updating of multiple objects.

    - Attributes:
        objects : List[Structure[oid:OID, obj:PersistentObject]]

    - Operations:
        newObject (obj:PersistentObject) : OID
        getObject (oid:OID, type:Class) : PersistentObject
        storeObject (obj:PersistentObject)
        removeObject (obj:PersistentObject)

- **PersistentObject**: Abstract class from which all persistent PDC objects inherit their unique object ID and the generic behavior of persistent objects (e.g., communication with their corresponding *database objects*).

    - Attributes:
        myDbObject : DatabaseObject
        objectID : OID

    - Operations:
        save ()
        remove ()

- **DatabaseObject**: Abstract class which is a superclass of all concrete database classes. It establishes the protocols for the various database access operations.

    - Operations:
        DbRetrieve (oid:OID) : PersistentObject   {abstract}
        DbInsert (obj:PersistentObject) : OID   {abstract}
        DbUpdate (obj:PersistentObject)   {abstract}
        DbDelete (obj:PersistentObject)   {abstract}

The following object structure diagram shows the object classes of the pattern. The example object class **ExternalSeminar** and its associated database class are shown grayed. Class attributes and operations are shown in *italics*.

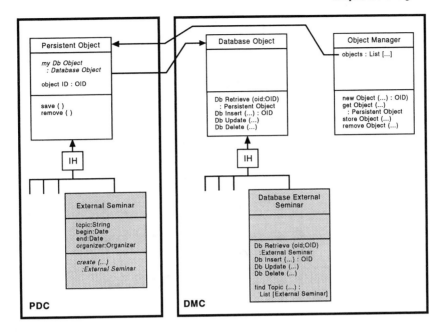

Figure 23-4: Persistent Object pattern for an RDBMS (object classes)

Each persistent object inherits two operations from **PersistentObject**: "save" to store the object's volatile state in the database and "remove" to delete the object both in volatile memory and in the database. In addition, each concrete persistent class requires a class operation *"create"* to initiate the consistent creation of a persistent object with its volatile and database states. For example, it could be defined as follows for the object class **ExternalSeminar**:

```
create (aTopic:String, anOrganizer:Organizer) : ExternalSeminar
```

where the arguments "aTopic" and "anOrganizer" take initialization values for the attributes "topic" and "organizer".

Each database class includes an operation "DbRetrieve" which supports finding an object by its object ID. Additionally, class specific queries can be implemented, e.g., a query which retrieves all seminars on a specific topic from the database:

```
findWithTopic (aTopic:String) : List[ExternalSeminar]
```

Object interactions of the pattern

The following object interaction diagram shows a number of possible scenarios for how persistent objects can be stored in and retrieved from the RDBMS. We use our example object class **ExternalSeminar** and its associated **DatabaseExternalSeminar** with both shown grayed. Class operations are shown in *italics*.

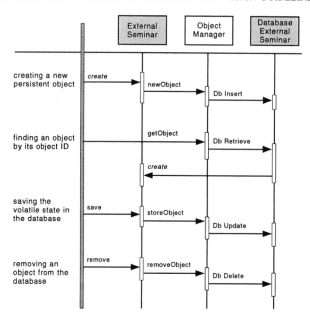

Figure 23-5: Persistent Object pattern for an RDBMS (object interactions)

Creating a new persistent object: The class operation *"create"* creates a new volatile object (initialized appropriately) and sends the "newObject" message to the object manager passing a reference to the new instance as an argument. The object manager now uses the "DbInsert" database access operation of the associated database object to create the persistent object in the database (database state). The database object is also responsible for generating a new object ID for the new object and for structure conversion of the volatile object into the database state. If the database transaction commits, the object manager registers the new object in its internal list and the operation *"create"* returns a reference to the new instance. Otherwise, if the transaction aborts, the new volatile object must be destroyed.

Finding an object by its object ID: A commonly required service provided by the object manager is to return a persistent object of which the unique object ID is known. The "getObject" operation takes an object ID and a reference to an object class as arguments. If the object ID is in the internal list, the object manager directly returns a reference to the object. Otherwise, it uses the "DbRetrieve" database access operation of the associated database object to retrieve the database state. The object manager can now create the corresponding volatile object and register this in the internal list. Finally, a reference to the object is returned.

Saving the volatile state in the database: When a persistent object currently existing in volatile memory receives the "save" event, it sends a "storeObject" message to the object manager passing a reference to *self* (current object) as an argument. The object manager now uses the "DbUpdate" database access operation of the associated database object to update the database state (= volatile state). The database object is also responsible for structure conversion between the volatile and the database states. These actions can occur together with other updates within a single database transaction, which at the end can either "commit" or "abort".

Removing an object from the database: On receiving a "remove" event, a persistent object currently existing in volatile memory sends a "removeObject" message to the object manager passing a reference to *self* (current object) as an argument. The object manager now uses the "DbDelete" database access operation of the associated database object to delete the associated database state from the database. At the end, if the database transaction commits, the object manager de-registers the persistent object from its internal list and the object can be destroyed in volatile memory.

How to apply the pattern

To use the Persistent Object pattern for an RDBMS in a project, proceed as follows:

1. Make the framework available for use. Implement the object classes **PersistentObject**, **DatabaseObject** and **ObjectManager**, if these object classes are not already available for reuse from previous projects or from a class library.

2. Make each persistent class a subclass of **PersistentObject**. For each, implement a class operation *"create"* which initiates the consistent creation of persistent objects of that class. Consider using *weak pointers* instead of direct pointers for the relationships between persistent objects.

3. For each persistent class, implement the associated database class as a subclass of **DatabaseObject**. This class forms part of the database access layer of the application and implements the access to the corresponding database tables. Implement any required specific queries for the class.

The State Machine Pattern

Alternatives for the implementation of control within a system are discussed in the sections "Choosing a control style for the system" and "Implementation of object life cycle models" in Chapter 15. The advantages of using state machines for the implementation of object life cycle models - the event-driven approach - mainly result from its contribution to system maintainability.

We describe in detail how to implement a state machine as an "object life cycle diagram interpreter". The main ideas are taken from Shlaer and Mellor.

The following diagram shows an object life cycle diagram for an object class **Registration** of the Seminar Registration System. It will serve as an example throughout this section.

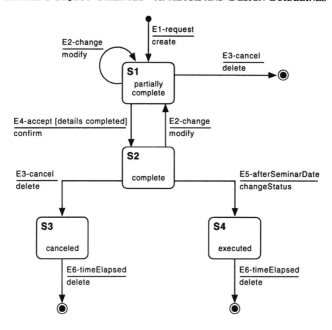

Figure 23-6: Example of object life cycle diagram for object class Registration

Description of the pattern

The main idea is that each object class with a complex behavior pattern described in an object life cycle diagram has an associated so-called *FSM object* (FSM = *finite state model*) that controls all state transitions of all instances of the object class.

For example, the FSM object associated with our **Registration** object class is responsible for processing all events received by any registration object. It embodies a list of the valid transitions as shown in the following table:

old state	event	new state	action
initial	E1	S1	create
S1	E2	S1	modify
S1	E3	final	delete
S1	E4	S2	confirm
S2	E2	S1	modify
S2	E3	S3	cancel
S2	E5	S4	changeStatus
S3	E6	final	delete
S4	E6	final	delete

Table 23-1: Example: valid state transitions for registration objects

The object classes of the pattern

The pattern is based on the following object classes:

- **FiniteStateModel**: Concrete class which serves to tie together all transitions belonging to a single object life cycle diagram. There is exactly one instance of this object class, the FSM object, for each object life cycle model.

  - Attributes:
    transitions: List[Transition]

  - Operations:
    create () : FiniteStateModel
    traverse (obj:ActiveObject, cur:State, ev:Event)
    addTransition (old:State, ev:Event, new:State, ac:Action)

- **Transition**: Concrete class that encapsulates the data describing each individual transition in all the state models of the system. For example, the rows of Table 23-1 represent instances of this object class.

  - Attributes:
    oldState : State
    event : Event
    newState : State
    action : Action

  - Operations:
    create (old:State, ev:Event, new:State, ac:Action) : Transition
    match (old:State, ev:Event) : Structure[new:State, ac:Action]

- **ActiveObject**: Abstract class from which each object with an object life cycle model inherits the ability to communicate with its corresponding FSM object in order to perform the appropriate state transition on each possible event.

  - Attributes:
    myFSM : FiniteStateModel
    transitions : String
    currentState : State

  - Operations:
    loadFSM ()
    doEvent (ev:Event)

The following object structure diagram shows the object classes of the State Machine pattern. Our example object class **Registration** is also shown (grayed). Class attributes and operations are shown in italics.

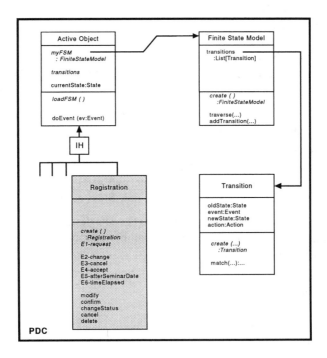

Figure 23-7: State Machine pattern (object classes)

Each object class with an object life cycle model is a subclass of **ActiveObject**. The class attribute *"transitions"* holds the class-specific object life cycle information which enables the class operation *"loadFSM"* to create and initialize an associated FSM object (i.e., an instance of **FiniteStateModel**). A class attribute *"myFSM"* points to that instance.

An object class with an object life cycle model contains a public event-taker operation for each event and a private action operation for each action of the life cycle model. We have chosen to use the event names for the event-taker and the action names for the action operations but, of course, each project can define its own naming conventions. Action operations implement the actual behavior of the object class while event-taker operations check guard conditions and then invoke the "doEvent" operation passing the current event name as an argument. Event-taker operations could potentially be generated. For example, the object life cycle diagram of our object class **Registration** specifies an event "E2-change" and an action "modify". So, our object class will contain a public operation "E2-change" and a private operation "modify".

One could ask why we have a separate event-taker operation for each event. Another solution is to have only one operation "takeEvent (ev:Event)". The solution proposed by our pattern helps to hide implementation details from clients of the object class. It is not usually desirable that clients should be aware whether the state machine pattern is being used or not.

In the example, the operations for the event "E1-request" and action "create" (on initial state) are modeled as class operations because a new registration object has to be created on this event. The operation "delete" performs any necessary cleanup before reaching the final state (where the object is deleted). Also, the operation "E4-accept", according to this pattern, will be responsible for checking the guard condition "details completed" which checks that the essential data for a registration has been provided. If the condition is not satisfied, no state transition is performed. We could have other transitions for this event "E4-accept" occurring while the registration is in state "S1" provided the corresponding guard conditions are mutually exclusive. So, another transition could be defined with a guard condition "details not completed" where the state would remain "S1" and an action "notifyReject" would be performed. Internally, the event "E4-accept" would be split into two events "E4-A" and "E4-B", one for each of the two guard conditions.

Object interactions of the pattern

The following object interaction diagram shows the interactions of the State Machine pattern. Again, we use our example object class **Registration** (grayed). In the upper half the creation and initialization of an FSM object for **Registration** is described. This typically happens when the application is initiated. The lower half explains the interactions required for processing an event (e.g., E2-change). Class operations are shown in *italics*.

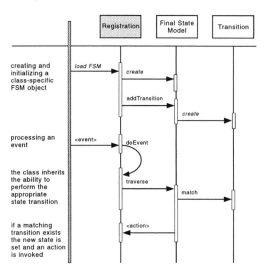

Figure 23-8: State Machine pattern (object interactions)

The "doEvent" operation is invoked by each individual "event-taker" operation and takes the current event as an argument. It invokes the "traverse" operation of the FSM object which takes as its arguments the current object, current state and current event and checks whether a matching transition exists in the internal table. The FSM object then sets the new state and invokes the corresponding action for the current object.

How to apply the pattern

To use the State Machine pattern, perform the following steps:

1. Make the framework available for use. Implement the object classes **ActiveObject**, **FiniteStateModel** and **Transition**, if these are not already available for reuse from previous projects or from a class library.

2. Make each object class with an object life cycle model a subclass of **ActiveObject** and add an event-taker operation for each event and an action operation for each action of the life cycle model.

3. Make the state model-specific information available so that the class operation *"loadFSM"* can initialize the associated FSM object. You can achieve this in more than one way: the information can be stored in a file or it can be defined using constant values in a class attribute.

Chapter 24

Guidelines for a Quality Design

The discussion in the earlier chapters of this book has implied that we will develop only one model of user requirements, and only one model of the logical and physical design of the system. Though we must choose a single model by the time programming begins, there are many possible models that will correctly implement a set of business requirements. But some models are better than others. How can application developers decide which model is the best one?

To some extent, the answer is based on prototyping and iterative development. An initial model may be proposed by the application developer, and diagrammed on a CASE workstation. But if the prototype proves unacceptable to the user, or unwieldy to the developer, it will be changed. Thus, many application developers argue that the best design is the one that works. Period.

But the real measure of goodness may not be apparent for several years after a system has been put into operation. Software lasts forever; many large organizations around the world are now maintaining application systems that are older than the programmers who maintain them! From this perspective, a good design is one that balances a series of tradeoffs in order to minimize the *total cost* of the system over its entire productive life span. Obviously, we want a system that is reasonably efficient, and we want it to be elegant, user-friendly, portable, and so forth. But we also want it to be reasonably easy to test, modify, and maintain. At least half of the total cost of the system—and often as much as 90 percent!—will be incurred *after* the system has been put into operation. It may not be glamorous or politically expedient, but that's where we should be focusing our attention.

How do we help the developer achieve an optimal design? One approach would be to rely more heavily on the idea of application-oriented design patterns, rather than the generic patterns we discussed in Chapter 23. Thus, if an organization eventually discovered (perhaps through trial and error) an ideal software architecture for the kind of systems it builds, it could then announce to its application developers, "Henceforth, *all* designs must look like this one!"

Of course, this presupposes that the organization only builds one kind of system—e.g., it does nothing but build payroll systems or flight control systems. For the organization that builds a wide variety of applications, the hard-nosed "one-size-fits-all" approach obviously won't work. However, a broader version of the "pattern" concept can be quite useful, as we will see later in this chapter. Indeed, much of the advice passed on from OO veterans to neophytes has to do with *bad* patterns: "Don't ever do *this*, because it leads to incredible problems!"

The object-oriented software field is gradually beginning to accumulate a storehouse of knowledge of this kind: guidelines, rules of thumb, warnings, and magic numbers that can be used to evaluate the goodness or badness of a proposed OO model. These guidelines are relatively informal. We have no statistical evidence or scientific experiments to confirm the validity of the various goodness criteria that will be discussed in this chapter.

Ironically, the same criticism was valid for structured analysis and design during the 1970s. It was only with the publication of David Card's book, *Measuring Design Quality,* some 15 years after the first book was published on structured design, that we saw the beginning of a serious, detailed, scientific effort to validate such concepts as coupling, cohesion, span of control, etc. Hopefully it won't take another 15 years for researchers to verify and quantify the goodness criteria for OO principles.

In the meantime, informal guidelines are better than nothing at all. The guidelines presented in this chapter may not be accurate in all cases; indeed, a few of them may eventually be proven wrong. But they reflect the real-world experiences of practicing OO analysts, designers, and programmers around the world And, as we will see, many of the OO guidelines are based on common software engineering principles that *have* been validated within the context of other analysis/design methodologies.

We begin with some general guidelines for object-oriented design and programming. All of these guidelines contribute to enhancing the extensibility, reusability and robustness of the application. Next, we summarize the OOD guidelines proposed by Coad and Yourdon, the design guidelines proposed by Tom Love, and those proposed by Kemerer and Chidamber.

General OO Design/Programming Guidelines

Information hiding

The implementation of the object class should be hidden from clients of the object class so that it can be changed without affecting any client object classes. For this reason, it is important to define all attributes and operations that are not intended for use outside the class as private or protected. This separates the interface (on which other object classes rely) from the implementation of the object class. Note: as to the question of whether *all* attributes should be private, we argue that there are attributes which can simply be accessed and can be treated as public. Where a programming language insists on the use of an operation to access attributes, public attributes identify attributes for which a standard, simple get operation is required.

We find it useful to distinguish, as C++ does, between private, protected, and public attributes/operations:

- A *private* attribute or operation may only be used by operations of the same object class and may not be used by the operations of any subclass.

- A *protected* attribute or operation may be used by operations of the same object class and any of its subclasses.

- A *public* attribute or operation may be used by any operation of any object class.

The difference between private and protected relates to inheritance. A protected attribute or operation is always visible in subclasses while a private one is not. Private attributes are only of interest for the internal implementation of an object class at a single node in the inheritance hierarchy. Public attributes and operations, of course, are always visible in subclasses.

Another aspect of information hiding concerns the extent of visibility of each operation. It contributes to the extensibility of the system if an operation has only limited knowledge of the object model as a whole. The Law of Demeter is useful in relation to this issue.

Controlling coupling with the Law of Demeter

This principle was outlined by Lieberherr and Holland. The law restricts the message sending structure of operations so that each operation can only send messages to a limited set of objects. The law states that an operation **m** of an object class **A** may only send messages to one of the following objects:

- the operation's argument objects (e.g., an object of class **C**),

- the *current* object (i.e., the object for which **m** was invoked) and the operation's object class (i.e., object class **A**),

- any object the current object has immediate knowledge of (e.g., an object of class **B** to which the current object has a pointer),

- any object created directly within the operation, or

- any object accessible via a global variable.

The following diagram illustrates the law. The communication associations allowed are shown using gray arrows.

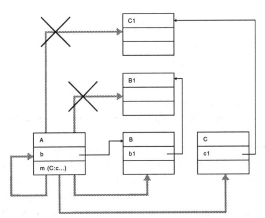

Figure 24-1: Controlling coupling with the Law of Demeter

Compliance with this law has to be checked by the application developer. In its strict form, it cannot usually be checked automatically at compilation time. There is a (so called) class form of the law which attempts to formulate the law in a form in which it could be checked by a compiler. But this version of the law does not express the real principle and we therefore do not discuss it further here.

Applying the Law of Demeter contributes to extensibility by assuring low coupling between object classes, information hiding and localization, and by decreasing operation complexity and nested message sending.

Applying the law can also increase the number of operations and possibly also the number of operation arguments. This can be disadvantageous. So, violations of the law should be allowed in some cases. In particular, direct communication can be allowed where the object class in between is stable. Lieberherr and Holland recommend the documentation of violations of the law by listing the required acquaintance object classes for each operation. This list shows the object classes with which the object class requires acquaintance because of violations of the law.

Factoring out common code

Where a common superclass is available, you can sometimes increase the amount of shared implementation by factoring out common code using either of the mechanisms described below. Object classes **B** and **C** are subclasses of an object class **A**:

- The operations **m1** of subclass **B** and **m2** of subclass **C** share common code by both calling operation **m** of superclass **A** (subroutine call).

- An operation **m** of superclass **A** calls an operation **m1** which is abstract (unimplemented) in object class **A** but has two different implementations in the subclasses **B** and **C** (operation factoring).

Note that minimizing code duplication can have the undesirable effect of increasing the coupling between object classes.

In situations where there is no common superclass, the sharing of implemented code can also be achieved using delegation, discussed below.

Using delegation to avoid "implementation inheritance"

Chapter 20 discusses in detail how to design and adjust inheritance in a well-designed object-oriented system; see also Chapters 13, 14, and 15 for additional discussions.

At the physical design level, especially when reusing code from a class library, it is important to avoid so-called "implementation inheritance". If subtyping is not possible, using delegation is an alternative way to share implementation. Delegation means the following: if an object class **A** needs to use part of the implementation contained in object class **B**, you make **B** a part of **A** (as an attribute or via aggregation) so that **A** can delegate specific service requests to **B**.

For example, suppose you have in your class library an object class **List** and you need to build an object class **Stack**. **List** can handle a variable number of objects (elements) and has operations for arbitrarily adding/removing elements as well as for identifying the first and last elements. **Stack** should have operations for pushing/popping elements. Making **Stack** into a subclass of **List** would have the disadvantage that **Stack** would inherit unwanted operations such as the ability to add/remove elements from arbitrary positions. That is to say, **Stack** would not be substitutable for

List. (See Chapter 20 for an explanation of substitutability.) Instead, **Stack** should be made an aggregate with **List** as a component. Then, the pop/push operations can be implemented by calling the *last* and the *add/remove* operations of its list component.

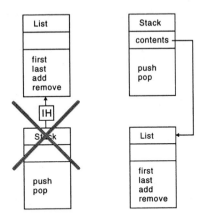

Figure 24-2: Example of using delegation instead of "implementation inheritance"

The Kemerer/Chidamber Guidelines

Next, we mention the guidelines proposed by Chidamber and Kemerer of MIT. It is interesting that the two researchers characterize their guidelines as "metrics":

> *This paper presents theoretical work that builds a suite of metrics for object-oriented design (OOD). In particular, these metrics are based upon measurement theory and are informed by the insights of experienced object-oriented software developers.*[1]

The guidelines or metrics, fall into six categories.

1. *Weighted methods per class, with a weighting factor based on static complexity of the individual methods.* "Objects with large numbers of methods are likely to be more application-specific, limiting the possibility of reuse." In addition, Coad and Yourdon's OOD guidelines note that a bad design often has an excessive number of attributes in the classes. There should be no more than one or two attributes, on average, for each operation, of which 2/3 should be traceable all the way back to the system requirements analysis model. A bad design also tends to have an excessive number of operations in each class. One typically finds no more than 6-7 public operations per class, in addition to whatever private operations are necessary for internal housekeeping, etc.[2] And a bad

---

[1] Shyam R. Chidamber and Chris F. Kemerer, "Toward a Metrics Suite for Object Oriented Design," *OOPSLA '91 Conference Proceedings*, pages 197-211.

[2] Of course, this can vary substantially, depending on the nature of the application.

design tends to have excessive collaboration between objects. While it's understandable that an object may not be able to respond to an external event by itself, it should not be necessary to interact with more than 7±2 other objects to accomplish something.

2. *Depth of inheritance tree.* "The deeper a class is in the hierarchy, the greater the number of methods it is likely to inherit, making it more complex." Coad and Yourdon note that good designs are neither too deep nor too shallow in terms of their class hierarchies. A medium-sized system with approximately 100 classes is likely to have class hierarchies with 7±2 levels of inheritance and aggregation structures. This may be affected by the programming language, by the use of single inheritance versus multiple inheritance, etc.—but it would be unusual (and probably a manifestation of a bad design) to see class hierarchies 20 levels deep, or only two levels deep. Excessive levels of subclasses often occurs with overly zealous first-time OOD practitioners who over-factor their design.

3. *Number of children.* "Generally, it is better to have depth than breadth in the class hierarchy, since it promotes reuse of methods through inheritance. The number of children gives an idea of the potential influence a class has on the design."

4. *Coupling between objects.* "Excessive coupling between objects outside of the inheritance hierarchy is detrimental to modular design and prevents reuse." Coad and Yourdon note that in an OO system, we are primarily concerned with the coupling between classes and objects that are *not* part of an inheritance hierarchy or aggregation. This coupling takes the form of message connections. Of course, the very principle of encapsulation is intended to minimize coupling, but we still look for ways to minimize the number of messages between objects, as well as minimizing the complexity and content of the messages themselves. Coupling is also created by inheritance in class hierarchies, but this is usually evaluated in terms of separate cohesion guidelines.

5. *Response for a class.* "If a large number of methods can be invoked in response to a message, the testing and debugging of an object becomes more complicated."

6. *Lack of cohesion in methods.* "Cohesiveness of methods within a class is desirable, since it promotes encapsulation of objects." Coad and Yourdon note that in OO models, we are concerned about cohesion at three levels: (a) the cohesiveness of individual operations, (b) the cohesiveness of the attributes and operations encapsulated within a class and object, and (c) the cohesiveness of an entire class hierarchy. At the microscopic level, operation cohesion can be evaluated just as it is with structured design. An operation should carry out one, and only one function, and it should be possible to accurately describe its purpose with a simple sentence containing a single verb and a single object. At the intermediate level, it can be evaluated using various guidelines discussed above; and at the class hierarchy level, it can be evaluated by examining the extent to which subclasses override or delete attributes and operations inherited from their superclasses.

Again, it is interesting to note the overlap between these guidelines, the ones proposed by Tom Love, the Coad-Yourdon guidelines, and the general guidelines discussed at the end of this chapter. Coupling and cohesion, for example, are evidently fundamental concepts that OO software engineers should watch carefully in their designs.

But it must be emphasized again that all of these guidelines are still at the proposal stage. Chidamber and Kemerer conclude their list of metrics with the comment:

> *...this set of six proposed metrics is presented as a first attempt at development of formal metrics for OOD. They are unlikely to be comprehensive, and further work could result in additions, changes and possible deletions from this suite. However, at a minimum, this proposal should lay the groundwork for a formal language with which to describe metrics for OOD. In addition, these metrics may also serve as a generalized solution for other researchers to rely on when seeking to develop specialized metrics for particular purposes or customized environments.*

The Coad/Yourdon OOD Guidelines

The Coad/Yourdon OOD guidelines are based on extensive discussions and interviews in 1989-1990 with software engineers throughout North America, Europe, and Australia. Some can be categorized as hard guidelines, with quantitative metrics; others are soft guidelines that must be interpreted by the designer on a case-by-case basis.

In addition to the points already noted in the discussion of Kemerer and Chidamber's research, the Coad/Yourdon guidelines include the following:

- *Focusing on the clarity of the design*—though it must be classified as a soft guideline, software engineers generally agree that if they can't understand someone's logical or physical design model, then they won't reuse it—and if they can't reuse it, it's bad (or, at least, worse than an alternative design that *can* be reused). Specific advice in this area includes using a consistent vocabulary for naming operations and attributes; avoiding excessive numbers of message templates, avoiding fuzzy class definitions; and adhering to existing protocols or behaviors of classes.

- *Keeping message protocols simple*—complex message protocols, as noted above, are a common indication of excessive coupling between classes and objects. If a message requires more than three parameters, it's often an indication of a bad design; the typical problem is that the class hierarchy has been poorly factored. Similarly, the existence of computer-science jargon in the message protocol typically means that the class is doing something other than what is in the problem domain.

- *Keeping operations simple*—with a reasonable high-level language, it should be possible to write the code for each operation in less than a page (which may require one or two screens on a workstation display monitor). With a language like Smalltalk, it is common to see operations implemented with less than 10 lines of code. If the operation involves a lot of code, look at it more closely. If it contains IF-THEN-ELSE statements or CASE

statements, it's a *strong* indication that the operation's class has been poorly factored—
i.e., procedural code is being used to make decisions that should have been made in the
inheritance hierarchy.

- *Minimizing the volatility of the design*—a bad design exhibits considerable volatility all
  during the development phase of the project, as well as during the ongoing maintenance
  efforts. A small change in one class, in order to fix a bug or add a new feature, causes a
  ripple effect throughout many other classes. It may not be clear what the cause of the
  volatility is (though it is usually the result of coupling problems), but it can nevertheless
  be used by the project manager as an unbiased assessment of the quality of the design.
  With a good configuration management system, the manager should be able to track the
  impact analysis associated with a change to an individual class, and it should be possible
  to detect a trendline of ever-increasing stability as the project inches closer to its
  deadline.

- *Minimizing the overall system size*—small is beautiful, big is ugly. A medium-sized
  application should require no more than a few dozen class hierarchies, each of which
  may involve a dozen subclasses. If each of the individual classes has half a dozen
  operations, and if each of those operations involves 10-20 lines of code, the aggregate
  amount of software is pretty substantial.

- *Emphasizing the ability to "evaluate by scenario"*—it should be possible to evaluate a
  design with a role-playing exercise, in which the reviewers act out the behavior of
  individual classes and objects. One reviewer might say to another, "Okay, I'm the XYZ
  object and I'm sending an 'abc' message to you; what are you going to do with it?" If
  this kind of exercise proves impossible to conduct, it may indicate that the
  responsibilities of the various classes have not been well described, or well thought out.

Tom Love's OOD Patterns

In a recent article, consultant Tom Love suggests that Christopher Alexander's principles of
timeless design can be applied specifically to object-oriented systems:

> *As I read three of Alexander's books, it occurred to me that we have an unusual*
> *opportunity in the software industry. As we are making changes in the*
> *development process to accommodate objects, we could simultaneously*
> *introduce some of the ideas of timeless design. At the very least, we could use*
> *this approach to derive some of the patterns of good object-oriented software*
> *design within our respective organizations and agree to adhere to them.*[1]

---

[1] Tom Love, "Timeless Design of Information Systems," *Object Magazine*, November-December, 1991,
page 46. For a more complete discussion of Alexander's concept of patterns and "timeless design," see
Christopher Alexander, *The Timeless Way of Building*, New York: Oxford University Press, 1979.

Love then proposes the following list of 22 patterns of good OO designs. Note: Love uses method in the same manner we have used operation.

1. Objects should not access data defined in their superclasses.

2. Classes should be grouped into defined collections of about twenty classes that have restricted visibility from other classes in the system. All methods should not be made available to all users. (Note: in our methodology, we propose the use of modules for this purpose. See the discussion in Chapter 8 for details.)

3. Classes near the root of an inheritance tree should not depend upon classes further down in the tree.

4. Methods of the same name in different classes should mean the same thing.

5. Methods with different names should mean different things.

6. Methods should do some work, not just pass the buck to another method. Avoid spaghetti code.

7. An inheritance tree should be a generalization/specialization tree with more specialized capabilities near the leaves of the tree. (Note: see also the discussion in Chapter 20, where we suggest that it is not sufficient to use generalization-specialization as the basis for inheritance; subclasses should also be substitutable.)

8. OO code should have a minimum number of branching statements, no more than one branching statement for every five lines of code.

9. Classes should be easy to describe and visualize. It should be possible to draw a picture of each class to convey its purpose or intent.

10. Classes should have minimum coupling with other classes and maximum internal cohesion.

11. A class tester should be written for every class that fully exercises that class and determines if it does what its specification claims.

12. There should only be one set of user interface classes within a single application or system.

13. The ergonomics group or a designated user shall approve all user interfaces including the choice of graphics, font, and color.

14. A focus group of real users should be assembled every four months during any development project. The project manager must explicitly address any usability issues raised in this meeting.

15. The application or system context should be visible to the user at any time. I should know where I am, where I have been, and where I can go.

16. Even large development projects should proceed in a piecemeal or spiral fashion—every six months a major new capability should be provided in the form of a working system. In other words, development should proceed by iterative enhancement with each iteration taking no more than six months.

17. At any given time, there should always be a list of new features and functions, as well as a list of improvements.

18. Methods should set the value of their instance variables by sending a message—to eliminate coupling among inherited classes.

19. Detailed estimates of runtime performance and memory utilizations should be made for each class (or ensemble of classes) at design time and tracked throughout development.

20. Testing of OO systems should strive to remove the most objectionable error first—looked at from the user perspective.

21. A printed design should require no more than 10% of the ink of the complete system.

22. A design should be machine checkable, executable, and analyzable.

Obviously, some of these patterns are not unique for object-oriented projects, and could just as well be used with other methodologies. And others—such as numbers 13, 14, and 16—are not so much concerned with *any* design methodology as they are with larger issues of project management and system development life cycles. It is also interesting to note that many of the specific design-level suggestions are compatible with the guidelines concerning coupling and cohesion that were discussed earlier in this chapter.

Appendix A

Related Approaches to Object-Oriented Development

There are now several dozen published object-oriented methodologies, of which nearly a dozen are fairly widely used and supported by textbooks, training courses, and CASE tools. The reader may well wonder why we have decided to add yet another method to this collection. Appendix A summarizes our reasons.

It should be emphasized that we have not attempted to develop an utterly new approach, unrelated to any existing work in the field. On the contrary, we feel that the methodology described in this book represents a synthesis of the best features of the currently popular methodologies, and hopefully avoids their shortcomings as well.

Key Requirements for an Object-Oriented Development Approach

Our key requirements were straightforward. The fundamental requirement for an object-oriented development approach was that it should work. Ideally it should be a tried and tested approach, using techniques with a track record behind them. It should be a genuinely practical approach which really can be used to develop applications in the real world.

It should be suited to the development of the type of system Software AG's customers develop — mainstream commercial applications that are mission-critical for the organization, involving the use of client-server concepts, graphical user interfaces and distributed software and data.

A further key requirement was that our approach should be acceptable to large-scale commercial users, rather than the research community.

What should an object-oriented development approach include?

When we considered what we thought an object-oriented development approach needed to include — what its scope should be, we arrived at the following requirements.

A complete development approach should include at least the following basic components:

- modeling concepts and techniques,
- diagram types to support these techniques,
- development procedures (worksteps and deliverables),
- quality assurance rules (checks for consistency and completeness), and
- design guidelines.

In addition, it should also fulfill a number of further requirements with respect to coverage.

- The development approach should cover the whole project life-cycle from project planning to application support during the operation phase of the life cycle.

- Moreover, the development approach should be scalable and flexible, so that development phases can be defined in accordance with the needs of individual projects, depending on the size of the project and its individual requirements. The approach to the project life cycle should therefore not be too rigid.

- The question of the type of project life cycle to be used should be addressed. Issues such as the merits of an evolutionary life-cycle and the role of prototyping should be addressed.

- Support for reuse should be considered. Reuse and the component-based building of systems is a primary benefit claimed for an object-oriented development approach, and yet development approaches tend to describe system development in terms of how to develop a new application. This is justifiable to the extent that even a system which reuses many components is a new system. However issues related to reuse must be addressed within the description of the building of a new system, e.g., when to look for candidate components for reuse and how to find them, and how to develop reusable components. The issues of organizing for reuse should be addressed as well as the relevance of good tool support.

- Issues relating to interfaces between systems, object-oriented or not, also need to be addressed as well as implementation issues related to data access and storage.

What are the characteristics of a good object-oriented approach to system development?

In addition to having specific contents, a good object-oriented development approach needs to have certain qualities. The qualities we regard as important are as follows.

- The approach should be simple with as few constructs as possible. This eases use and minimizes memory load on users of the method. In support of this objective:

  - Diagram types should be as familiar as possible, within the object-oriented or the general computing community, and diagramming notations should be as close to already accepted norms as possible.

  - Terminology should be selected first and foremost to ensure clarity. Where possible, the terms should be those most widely accepted within the object-oriented community or those adopted by the Object Management Group. Where there is no clearly accepted term, the terms selected should be those most readily comprehensible to other members of the IT community.

- The approach should be consistent and complete. There is inevitably a trade-off between completeness and simplicity and an effort should be made to avoid over-complexity.

- Relevant standards should be taken into account, particularly those of the OMG.

- One major factor is that the models defined during development should be stable in the face of change, both as the project progresses and during maintenance. The method should minimize the amount of reworking required when changes are made.

- Good traceability from requirements through to implementation is important. Object-orientation offers the possibility of a single development paradigm from analysis through to implementation. This allows an additive development process, in which information is added to the system definition in each development phase, and information from previous phases is carried forward and remains part of the system definition. Since the object-oriented paradigm offers the possibility of an additive development process, with benefits for traceability, a good object-oriented development approach should maintain this benefit and not introduce unnecessary transitions.

General Comments on Popular OO Methodologies

All of the popular methodologies assume the pre-existence of a problem description as the starting point for developing an application. This description is either a written textual document or verbal information provided by the users, etc. From this description, objects are identified and object structure and object behavior models are developed.

Note that this assumption does *not* automatically prescribe a waterfall-oriented or prototyping approach to the development of the system. We discuss that choice, and the various issues associated with it, in Part III of this book. But the popular OO methodologies *do* typically assume that (a) users have some reasonably well-formed opinion of their requirements for the system, and (b) users and application developers jointly agree that it's worth the time and effort to document those requirements and express them in a document of some kind—rather than having a few moments of informal conversation, followed by a period of extemporaneous coding to build a prototype.

Where most methodologies assume the pre-existence of such a statement of requirements, the Jacobson OO methodology introduces an additional step before building a formal object model: it carries out a requirements analysis in a use case model. This is, quite literally, a model of the way(s) in which the user interacts the system, which we believe is a good idea. We believe the modeling of user requirements should be included within an object-oriented development approach and we have therefore adopted the concept of a use case in our methodology, with the definition that it is a sequence of related transactions performed by a user.

Indeed, many OO methodologists have adopted Jacobson's use-case concept in one form or another, though it is not highlighted in most of the current published books on the subject. Rumbaugh, for example, has a similar concept with the notion of scenarios, however, Rumbaugh's scenarios differ from use cases in that they describe specific possible courses of events, whereas use cases describe system usage in a more generic way. Moreover, Rumbaugh's scenarios, and the events mentioned by other OO methodologists, typically don't have a prominent place in the methodology, and are often used only as a means of identifying the required operations. Rumbaugh implies that the experienced analyst can do without scenarios. We (following Jacobson's leadership) have given them a position of importance.

Rumbaugh's object model is an extension of the Entity-Relationship model. This has the advantage for us that it provides a convenient migration path for developers already familiar with E/R modeling. But Rumbaugh's modeling of operations appears unnecessarily complex, with its division of operations into activities and actions seems to us unnecessary.

Jacobson's methodology makes another useful contribution by distinguishing between three different object types: entity objects, interface objects, and control objects. The idea is to identify elements of the user interface early in the development process and place them in interface objects. Entity objects are the application-related objects which contain business logic and business data. Control objects contain functionality that is not naturally tied to any other single object. A control object is typically involved in coordinating or synchronizing the behavior of other (interface and entity) objects.[1]

Our object structure model is a combination of Rumbaugh's and Jacobson's methodology, which also covers the Coad/Yourdon approach. The Martin/Odell methodology is also quite similar, but it includes additional complexity — e.g., the notion of computed object types, reality object types, changeable versus immutable object types, etc. — which we have not adopted.

In our opinion, none of the currently popular OO methods has a thoroughly convincing system-wide behavior diagram. Jacobson's use case diagrams don't have much information content, while Rumbaugh's event-flow diagrams and Coad/Yourdon's service-layer diagrams show all messages passing between objects, and are likely to be unreadable for large systems. Wirfs-Brock has the most promising solution in this area, with diagrams that show subsystems and the contracts between them.

Both Jacobson and Rumbaugh contain similar use-case/scenario-level diagrams and object life cycle diagrams, which we have incorporated in our method. In contrast, the Coad/Yourdon OOA methodology mentions the use of object life history diagrams as a means of discovering necessary operations, but does not emphasize them heavily.

Traditional functional-decomposition concepts, represented by dataflow diagrams (DFDs), are presented in Rumbaugh and Martin/Odell. We don't feel they are appropriate in an OO methodology, since they are likely to tempt the unwary application developer into non-object-thinking. In any case, their relevance is not clear, and we avoided their use in our methodology.

All of the popular methods have some concept of a subsystem. The names and details vary; for example, the Coad/Yourdon methodology refers to subsystems as subjects. There are also differences of opinion as to the number of levels of subsystems that are needed. All of the OO methodologies use the subsystem concept simply as a grouping, or abstraction, mechanism.

---

[1] The Coad/Yourdon approach focuses on the same issue, but not until the design stage of OOD. Rather than identifying different "types" of objects, it encourages the designer to separate interface-related objects, application-related objects, and task-management-related objects into separate "components" of the overall design model. A fourth component is responsible for mapping appropriate objects from the application software to the DBMS (e.g., mapping objects onto relational rows and tables).

Jacobson and Rumbaugh both provide good explanations of the notion of subsystems. Wirfs-Brock adds a useful additional concept with her notion of contracts between subsystems.

None of the popular methods has much to say on the subject of GUI-based or distributed, client-server systems. This is ironic, as these are precisely the kind of environment in which an object technology is most often used.

Strengths and Weaknesses of Some Popular OO Methodologies

A brief summary of the strengths and weaknesses of several popular OO methodologies is provided below.

The Rumbaugh method

The strengths of the Rumbaugh method lie in its use of E-R concepts and in its detailed description of how to map an object-oriented design to both traditional and OO-compatible DBMS packages and programming languages. The Rumbaugh method is similar to Jacobson in the way it analyzes the behavior of a system using scenarios. It provides a link between the system's functional requirements and the identification of operations required to support them; however, this link is given more emphasis and a more convincing treatment in Jacobson.

The weaknesses of the Rumbaugh approach are an overly complicated division of operations into activities and actions (with four different types of actions), and an attempt to relate traditional DFDs to object-oriented analysis and design.

The Jacobson method

Jacobson describes his method as a use case driven approach. Use cases are a very important part of the method: they are used heavily when finding objects, associations and operations. Jacobson claims that systems designed using use cases have a modular structure which is more robust to changes than those developed with "simple" OO techniques.

One negative point is that there appears to be a change of concepts as one moves from the analysis stage to the design stage in the Jacobson approach. The Jacobson analysis model identifies three different object types: entity, interface, and control. But in the design model, these are all converted into blocks.

Jacobson describes the issue of the human interface briefly in the analysis portion of his methodology, but it is not elaborated further in the design model. This is becoming a more and more practical problem in the field today, because application developers typically want to transform an analysis model of the user interface into a design model that will be implemented with a particular "GUI-builder" tool or a commercially-available set of class libraries.

Finally, we note that Jacobson uses state transition diagrams (for modeling the behavior and life cycle of objects) that are quite detailed in nature. These may be necessary for real-time applications, but they are probably too complex for many business applications.

The Martin/Odell method

A major problem with the Martin/Odell method lies in the exposition provided in the descriptive textbook. The overview discussion and detail-level discussion are not always consistent. For example, a process dependency diagram is introduced in the overview discussion, but never discussed further elsewhere in the book. The textbook also discusses a number of optional approaches, but it is not clear which ones must be (or should be, or might be) included in the method. And the explanations of concepts within the method are often tortuous. For example, attributes and associations are first introduced as examples of functions, which many business-oriented application developers are likely to find counter-intuitive.

The Martin/Odell method uses information engineering as its basis, in the same way that Rumbaugh and Coad/Yourdon use structured analysis as their basis. Martin/Odell include E-R analysis, and include more E-R modeling features than Rumbaugh or Coad/Yourdon. For example, the methodology allows N-ary relationships between objects (while Coad/Yourdon only allow binary relationships), as well as relationships between relationships.

Some of the Martin/Odell diagrams are distinctively different from those in other methods. The event schema diagrams, for example, are a distinctive type of state transition diagram on which events and operations are noted. The scope of the diagram is not made explicit, and it seems reasonable to suppose that the diagram may show behavior belonging to more than one object class. The Object Flow diagram, which shows products and activities, is a system-wide diagram, but it is difficult to relate it to an object-level view of the system.

The Coad/Yourdon method

The Coad/Yourdon method, originally published in 1989, is similar to Rumbaugh in its emphasis on E-R modeling. It has the benefit of relative simplicity and clear exposition, with an attractively clear categorization of the components of a design model: the "problem-domain" (application) component, human interaction component, task management component, and data management component. This method is now more properly called the Coad method, as it is not longer being developed by the two authors in collaboration.[1]

Like Rumbaugh, the Coad/Yourdon diagramming scheme can lead to excessively cluttered diagrams, making it very difficult to understand the message interactions between collaborating objects for various use cases. Jacobson, on the other hand, provides an elegantly simple diagram known as a fence or fencepost diagram that clearly illustrates the interaction between objects for the processing of a use case.

---

[1] See, for example, Peter Coad and Jill Nicola's, *Object Oriented Programming* and Edward Yourdon's, *Object-Oriented Systems Design: An Integrated Approach*; and Peter Coad, with David North and Mark Mayfield, *Object Models: Strategies, Patterns, and Applications* (Englewood Cliffs, NJ: Prentice-Hall, 1995).

The Coad/Yourdon method provides no straightforward mechanism to show the link between the system's functional requirements and the operations within various objects. The primary strategy for discovering operations is to analyze the state-transitions in an object life-history diagram (although that diagram is not a formal part of the method, and is not included as part of the permanent documentation of the user requirements). But it is often difficult to identify operations so directly; in addition, it means that the link between each system requirement and the operations that implement it is not documented.

Despite the existence of a separate Coad/Yourdon book on object-oriented design, there is not much detail in the methodology for mapping objects, inheritance hierarchies, and operations to OO and non-OO databases and programming languages. Also, the graphical notation, which is appropriately spare and simple for analysis models in OOA, is also used in the OOD design activity, where it fails to provide mechanisms for documenting a number of detailed implementation issues (e.g., for distinguishing between public and private methods).

The Booch method

Grady Booch is reported to regret today that his method was originally named an "object-oriented *design*" approach, because it also includes a number of typical analysis activities, such as discovering and modeling classes. Booch emphasizes two different views of a system; the first is a logical view, with class and object diagrams which describe the static semantics of the application, and state transition and timing diagrams which describe the dynamic semantics. The second view provided by Booch is a physical one, with module and process diagrams which describe the design and implementation of the system.

Mapping the logical view to the physical design is a strength of Booch's method, and one reason it is so popular with programmers and designers. Booch describes concepts for object visibility and synchronization. Timing diagrams are used to show the object interactions for time-critical activities. The allocation of logical classes to physical modules, and the allocation of processes (operations) to processors (CPUs) are also modeled in diagrams within the Booch methodology.

It is interesting to note that Booch includes a concept for free processing components (subprograms, or modules) which he calls class utilities. These subprograms do not belong to any class, but are globally available to all of the classes in a system

The Wirfs-Brock method

The Wirfs-Brock responsibility-driven design approach is one of the first object-oriented methods published. It is very simple, with few concepts and few diagrams. It cannot be seen as a complete method with the level of detail that Booch, Rumbaugh, Coad/Yourdon, or Martin/Odell have defined in their approach, but it nevertheless remains valuable as a means of teaching object think. The interesting part of the methodology is the description of objects, with an emphasis on the *roles* and *responsibilities* of the objects. This is done for each object by considering its interactions with other objects. The fundamental paradigm in the Wirfs-Brock approach is that objects work together (collaborate) to fulfill a task.

An object is described with its responsibilities—i.e., "the knowledge an object maintains and the actions an object can perform." Responsibilities are grouped into *contracts*; a contract describes a cohesive set of responsibilities that a client can depend upon. This is a pure object-oriented view, and provides useful concepts for supporting a client-server architecture.

Classes, contracts, and collaborations (message connections) are diagrammed in so-called "collaboration graphs." Using the concept of subsystems (which are also objects, and also have contracts), fairly large systems can be viewed in their entirety.

The FUSION method

Fusion, like our methodology, also represents a second-generation OO methodology; it is the result of some significant methodological research at Hewlett-Packard. Like the Software AG approach described in this book, it draws from many of the good ideas published by Booch, Rumbaugh, Jacobson, et al, and it contains some very practical discussions of project management and reuse. There are some minor notational differences between FUSION and our OOAD (e.g., FUSION's basic object diagrams don't show the operations within a class); but more importantly, the formal notation does not include the object life cycle diagrams that we include in Chapter 7. And while FUSION refers to the concept of "scenarios," the formal notation does not include the transaction sequence diagrams and object interaction diagrams described in this book. This we find to be a major limitation; on the other hand, we found FUSIONS's notion of "visibility graphs" to be a useful addition to the collection of OO methodology concepts.

The Shlaer-Mellor method

The Shlaer-Mellor method has been published in two parts as of the end of 1994, and a third part is in progress. The original part, published in 1988,[1] presented an OOA approach that was based almost entirely on an E-R modeling technique. Indeed, the approach used E-R diagrams and data flow diagrams, with no distinct graphical notation at all to represent objects.

A more recent component of the Shlaer-Mellor method presents a "real-time" flavor of OOA and OOD, with a commendable emphasis on the dynamic behavior of objects by describing life cycle diagrams for objects in great detail. The more recent component of the method also provides adequate detail on the transition from an OOA model to an OOD model, but does not fully describe the recursive design approach that the authors practice in their training and consulting activities. A third component of their method, which is expected to be published in the 1995-96 timeframe, will expand on the details of OOD.

Meanwhile, the Shlaer-Mellor method seems to have de-emphasized a number of traditional OO concepts; there is very little mention of inheritance or polymorphism, for example, and it is not easy to see the connection between objects, operations, and messages.

---

[1] Sally Shlaer and Stephen Mellor, *Object-Oriented Analysis: Modeling the World in Data* (Englewood Cliffs, NJ: Prentice Hall, 1988)

Conclusion

We decided to base our object-oriented development approach on a combination of object structure modeling techniques, extended with E-R-based concepts, and object life cycle modeling techniques, as described in detail by Rumbaugh and Coad/Yourdon, with Jacobson's functionally-strong use-case approach. Our approach incorporates all of the major features of the Coad/Yourdon method, with additional material from Rumbaugh, as the Rumbaugh method has a wider scope and more detail. On the other hand, we have not included all Rumbaugh's concepts, where we considered these unnecessary or overcomplicated. We cover the Martin/Odell approach to the extent that E-R modeling is covered.

In addition to these techniques, we find subsystem modeling as outlined in many other methods useful, particularly when enhanced with the concept of services which we derive from Wirfs-Brock's concepts of contracts and collaborations.

The approach that we have taken will not surprise many readers, for a similar effort to integrate and synthesize popular OOAD methodologies has been underway in many companies. Indeed, it would not surprise us to see a convergence of commercially available OOAD methodologies to a few minor variants on the common themes we have outlined in this chapter — just as the commercially popular structured analysis/design methodologies converged to a common set of notations and strategies by the mid-1980s.

Glossary

Abstract class
Abstract classes are superclasses for which no object exists which does not belong to a subclass.

Action
Actions are associated with state transitions. When an object class in a given state receives a given event, it executes an action resulting in a state transition. The same action may be associated with more than one state transition.

Activity
An activity groups a sequence of object interactions.

Activity Flow Diagram
Activity flow diagrams are used in conjunction with object interaction diagrams to describe business processes and transaction sequences. Their specific use is to document how control flows between activities. They document decisions, iterations and parallel/random processing.

Actor
Actors are external agents who interact directly with the system. They may represent human users or interfaces with other systems. Each actor represents a role which a class of users play with respect to the system rather than an individual user. Any individual user may play a number of roles and may therefore be represented by a number of different actors.

An inheritance hierarchy may be defined for actors. Thus, actors may have subtypes and supertypes.

Additive Development Process
The results of each phase are used as input to the next phase and updated/extended as appropriate. This is in contrast to methodologies that are transformational, such as structured analysis and design.

Aggregation
Aggregation is used to model whole-part structures. The whole is called a **composite object** or **aggregate** and the parts are called **component objects**. Both the aggregate and its components are modelled as object classes.

Association
Objects can be associated via inheritance, aggregation, static relationships and communication associations. See also the entries for inheritance, etc.

Attribute
Attributes are data values associated with objects belonging to an object class. The values of attributes are pure data values without identity.

Attribute Type
Attribute types provide a standard definition for the format, length and range of values of attributes of the same type, e.g., for quantity, price, name, address, zipcode or postcode. Inheritance and aggregation can be used within attribute type definitions.

Business Process
A business process is a collection of activities that takes one or more kinds of input and creates an output that is of value to the customer.

Cardinality
Cardinality identifies the minimum and maximum number of objects in one object class that are related to a single object in the second object class.

Class Attribute
An object class can be considered as an object in its own right and hence can itself have attributes. These are called class attributes. Class attributes are used for data values which are associated with the object class as a whole. Class attributes can, for instance, be used to contain statistics (number of objects in class, average values) for all objects in the class.

Class Operation
Class operations handle behavior which cannot be associated with individual objects in a class. For example, an operation **Find Customer**

Object could be defined as a class operation for the object class **Customer**.

Cohesion

Cohesion describes the strength of the relationships between the elements within a system component. Within a system component, high cohesion is desirable.

Common Sequence

A common sequence is a sequence of events which occurs in more than one transaction sequence.

Communication Association

A communication association shows that objects of an object class send messages to objects of another or the same class.

Constraint

A constraint is a rule which controls the value of an attribute or relationship.

Control Object

Control objects are used to package task-related behavior, i.e., transaction sequence-specific behavior. They contain behavior which does not naturally belong to entity and interface objects.

Coupling

Coupling describes the strength of the relationships and interdependencies between separate system components. Between system components, low coupling is desirable.

Encapsulation

Encapsulation is any mechanism that hides the implementation of an object, so that other components of the system do not need to be aware of the internal structure and details of the object.

Entity Object

Entity objects are usually problem domain objects. They package attributes, relationships and behavior and are usually persistent. In addition to problem domain objects, entity objects are used for application objects which are used for the persistent storage of system-related information, e.g., audit information.

Event

An incident which requires some response. An event causes a specific state change within an object. An event may be external or internal. External events are sent by an actor. Internal events are sent by an object class. Events may be temporal, e.g., triggered at a specific time. Temporal events have a frequency, but no sender or carried data.

Guard Condition

A guard condition is used in combination with an event to determine what an object's next state should be when a given event occurs. This is useful where the object's current state and the event received are not sufficient to determine what the object's next state should be. Guard conditions are formulated so that they are either true or false. All guard conditions for an event are mutually exclusive. When an event associated with guard conditions occurs, the subsequent state transition is that for which the guard condition is true.

Identifying Attributes

An object can have one or more sets of identifying attributes. A set of identifying attributes consists of an attribute or a group of attributes and/or relationships which uniquely identify the objects in an object class.

Inheritance

Inheritance is an association between object classes which allows an object class to include the attributes and operations defined for another more general object class. The more general class is called the superclass and the more specific class is called a subclass.

Interface Object

Interface objects are used to handle communication between the system's environment and the system. They are environment-dependent. They isolate behavior relating to interfaces so that changes in system presentation or in external communications affect only interface objects.

Message

A message is sent by one object to another object to invoke an operation belonging to the receiving object. The message contains the operation name and a list of input and output argument values.

Method

A method is a specific implementation of an operation for an object class.

Multiple Inheritance

With multiple inheritance, an object class may inherit from more than one superclass.

Object

An object is an instance of an object class. An object combines data structure and behavior. It has an object state, consisting of its data values, and is capable of responding to messages, using the operations defined for the object class.

Object Behavior Model

The object behavior model describes the dynamic aspects of objects using operations, states and events.

Object Class

Object classes are used to provide descriptions of groups of objects which can be regarded as being of the same type. Objects belonging to an object class have similar behavior, a common data structure and common semantics.

Object Identifier

Each object has an internal object identifier which can be used internally within the system to retrieve the object.

Object Interaction

An object interaction involves the sending of message from one object to another.

Object Interaction Diagram

An object interaction diagram represents how the functionality required by a transaction sequence is provided by objects and communications between them.

Object Life Cycle Diagram

Object life cycle diagrams are similar to state transition diagrams and are used to describe the life cycle of objects of a given object class.

Object Structure Model

The object structure model describes the static aspects of objects, including inheritance, aggregation and relationships between objects.

Object Structure Diagram

Object structure diagrams are used to show object classes and the associations between them, i.e., inheritance, relationships, aggregation and communication associations.

Operation

An operation is processing which can be requested as a unit from an object. Objects of different classes may be able to perform the same operation. The operation defines the semantics and the signature of the operation. The operation's signature consists of the name and the argument list for the operation. Operations are implemented in methods.

Persistence

Persistent objects can survive longer than the process or computer session in which they are created. A persistent object exists until it is explicitly deleted. To achieve persistence, objects are stored in secondary storage, e.g., on disk. Not all the attributes of a persistent object are necessarily persistent.

Polymorphism

The ability to take on many forms. When an operation is invoked, its caller does not need to know which implementation of the operation should be selected. Instead, the object-oriented system selects the version of the operation which is appropriate to the object in question.

Problem Domain

A problem domain is a real-world domain which a computer system is built to support.

Relationship

Relationships model intrinsic, semantic relationships between objects according to understood rules from entity-relationship modelling.

Service

A service is a group of related functions which share some common purpose and which a subsystem offers for use by other subsystems or by users.

Signature

The signature of an operation defines the parameters required when the operation is invoked.

Single Inheritance

Single inheritance means that an object class inherits from only one superclass.

State

States are used to represent a situation or condition of an object during which certain physical laws, rules and policies apply. The state of an object is defined by the set of the values of attributes and relationships associated with that object. Associated with each state are one or more events which cause that state to change. Only states which are significant in determining the behavior of the object are modelled.

State Transition

A state transition is a change in the state of an object caused by an event occurring to the object while it is in a given state.

Static Relationship

See Relationship.

Subclass

An object class which inherits the attributes and operations of another object class (its superclass).

Subsystem

A subsystem is a collection of interrelated object classes, together with associated relationships and operations, which offer a definable service to, and have a well-defined interface with, other subsystems. Subsystems should have high internal cohesion and low external coupling. By low external coupling, we mean that their interface with other subsystems should be small. Most interactions should be internal to a subsystem.

Superclass

An object class from which other object classes (subclasses) inherit attributes and operations.

System

A software system or application.

System-Wide Model

The system-wide model has as its purpose complexity management. System-wide modelling is achieved using subsystems, services and system overview diagrams.

Transaction Sequence

A sequence of related transactions initiated by an actor and then proceeding as a dialogue between one or more actors. A transaction sequence describes a standard flow of events which the system is able to handle. It describes a specific way of using the system.

Transaction Sequence Model

The transaction sequence model is used to define what capabilities the system is to provide for its users.

Visibility

Visibility defines which objects may access and use the attributes and operations of any given object. The visibility of attributes and operations can be defined as private, protected or public. Private attributes and operations may be accessed only by the object to which they belong, and moreover may not be accessed by operations defined in subclasses. Protected attributes and operations are like private attributes and operations except that they can be accessed by operations defined in subclasses. Public attributes and operations may also be accessed by other objects.

Bibliography

Berard E.V. (1993) *Essays on Object-Oriented Software Engineering, Volume 1.*
Englewood Cliffs, NJ: Prentice Hall

Booch G. (1994) *Object-Oriented Analysis and Design with Applications.*
Redwood City, CA: Benjamin/Cummings

Carmichael, Andy (editor) (1994) *Object Development Methods.* New York City, NY: SIGS Books

Cattell R. ed. (1994) *The Object Database Standard: ODMG-93.* San Mateo, CA: Morgan Kaufmann

Coad P., Nicola J. (1993) *Object-Oriented Programming.*
Englewood Cliffs, NJ: Yourdon Press/Prentice Hall

Coad P., North D., Mayfield M., (1995) *Object Models: Strategies, Patterns, and Applications.*
Englewood Cliffs, NJ: Prentice-Hall

Coad P., Yourdon E. (1991) *Object-Oriented Analysis* (2nd Edition).
Englewood Cliffs, NJ: Yourdon Press/Prentice Hall

Coad P., Yourdon E. (1991) *Object-Oriented Design.* Englewood Cliffs, NJ: Yourdon Press/Prentice Hall

Coleman D., Arnold P., Bodoff S., Dollin C., Gilchrist H., Hayes F., Jeremaes P. (1994)
Object-Oriented Development: The FUSION Method. Englewood Cliffs, NJ: Prentice Hall

Cox B. (1986) *Object-Oriented Programming: An Evolutionary Approach.* Reading, MA: Addison-Wesley

Date C.J. (1986) *An Introduction to Database Systems, Volume I, Fourth Edition.*
Reading, MA: Addison-Wesley

Embley D.W., Kurtz B.D., Woodfield S.N. (1992) *Object-Oriented Systems Analysis: A Model Driven Approach.* Englewood Cliffs, NJ: Prentice Hall

Firesmith D., (1993) *Object-Oriented Requirements Analysis and Logical Design.*
Reading, MA: Addison-Wesley

Gamma E., Helm R., Johnson R., Vlissades J., (1995) *Design Patterns: Elements of Reusable Object-Oriented Software.* Reading MA: Addison-Wesley

Graham I., (1994) *Object oriented methods*, 2nd edition. Reading, MA: Addison-Wesley

Hammer M., Champy J. (1993) *Reengineering the Corporation: A manifesto for business revolution.*
USA, HarperCollins

Henderson-Sellers B., Edwards J. (1994) *BOOKTWO of Object-Oriented Knowledge: The Working Object.*
Sydney, Austrailia: Prentice Hall of Austrailia

Jacobson I., Christerson M., Jonsson P. Övergaard G. (1992) *Object-Oriented Software Engineering: A Use Case Driven Approach.* Reading, MA: Addison-Wesley, ACM Press

Martin J., Odell J. (1992) *Object-Oriented Analysis and Design.* Englewood Cliffs, NJ: Prentice-Hall

McMenamin S.M., Palmer J.F. (1984) *Essential Systems Analysis.* Englewood Cliffs, NJ: Yourdon Press

Meyer, B. (1988) *Object-Oriented Software Construction.*
Englewood Cliffs, NJ: Prentice-Hall International

Pree W., (1995) *Design Patterns for Object-Oriented Software Development.*
Reading, MA: Addison-Wesley

Rumbaugh J., Blaha M., Premerlani W., Eddy F., Lorensen W. (1991)
Object-Oriented Modeling and Design. Englewood Cliffs, NJ: Prentice-Hall

Selic B., Gullekson G., Ward P.T. (1994) *Real-Time Object-Oriented Modeling.*
New York, NY: John Wiley & Sons

Shlaer S., Mellor S.J. (1988) *Object-Oriented Analysis: Modeling the World in Data.*
Englewood Cliffs, NJ: Yourdon Press/Prentice-Hall

Shlaer, S, Mellor S.J. (1992) *Object Lifecycles: Modeling the World in States.* Englewood Cliffs, NJ.
Yourdon Press/Prentice Hall

Taylor D. (1991)*Object-Oriented Technology: A Manager's Guide.* Reading, MA: Addison-Wesley.

Wilkie G., (1993) *Object-Oriented Software Engineering: The Professional Software Developer's Guide.*
Reading, MA: Addison-Wesley

Wirfs-Brock R., Wilkerson B., Wiener L. (1990) *Designing Object-Oriented Software.*
Englewood Cliffs, NJ: Prentice-Hall

Yourdon E., (1989) *Modern Structured Analysis.* Englewood Cliffs, NJ: Prentice-Hall

Yourdon E., (1994) *Object-Oriented Systems Design: An Integrated Approach.*
Englewood Cliffs, NJ: Yourdon Press/Prentice Hall

Index

Object Interaction Diagram ~ Fence

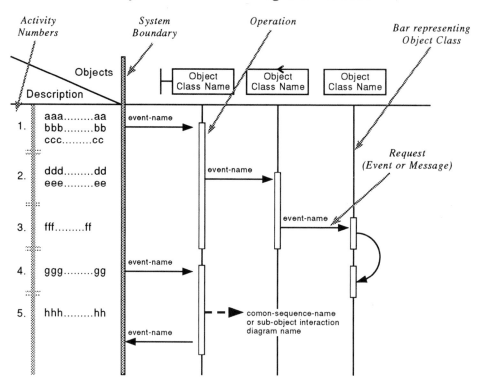

Object Interaction Diagram ~ Net

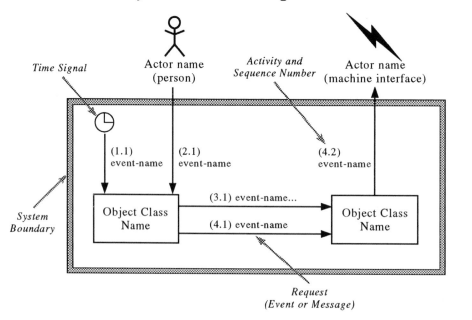